Public Debt and the Common Good

The American national debt stands at $20.49 trillion as of January 2018, or roughly $63,000 for every person in the United States. The national debt has grown six-fold in the past 25 years, and borrowing only has accelerated in recent administrations. What are the factors driving such unrestrained borrowing? Is American fiscal policy different now than in an earlier era? Is there a moral dimension to public debt and, if so, how can that dimension be measured?

Public Debt and the Common Good addresses these and other questions by looking to the fiscal policy of the American states. Drawing on classical themes and the longest quantitative review of state debt in the literature, James Odom expertly integrates institutional analysis with dimensions of culture to define the parameters of political freedom in a theoretically coherent way. In doing so, Odom argues that centralization and injustice, or the incapacity for the common good, can help explain state indebtedness.

Contributing to ongoing scholarly debates on public debt theory, this book will be of interest to students, scholars, and practitioners who work at the intersection of political philosophy and economics, as well as those who specialize in state public policy, state politics, and federalism more generally.

James Odom is Senior Policy Advisor to Texas State Senator Bryan Hughes. A recent Baylor University graduate, Odom has served as Director of Public Affairs at the same institution as well as a policy analyst with then-Sen. John Ashcroft of Missouri. In 2000, Odom was a candidate for the U.S. Congress from Oklahoma's fourth district.

Routledge Research in American Politics and Governance

14 The Latino Gender Gap in U.S. Politics
Christina E. Bejarano

15 Perspectives on Presidential Leadership
An International View of the White House
Edited by Michael Patrick Cullinane and Clare Frances Elliott

16 Super PAC!
Money, Elections, and Voters after *Citizens United*
Conor M. Dowling and Michael G. Miller

17 White Voters in 21st Century America
George Hawley

18 Candidate Character Traits in Presidential Elections
David B. Holian and Charles L. Prysby

19 The Social Process of Lobbying
Cooperation or Collusion?
John C. Scott

20 Congressional Communication in the Digital Age
Jocelyn Evans and Jessica Hayden

21 Reforming the Presidential Nominating Process
Front-Loading's Consequences and the National Primary Solution
Lisa K. Parshall

22 Public Debt and the Common Good
Philosophical and Institutional Implications of Fiscal Imbalance
James Odom

23 Removal of the Property Qualification For Voting in the United States
Strategy and Suffrage
Justin Moeller and Ronald F. King

Public Debt and the Common Good

Philosophical and Institutional Implications of Fiscal Imbalance

James Odom

Routledge
Taylor & Francis Group
LONDON AND NEW YORK

First published 2019
by Routledge

2 Park Square, Milton Park, Abingdon, Oxfordshire OX14 4RN
52 Vanderbilt Avenue, New York, NY 10017

Routledge is an imprint of the Taylor & Francis Group, an informa business

First issued in paperback 2020

Library of Congress Cataloging-in-Publication Data
A catalog record for this title has been requested

ISBN: 978-1-138-61816-9 (hbk)
ISBN: 978-0-367-66600-2 (pbk)

Typeset in Times New Roman
by Wearset Ltd, Boldon, Tyne and Wear

For the Lord Jesus Christ. None of his good promises have failed.
And for Wendy and Isaac.

Contents

	List of Figures	viii
	List of Tables	ix
1	Introduction	1
2	Justice as the Common Good	13
3	Of Keynes, Crisis, and Credit: An Overview of American Fiscal Trends in the Twentieth Century	40
4	Modeling Injustice	64
5	Interpreting Injustice	108
6	Progressivism and the Rise of the American Administrative State	124
7	Conclusion	150
	Appendix: Data Sources	160
	Index	164

Figures

3.1	Total Local and State Debt	46
3.2	Total Local, State, and Federal Debt	46
3.3	Total Local, State, and Federal Revenue	47
3.4	Measures of Centralization	47
3.5	Local, State, and Federal Debt Per Capita Relative to Tax Base	50
3.6	Local, State, and Federal Revenue Per Capita Relative to Tax Base	51
3.7	Mencken's Illustration of Durkheim	57
3.8	An Aristotelian View of Centralization	58
3.9	The Capacity For Political Freedom	59
4.1	Real State Debt Per Capita	85
4.2	Population Density	86
4.3	Percent Population Living in Cities Less than 100,000	90
4.4	State Revenue as a Percent of Total Local and State Revenue	90
4.5	Real Intergovernmental Aid to the State Per Capita	91
4.6	Protestant/Catholic Population	95
4.7	Real Income Per Capita	97
4.8	Total Number of Lawyers	98
4.9	Lawyers Per 1,000 Population	99
5.1	Last Occupation Prior to Service in the U.S. House (1789–1860)	116
5.2	Last Occupation Prior to Service in the U.S. House (1870–1900)	116
5.3	Last Occupation Prior to Service in the U.S. House (1901–1946)	117
5.4	Last Occupation Prior to Service in the U.S. House (1947–1996)	117

Tables

3.1	Local, State, and Federal Debt	42
3.2	Local, State, and Federal Revenue	43
3.3	Local, State, and Federal Debt Per Capita	45
3.4	Local, State, and Federal Revenue Per Capita	45
4.1	Descriptive Statistics	76
4.2	Regression of Real State Debt Right Censored on Select Variables	80
4.3	Regression of Real State Debt Right Censored on Select Variables	82
4.4	Regression of Real State Debt Right Censored on Select Variables	83
4.5	State Rank: Real State Debt Per Capita	85
4.6	State Rank: Population Density	87
4.7	Per Capita Fiscal Amounts by City Size	88
4.8	State Rank: Percent Population Living in Cities Less than 100,000	91
4.9	State Rank: State Revenue as Percent of Local and State Revenue	92
4.10	State Rank: Real Intergovernmental Aid to the State Per Capita	93
4.11	State Rank: Voter Turnout	94
4.12	State Rank: Protestant/Catholic Population Ratio	96
4.13	State Rank: Real Income Per Capita	98
4.14	State Rank: Lawyers Per 1,000 Population	99
5.1	Correlation of Lawyer Population with 2005 Litigation Data	109
5.2	Descriptive Statistics	111
5.3	Regression of Lawyer Population on Select Variables	112
5.4	Correlation of Lawyer Population with Mercatus Freedom Index	115

1 Introduction

> Credit is morality, and the exact measure of the soundness of the social state.
>
> —*Junius Tracts*, 1844

Money is imbued with moral meaning because, as the saying goes, money is condensed life. Money is food, shelter, clothing, and the means to other material goods that fill a human life beyond subsistence. As Michael Sandel has provided an important, recent reminder of ancient teaching, money cannot place a value on all things and can itself obscure a view of what is truly important.[1] Still, money is the means by which physical life is sustained and for that reason is of great significance.

If morality pertains to the proper manner of living, then credit does indeed have a moral dimension. When credit is taken, the means of living of one person are entrusted to another, and a pledge to return those means, usually with compensation in the form of interest, is received in turn. Not to honor the commitment to repay is to take the sustenance for life away. Hence, the debtor's reliability is revealed by his handling of the money entrusted, and his character is estimated by his creditworthiness.

Notions of reliability, faithfulness, and character may come to mind more quickly when assessing an individual borrower, particularly if one is the lender and relying on that borrower to repay. These concepts extend beyond interpersonal credit arrangements, however, to the fiscal behavior of nations. National currencies are issued and sustained with the full faith and credit of those governments. Societies have a national character, all that goes under the general and often nebulous word "culture." Furthermore, how nations handle their public accounts pertains to their national character. In "The Crisis of the Tax State," Schumpeter writes:

> The spirit of a people, its cultural level, its social structure, the deeds its policy may prepare—all this and more is written in its fiscal history, stripped of all phrases. He who knows how to listen to its message here discerns the thunder of world history more clearly than anywhere else.[2]

As with the individual, the handling of money by national governments reveals what truly animates that polity, its priorities and objectives, and, it will be argued, its moral character, or capacity for justice.

The American national debt stands at $20.49 trillion as of January 2018, or roughly $63,000 for every person in the United States.[3] A fiscal challenge of this magnitude has been most of a century in the making, under Republican and Democratic administrations and congresses. Norms of budget balance shared broadly by both parties came to be replaced by norms of deficit financing. For most of the postwar era, Democrats consistently have pushed for the expansion of social programs, and Republicans have favored tax cuts without commensurate spending reductions. The net result of both these enduring party objectives has been the sustained and, more recently, rapidly accelerating growth of the national debt under the Bush, Obama, and Trump administrations.

The ability to repay official debt totals is complicated by the question of currency valuation and unfunded liabilities of various social programs. "Quantitative easing," much of which has been used to finance new government debt since the Great Recession of 2008, has not been accompanied by inflation, but it is not a foregone conclusion that the dollar's value will hold, especially if political exigencies undermine the independence of the Fed. Alberto Giovannini discusses the dangers of central banks being responsible for the simultaneous management of monetary and debt policy.[4] In addition, the magnitude of demands on fiscal coffers is understated by social program liabilities that are not counted in official debt totals.

Rising debt levels have been accompanied with diminished political will to curtail spending. Debt ceilings are repeatedly increased, and significant spending reductions forestalled. President Obama did not mention the national debt in his last State of the Union address (although he did mention reducing the deficit once), and President Trump did not mention it in his first.

To be clear, public debt is not inherently immoral, or, to use a more theoretically durable term, "unjust." Public debt has financed many of the social improvements underlying the modern economy that sustains a high standard of living in America. For these reasons and others, economists and social scientists may not be among the most eager to discuss the national debt in moral terms. The injustice of public debt is a persistent theme in the popular debate, however, and this theme can be better grounded in scholarship.

Perhaps the phrase with connotations of justice most often heard from elected officials and others concerned with the national debt is, "Mortgaging our children's future." In this description of national debt is implicit the fundamental elements of a credit relationship described above, but between generations of Americans instead of individual persons. Public borrowing is taking the means of livelihood of younger and future generations of Americans (not to mention overseas investors who buy U.S. debt instruments), and, to the extent these creditors are not repaid, breaking faith with them or treating them unjustly. The increasingly tenuous fiscal position of the federal government indicates that such a breach of faith is occurring. On its current course, the fiscal trajectory of the U.S. is not sustainable, and national indebtedness has become an injustice threatening the country's future well-being.

A Note on Terminology

Defining terminology is important for any argument. Gary Lawson's discussion of a widely used economic term, "social efficiency," is illustrative.[5] After reviewing different meanings for social efficiency, he shows that all such definitions are deficient. His conclusion, entitled "Enough is Enough," cautions against overstating a term's precision in scholarly research. Keeping Lawson's advice in mind, "unsustainable" is a term that already has been used and is open to definitional problems. What does it mean to say that public debt is unsustainable? A scholarly answer will not be ventured to this question, for "efficiency's" sake but also because it is not essential to the analysis herein, which is focused more on factors that contribute to public debt rather than defining a tipping point of insolvency.

It is central to this book, however, that public debt has become unjust. To be sure, the injustice of public debt is related to its unsustainability, but the bulk of this analysis is intended, again, to advance an understanding of unsustainability grounded in mores and institutions rather than cumulative debt totals that pass a point of no return. Regarding unsustainability, it will be enough to say that the national debt cannot continue to increase almost six-fold every 25 years, which was the case from 1990 to 2015 (from $3.23 to $18.15 trillion nominal dollars).[6] What justice is and what transgresses it in terms of indebtedness will be covered in some detail, however, and a quantitative measurement of injustice in the American states will be proposed, integrated into statistical modeling, and evaluated for possible meaning.

Methodological Perspective

One approach to studying American politics is to review policy at the national level over time, as Sidney Milkis does in *The President and the Parties*.[7] His account is not focused on debt per se, but on the expanding scope of the national government and how that expansion at once reflects and influences the character of the American people, a nation he finds more self-interested and less communal with a mature administrative state driven by parochial concerns rather than a sense of the national interest.

Another approach, the one used here, is to step back from policy at the federal level and evaluate the American states. Alexis de Tocqueville, perhaps the greatest commentator on American democracy, took this approach. He believed that the character of the national government could be discerned best by looking at the American states.[8] From a quantitative standpoint, a review of the states has the obvious benefit of comparative analysis that a review of the federal government in isolation does not. Because the states comprise one country, inferences can be drawn about debt in an American context to inform what may be happening at the federal level. The methodology and focus of this analysis is thus different than Milkis', but similar themes are reiterated relating to the effect of changing fiscal norms and centralization.

Political Culture

The American federal system was a unique creation of the Founders to address the immediate political exigencies of forming a national government and the longer-term challenges of governing a large republic. The national government would be supreme in its sphere of enumerated powers, and the states would retain those powers not delegated. The centralization of power at the national level has been a prominent feature of American federalism since the Founding, but the states still retain significant discretion on a number of policy fronts, to include budgeting. This has allowed the states to take different paths in how they handle fiscal affairs.

In addition to the institutional features of fiscal independence, the states have different socioeconomic traits that can be incorporated into an analysis of public debt levels. The study of state "culture" has been an enduring component of federalism scholarship since Daniel J. Elazar's seminal work *American Federalism: A View From the States*.[9] Elazar argues that the marketplace and the commonwealth are the major paradigms by which Americans seek to integrate the two central issues of civil society: the use of power and the attainment of justice. These paradigms are expressed in three essential national subcultures—individualistic, moralistic, and traditionalistic—that influence how a state perceives the purpose of government, determines who will participate in politics, and conducts actual government operations.[10]

The individualistic culture views politics as a marketplace and government as a utilitarian agent to meet the needs of citizens. Elazar states,

> A government need not have any direct concern with questions of the good society, except insofar as it may be used to advance some common conception of the good society formulated outside the political arena just as it serves other functions.[11]

Government intervention in society is limited and designed to encourage private initiative. Bureaucracy is viewed in ambivalent terms: negatively, it interferes with the personal relationships that drive politics in an individualistic culture, or, positively, it increases efficiency that mirrors the marketplace. Politics is viewed in non-ideological terms as the domain of professionals who must traffic in a certain degree of corruption that necessarily attends the work of government. As long as that corruption does not become excessive, those political professionals can advance without public censure. In the absence of other unifying forces, political parties are the primary means of organizing political activity in individualistic cultures and thus maintain a high degree of cohesiveness.[12]

The moralistic culture views politics as "the search for the good society—a struggle for power, it is true, but also an effort to exercise power for the betterment of the commonwealth."[13] Non-governmental activity is favored to improve society, but government itself is a positive instrument for social change and more willing to intervene on economic and social policy. Politics can be seen in more ideological terms that diminishes the importance of party allegiance. Political participation is open to all and should be pursued with public instead of individual interests in mind. As such, there is much less tolerance for corruption in politics. Bureaucracy can be viewed negatively as conflicting with the communitarian emphasis on local politics often present in moralistic cultures or positively as a means to enhance government neutrality.[14]

The traditionalistic culture is organized around the dominance of political elites. Elazar writes,

> It reflects an older, precommercial attitude that accepts a substantially hierarchical society as part of the ordered nature of things, authorizing and expecting those at the top of the social structure to take a special and dominant role in government.[15]

Government has a positive role in society but is inherently conservative in nature, limited to the preservation of the elite power structure. Political parties are less important than informal relationships. As such, one party predominates, and party politics are between factions within this party. Political participation is limited and bureaucracy is severely constrained, viewed as antithetical to the elite relationships that drive traditionalistic politics.

Shortly after Elazar initially proposed his typology for political culture, Ira Sharkansky noted its "curious juxtaposition" alongside the prevailing trend toward quantitative analysis in the study of the states.[16] Purely quantitative analysis tends to ask whether something happens or not and under what conditions. A cultural lens allows the investigator to ask the more value-laden question of why something happens, with an attendant judgment on the outcome. As Joel Lieske writes, culture "shapes people's basic racial, ethnic, religious, and social identities. It provides norms and rules on how they should behave and relate to others. And it determines what kinds of social relationships and institutions are acceptable and legitimate."[17]

An argument that public debt has become unjust clearly uses culture as a pretext to assess norms influencing public policy. Elazar is mentioned therefore not because his typology serves as a guide for this analysis but because the durability of his framework and the literature it spawned provide a defensible position from which to assume that norms matter and that certain outcomes are more or less desirable. A validation of Elazar's general cultural categorization of the states is not sought, but the analysis herein does show how various attributes of the three cultures influence state debt levels and that these influences can be countervailing.

Elazar's consideration of political culture draws on a persistent strand of political thought. Aristotle, Tocqueville, and John Rawls, three thinkers featured in the next chapter, come from different eras of political theory (the classical, modern, and contemporary, respectively), but each acknowledges the importance of norms related to governance. Aristotle argues that unwritten customs are more authoritative than written laws.[18] Tocqueville offers a more precise definition of culture in his discussion of "mores"; he applies this term "to the different notions that men possess, to the various opinions that are current in their midst, and to the sum of ideas of which the habits of the mind are formed."[19] In short, mores constituted "the whole moral and intellectual state of a people."[20] Even more fundamental for Tocqueville than mores is the "social state" of a people. It is the "first cause of most of the laws, customs, and ideas that regulate the conduct of nations."[21] As does Aristotle, Rawls recognizes that constitutions may be written or unwritten.[22] Furthermore, political liberalism has norms, what Rawls might call "our firmest considered convictions," that rule out certain regime types, set boundaries for deliberation within the original position, and guide subsequent regulation of the basic structure.

Initial Considerations Regarding Justice and Overview of Chapters

Justice is a particularly useful concept around which to discuss the difficulties in making value judgments in academic research. As a fundamental value of democratic civil society, justice is a ubiquitous theme in public discourse. But what does justice mean and what is its value? This question may be answered on two levels: what is justice and to what does it pertain. Contemporary views of justice may see it as a proxy for or little more than an accessory to equality. Consider Stephen L. Gardner's definition at the end of his eloquent essay considering, among other things, the role of debt in aggravating democratic nihilism: "'Equality of conditions' … is a demand of justice. But the less discerning advocates of equality fail to understand that justice is not a social bond and does not make social life or, for that matter, integral community."[23] For Gardner, justice is a somewhat sterile notion that seems to enable equality but is not something around which human relationships are formed. Gardner's view would not be atypical in contemporary scholarship and is informed by an undercurrent of Rawlsian liberalism that distinguishes between democratic society and community. In democratic society, public reason restrains the influence of value judgments and buttresses what Sandel calls a "procedural republic."[24] Community, by contrast, is where comprehensive doctrines organize social life around the values of that particular group of people.

As will be argued in the next chapter, this tendency of political liberalism to differentiate between democratic society and community effectively severs a consistent view of justice at once applicable at the private and public level. Justice becomes something that courts dispense and philosophers expound upon rather than what two people demonstrate in their dealings with each other. Human dignity receives its most vigorous defense with political liberalism, but political liberalism may diminish considerations of virtue that contribute to that dignity and worth. While seriously deficient in its view of human equality, classical philosophy offers a more coherent view of justice. Aristotle viewed justice as the common good that is manifested in sustainable society, or the durability of human relationships. This ancient view of justice can be incorporated into modern statistical analysis, for various aspects of societal health can be measured and certainly have been measured in groundbreaking ways by recent scholarship. Putnam's social capital index is Aristotelian in nature. Other concepts such as social trust and political efficacy also are informed by Aristotelian themes. Not without its own shortcomings, classical philosophy can provide a helpful, alternative perspective by which to assess the cultural and institutional factors contributing to public indebtedness.

To what does justice pertain is a second and perhaps easier question. Obviously, in this book, justice is being discussed from the vantage point of debt: justice as it pertains to fiscal policy is that which results in sustainable levels of public debt that do not benefit present taxpayers at the expense of future generations. Certainly, justice could be guided by other considerations. Justice could be measured in terms of education spending or veterans' benefits or retiree healthcare. All of these claims have merit in terms of justice, but to a degree all of them are subsumed in an overarching concern for sustainable fiscal behavior. To the extent that the entire fiscal edifice is endangered due to unsustainable public borrowing, none of these other worthy policy goals will be achieved. This book approaches public debt in this light. It does not seek to differentiate between contending programs for public funds but to look at factors that support or undermine overall fiscal health. What policymakers do with public revenues is important but not as fundamental as the implications of sustained imbalance between revenue and expenditure.

Following a discussion of justice's meaning and relevance to the issue of public indebtedness, twentieth-century fiscal trends and economic thought on public debt are reviewed. The "fiscal revolution" usually attributed to John Maynard Keynes, upon closer inspection, took important steps prior to the publication of his *General Theory* and continued with diminished support after Keynesianism suffered theoretical setbacks in the midst of simultaneous high unemployment and high inflation in the 1970s. The dominance of Keynesianism, it will be argued, may be due more to the compatibility of its assumptions with aims of the modern administrative state than to the empirical relevance of its theory. Keynesianism offered a theoretical rationale for debt issuance by governments inclined to borrow. Robert J. Barro constitutes the second major strand of thought on public debt by contemporizing the Ricardian equivalence theorem, which postulates that public debt issuance today is in essence the same as a tax tomorrow. Mathematically irrefutable, the theorem has fairly severe empirical limitations. From the standpoint of fiscal conservatism, Barro can be seen as arguing that the bill will come due, that debt must be paid. In the context of political reality where it is easier to issue debt than raise taxes, the empirical effect of Barro is Keynesian: a greater proclivity to issue debt. A third strand of thought on debt is represented by James Buchanan and draws on classical (not as in Greek but as in economic thought of the eighteenth and nineteenth centuries) themes to attack the central assumptions of Keynesianism. Taking a collective view, Keynesians like Abba Lerner argue that debt does not disadvantage future generations because "we owe it to ourselves," that is, one part of society is merely repaying another part of society. Buchanan argues convincingly that this may not be the case. Public debt may do good if used prudently but also may result in a transfer of wealth from the future to the present.

After fiscal trends and economic thought on public debt are reviewed, statistical modeling is conducted to assess the determinants of state per capita debt levels. U.S. Census records are the source for most of the data. As with many social science statistics, Census records are much more complete after World War II, but enough data is available prior to the war to construct decennial measurements. This study is based on such decennial measurements from 1920 to 1990, the longest such review of state debt in the literature. Independent variables typical of other studies are included, such as personal income, state revenue, intergovernmental revenue, measures of centralization, ideology measures, and budget rules. Additional variables that have not received much consideration in similar models also are included: religious makeup, voter turnout, and the distribution of city size. Importantly for this study, a synthetic variable is derived that uses criminal and civil faction as a measure of injustice, or the lack of the common good, with the assumption being that citizens less capable of preserving the common good among themselves are less likely to attain the common good between themselves and future generations; they are more likely to use debt to benefit the present at the expense of the future. One of the best ways to measure criminal and civil faction is the number of criminal and civil court proceedings by state. Such data is available for recent years but not far back into the twentieth century. It is argued that the size of the state bar (numbers which are available from the latter nineteenth century) can serve as a synthetic measure of societal injustice as reflected in criminal and civil faction, not that attorneys cause injustice but that they are its handlers, and the level of criminal and civil faction can be correlated with the number of lawyers per state. Many of these variables are found to be significant in explaining state debt levels, including the measure of injustice.

The significance of the injustice variable leads to a discussion of several possible meanings for the variable. The size of the state bar convincingly is shown to have historically durable correlations with various measures of societal dysfunction or injustice or the lack of the common good. The lawyer population itself is used as a dependent variable in a separate model and is found to be driven by factors of societal dysfunction. Alternatively, the lawyer variable could be seen as a measure of legal complexity. Peter H. Schuck provides an excellent overview of legal complexity and its ramifications for various aspects of good government. Complexity is not necessarily a bad thing, Schuck readily admits, but it can diminish faith in government to the extent that it makes the law inaccessible and arbitrary in light of common standards of justice. Finally, the size of the state bar can be understood as reflective of the dominance of attorneys in state legislatures. Data on the composition of the U.S. House of Representatives is reviewed to show the high percentage of legislative seats occupied by attorneys over the course of American history. A similar database apparently is not available for state legislatures, but the assumption is that the size of the state bar translates into greater dominance of attorneys in state legislative councils. This is not a problem because the legislators are attorneys but because as attorneys they bring a particular set of interests to bear on public policymaking, just as any other professional group would be wont to do. The general public would be concerned if 50–60 percent of U.S. House seats were occupied by doctors over the past two centuries, not because these legislators are doctors but because the interests of doctors would be overrepresented in the policymaking process. Public reticence regarding the legislative service of attorneys may be less acute because attorneys are trained in the law. Attorneys have their own distinct interests, however, and this cursory review of their dominance in the U.S. House points to the need for more research to better understand how the norms of the bar influence American politics.

As deficits preceded Keynes, so the impetus for centralization preceded the New Deal. In the years leading up to and during the Progressive Era, the American people began to empower government to exert more public stewardship over a society being transformed by industrialization and urbanization. With the significance of centralization established in quantitative modeling in Chapter 4, Chapter 6 reviews the rise of the American administrative state, with emphasis on Progressive Era reforms that were consolidated during the New Deal.

An ambitious agenda outlined by the Progressive Party in the 1912 election implied an administrative apparatus out of step with traditional American views of limited constitutional government. Through its separation of powers, enumerated powers, federal structure, and natural rights tradition, limited constitutional government necessarily considers both the equal and the unequal in seeking a just society. The United States thus could be founded on the proposition that all men are created equal and then constitute a government whose "first object," according to Madison, is to protect the diverse faculties of its citizens that result in unequal outcomes.[25] The development of the American administrative state necessarily involved the diminishment of constitutional forms that provided various political platforms from which to advance varying, "unequal" viewpoints. Social welfare initiatives pursued in centralized fashion also conflicted with a natural rights tradition that emphasized equality of opportunity rather than equality of outcome. The growth of the administrative state was accompanied by a heightened emphasis on collective opinion as a substitute for the constitutional structure that was being abandoned. American democracy came to rely more on a central figure to discern and lead that public opinion, as Tulis recounts of Wilson and subsequent American presidents.[26] While not dismissing the successes of the modern American administrative state, this chapter applies the theoretical arguments of Chapter 2 to the historical narrative of Progressivism to show how centralized administration more capable of programmatic achievement may be less capable of the justice that accompanies self-government.

Conclusion

As the methodological framework implies, this book deals with two topics that must be handled with care: culture and justice. An assumption that state political culture matters is an assumption that can be made with confidence due to the work of Elazar, the literature that follows him, and the political thought that precedes him. An assumption that culture matters is the pretext for the value judgment of justice, but justice has to mean more than it does in political liberalism to be used in this way. It is a term imbued with moral meaning, but contemporary political thought has done much to hollow out the moral core of justice, leaving a form of moral value that draws what substance it can from shifting views of equality. Gardner says that justice is not the basis for community, but it is, rather, equality that cannot serve in this way. As Tocqueville shows, equality can take the degraded form of subservience under political oppression. Equality is thus different from political freedom that comes with the exercise of civic powers for self-government, a self-government that only can be learned and practiced in the context of community. An Aristotelian view of justice as the common good thus has much to contribute to contemporary notions of democracy and the threats that imperil it, among the first of which is public debt.

Notes

1 Michael J. Sandel, *What Money Can't Buy: The Moral Limits of Markets* (New York: Macmillan, 2012).
2 Joseph Schumpeter, "The Crisis of the Tax State," in *The Economics and Sociology of Capitalism*, ed. Richard Swedberg (Princeton, NJ: Princeton University Press, 1991), 101.
3 U.S. Department of Treasury, "The Debt to the Penny and Who Holds It." Accessed March 7, 2018 at https://treasurydirect.gov/NP/debt/current.
4 Alberto Giovannini, "Government Debt Management," *Oxford Review of Economic Policy* Vol. 13 No. 4 (Winter 1997): 43–52.
5 Gary Lawson, "Efficiency and Individualism," *Duke Law Journal* Vol. 42 No. 1 (October 1992): 52–98.
6 U.S. Department of Treasury, "Historical Debt Outstanding: Annual." Accessed November 3, 2016 at http://treasurydirect.gov/govt/reports/pd/histdebt/histdebt.htm.
7 Sidney M. Milkis, *The President and the Parties: The Transformation of the American Party System Since the New Deal* (New York: Oxford University Press, 1993).
8 Alexis de Tocqueville, *Democracy in America*, trans. Harvey C. Mansfield and Delba Winthrop (Chicago: University of Chicago Press, 2000), 56.
9 Daniel J. Elazar, *American Federalism: A View From the States* (New York: Crowell, 1966).
10 Daniel J. Elazar, *American Federalism: A View From the States*, Third Edition (New York: Harper & Row, 1984), 112.
11 Ibid., 115.
12 Ibid., 115–116.
13 Ibid., 117.
14 Ibid., 117–118.
15 Ibid., 118.
16 Ira Sharkansky, "The Utility of Elazar's Political Culture: A Research Note," *Polity* Vol. 2 No. 1 (Autumn 1969): 67.

17 Joel Lieske, "The Changing Regional Subcultures of the American States and the Utility of a New Cultural Measure," *Political Research Quarterly* Vol. 63 No. 3 (2010): 538.
18 Aristotle, *Politics*, trans. Carnes Lord (Chicago: University of Chicago Press, 2013), 1287b5–10.
19 Tocqueville, *Democracy in America*, 275.
20 Ibid.
21 Ibid., 45.
22 John Rawls, *Justice as Fairness: A Restatement*, ed. Erin Kelly (Cambridge, MA: Belknap Press, 2001), 41.
23 Stephen L. Gardner, "Democracy's Debt: Capitalism and Cultural Revolution," in *Debt*, eds. Peter Y. Paik and Mary Wiesner-Hanks (Bloomington: Indiana University Press, 2013), 114.
24 Michael J. Sandel, *Democracy's Discontent: America in Search of a Public Philosophy* (Cambridge, MA: Belknap Press, 1996), 4.
25 Alexander Hamilton, James Madison, and John Jay, *The Federalist* (New York: Barnes & Noble, 2006), 53.
26 Jeffrey K. Tulis, *The Rhetorical Presidency* (Princeton, NJ: Princeton University Press, 1987).

Bibliography

Aristotle. *Politics*. Translated by Carnes Lord. Chicago: University of Chicago Press, 2013.

De Tocqueville, Alexis. *Democracy in America*. Translated by Harvey C. Mansfield and Delba Winthrop. Chicago: University of Chicago Press, 2000.

Elazar, Daniel J. *American Federalism: A View From the States*. New York: Crowell, 1966.

Elazar, Daniel J. *American Federalism: A View From the States*, Third Edition. New York: Harper & Row, 1984.

Gardner, Stephen. "Democracy's Debt: Capitalism and Cultural Revolution." In *Debt*, edited by Peter Y. Paik and Mary Wiesner-Hanks, 94–115. Bloomington: Indiana University Press, 2013.

Giovannini, Alberto. "Government Debt Management." *Oxford Review of Economic Policy* Vol. 13 No. 4 (Winter 1997): 43–52.

Hamilton, Alexander, James Madison, and John Jay. *The Federalist*. New York: Barnes & Noble, 2006.

Lawson, Gary. "Efficiency and Individualism." *Duke Law Journal* Vol. 42 No. 1 (October 1992): 53–98.

Lieske, Joel. "The Changing Regional Subcultures of the American States and the Utility of a New Cultural Measure." *Political Research Quarterly* Vol. 63 No. 3 (2010): 538–552.

Milkis, Sidney M. *The President and the Parties: The Transformation of the American Party System Since the New Deal*. New York: Oxford University Press, 1993.

Rawls, John. *Justice as Fairness: A Restatement*. Edited by Erin Kelly. Cambridge, MA: Belknap Press, 2001.

Sandel, Michael J. *Democracy's Discontent: America in Search of a Public Philosophy*. Cambridge, MA: Belknap Press, 1996.

Sandel, Michael J. *What Money Can't Buy: The Moral Limits of Markets*. New York: Macmillan, 2012.

Schumpeter, Joseph. "The Crisis of the Tax State." In *The Economics and Sociology of Capitalism*, edited by Richard Swedberg, 99–140. Princeton, NJ: Princeton University Press, 1991.

Sharkansky, Ira. "The Utility of Elazar's Political Culture: A Research Note." *Polity* Vol. 2 No. 1 (Autumn 1969): 66–83.

Tulis, Jeffrey K. *The Rhetorical Presidency*. Princeton, NJ: Princeton University Press, 1987.

U.S. Department of Treasury. "The Debt to the Penny and Who Holds It." Accessed November 20, 2017 at https://treasurydirect.gov/NP/debt/current.

U.S. Department of Treasury. "Historical Debt Outstanding: Annual." Accessed November 3, 2016 at http://treasurydirect.gov/govt/reports/pd/histdebt/histdebt.htm.

2 Justice as the Common Good

> For all fasten on a certain sort of justice, but proceed only to a certain point, and do not speak of the whole of justice in its authoritative sense … For the ones, if they are unequal in a certain thing, such as goods, suppose they are unequal generally, while the others suppose that if they are equal in a certain thing, such as freedom, they are equal generally. But of the most authoritative thing they say nothing.
>
> —Aristotle, *Politics*

The strength of political liberalism is its grasp of the inherent dignity and worth of each human being. Referencing Rawls, perhaps the most important political philosopher of the twentieth century, equality is based on the two moral powers that every person possesses: "the capacity for a sense of justice" and "a capacity for a conception of the good … set within, and interpreted by, certain comprehensive religious, philosophical, or moral doctrines."[1] Through concepts such as the original position, the veil of ignorance, and the overlapping consensus, Rawls does much to strengthen contemporary democracy by taking seriously society's need for justice and placing that need within a theoretical framework for a "fair system of cooperation."

Rawls' "justice as fairness" would equip every human being with the basic liberties and primary goods necessary to pursue the good life, while advancing a notion of public reason that leaves open the question of what the good life is. Comprehensive doctrines around which concepts of the good are formed are restricted in political discourse, especially on matters of constitutional essentials. Positively, this restriction may point citizens toward public reason that facilitates political cooperation. Negatively, as Kraut points out, it may bifurcate the good into private and public spheres, diminishing politics by excluding the most important questions of value.[2]

To the extent that political liberalism privatizes concepts of the good, it may deal with justice in an incoherent way. Justice is a foundational concept in civil society. It also is a term imbued with moral meaning, based on an assumption that rightness can be discerned and should be defended. This places political liberalism in a difficult position: it must deal with justice but has a certain discomfort with all that justice implies. Sandel describes the outcome as a "procedural republic,"[3] where justice is defined in terms of conditions that afford more equal opportunities rather than as a concept distinct from equality and related to virtue.

A different cultural lens allows contemporary democracy to see its strengths and weaknesses more clearly. Classical philosophy preserves the link between virtue and justice in a way that more consistently integrates private and public life, and this perspective can help citizens of contemporary democracies better see the personal relevance of political issues and the obligations that accompany self-government. Highlighting what will be argued is a positive contribution of classical philosophy should in no way obscure severe deficiencies in the classical view of human equality. Aristotle argued for natural slavery and excluded wide swathes of society from the decision and office that comprise citizenship. The corrective to these deficiencies offered by political liberalism should be kept in mind even as this chapter focuses on the classical contribution to a contemporary understanding of justice.

Aristotle

Modern Relevance

Modern political thought generally is regarded as beginning with Machiavelli. With the following statement, Machiavelli expresses the essence of modernity's dismissal of much of classical political theory. In *The Prince*, Machiavelli writes,

> And many have imagined republics and principalities that have never been seen or known to exist in truth; for it is so far from how one lives to how one should live that he who lets go of what is done for what should be done learns his ruin rather than his preservation.[4]

Yet such a statement mischaracterizes Aristotle and misses the modern relevance of his teaching.

In the *Politics*, Aristotle provides a detailed taxonomy of regimes, arguably better than Machiavelli himself. He discusses regimes based on virtue (kingship and aristocracy) but readily acknowledges that most governments do not aspire to and cannot attain virtue. It is the common good that defines the best regimes and rule for private interest that typifies the corruption of government. Machiavelli takes a very similar line:

> But above all it is very marvelous to consider how much greatness Rome arrived at after it was freed from its kings. The reason is easy to understand, for it is not the particular good but the common good that makes cities great. And without doubt this common good is not observed if not in republics, since all that is for that purpose is executed … In this mode, as soon as a

> tyranny arises after a free way of life, the least evil that results for those cities is not to go ahead further nor to grow more in power or riches, but usually—or rather always—it happens that they go backward.[5]

Machiavelli thus shares Aristotle's admiration for a free way of life and his wariness of the corrosive effects of tyranny. Aristotle offers a more coherent theoretical defense of the common good than Machiavelli, however, and bases that common good on notions (albeit narrower) of equality and of political rule defined by ruling and being ruled in turn.

Aristotle surrenders little if anything to modern thought in terms of a realistic view of politics and anticipates many of the specific issues that modern thinkers wrestle with and comment upon. Anticipating a Madisonian cacophony of claimants on the regime, he lowers expectations for government by arguing that virtue is just one of many claimants. He makes a clear distinction between claimants on the regime, of which there are many, and the claimants on the good man, which are education and virtue alone.[6] In addition to lowering expectations for government, this notion of different claimants upon the city and good man anticipates a more modern understanding of the space between the government and the citizen.

Assortedly, he foresees and takes exception to Bentham's argument on the commensurability of goods.[7] Aristotle anticipates Tocqueville by noting that democracy pursues equality above all else.[8] He presages Machiavelli's argument on ingratitude to the excellent by acknowledging that noteworthy men may need to be eliminated.[9] Aristotle anticipates a modern judicial function by saying that judges fill in the gaps where law does not speak, an argument that also applies to use of the executive's prerogative power.[10] He anticipates Tocqueville in the role of associations forming a "single human being" that is greater than any of its members.[11] He anticipates Mill on the need for one ruler to have many subordinates because it is hard for one opinion to be informed.[12] His argument that larger cities have less faction shares an affinity with Madison's argument on the large republic.[13] As will be discussed below, he anticipates middle-class democracy that has come to define the modern liberal state. He offers a better theoretical basis for this than modern thinkers, however: the rich will not be ruled and the poor are subservient, comprising a city of masters and slaves who despise each other, contrary to the affection needed for a community.[14] Inequality is thus a source of factional conflict.[15] He anticipates political liberalism's openness to various concepts of the good by discussing a defining characteristic of democracy: living as one wants.[16] He anticipates Tocqueville on the character of the many versus the excellent and Machiavelli on the many being better judges.[17] His distinction between natural and conventional justice anticipates Tocqueville's distinction between morality and honor.[18] He anticipates the debate over term limits by saying that periods of rule should be short to facilitate ruling and being ruled in turn.[19] He anticipates the debate over the need for private character in public office by arguing that virtue is important for a ruler generally but that its importance varies according to the office held.[20] He anticipates the debate over welfare to work by arguing that public aid to the poor should not be indiscriminate but equip them with a trade or other means to secure a living.[21] He would caution against certain strands of American progressive thought that would undermine political institutions in favor of ever more democracy (a theme discussed in greater detail in Chapter 6).[22] He anticipates institutional analysis by discussing how institutions shape regimes and the character of the people.[23] He anticipates tort reform by arguing for penalties against frivolous lawsuits targeting the rich.[24] He offers enduringly relevant observations about how the geographic situation of a country and the nature of its terrain shape its politics. Colonies served as an outlet for the poor, a function that characterized the first settlement of and westward migration across America.[25] He anticipates Madison's criticism of Jefferson in *Federalist* 49 by saying that frequent change in the law weakens respect for it.[26] He anticipates Tocqueville on the advance of equality over time.[27] He anticipates Putnam in incorporating an essential view of social capital in his discussion of regimes. The tyrant, for example, does not permit "common messes, clubs, education, or anything else of this sort, but guard[s] against anything that customarily gives rise to two things: high thoughts and trust."[28] He has a functional rather than an abstract definition of the citizen. The citizen partakes in "decision and office."[29] He must be educated to the regime in which he lives, for the regime must have greater support than opposition to survive.[30]

His critiques of certain deficiencies in political life apply with force to aspects of modern political thought. His discussion of the neglect of land held in common encapsulates the capitalist argument against Marx and the excesses of communism.[31] His observation that people come together for more than property encapsulates the socialist argument against Locke and the excesses of capitalism.[32] His observation that the city is for more than avoiding injustice offers an implied critique of Kant.[33] Indicting Nietzsche, the person who stands outside of community is suspect; he is potentially at war with the city.[34]

Aristotle's theme of the mean is exponentially more powerful than any other economic, sociological, or philosophical principle. It integrates body and soul, orders the soul, integrates man to his fellow man, orders man's relationship to the city, and governs the regime of the city. Its durability is tied to its relativity. It is situational, depending on actors and circumstances involved, yet informed by an unshakeable telos of justice, or search for the common good.

Aristotle's View of Justice

Aristotle's view of justice is at once more earthy and elevated than contemporary notions. For Aristotle, justice is worked out in the give and take of human relationships and is thus dependent on virtue, the trust-building behavior that evaluates personal interest in light of another's well-being. It is not a lofty ideal but the flesh and blood attainment of the common good sought in the midst of mundane circumstance. Justice is virtue entire because it is virtue practiced, and its worth is proven in sustainable relationships.

Aristotle's view of justice has a sense of comprehensiveness that speaks to the legal, institutional, and cultural capacity of a society for good governance. Justice is law but more than law. It is order but more than order. It is institutions but more than institutions. For Aristotle,

> The political good is justice, and this is the common advantage. Justice is held by all to be a certain equality ... for they assert that justice is a certain thing for certain persons, and should be equal for equal persons.[35]

Justice is thus the capacity to recognize and attain the common good, both at the individual and the regime level.

At the individual level, justice is

> that by which the just person is said to be disposed to act according to his choice of what is just, and to distribute things to himself in relation to another (and to another person in relation to a third), not in such a way as to distribute more of what is choice worthy to himself and less to his neighbor, and of harm the reverse, but rather to distribute what is equal in accord with the proportion (and similarly also in the case of another person in relation to a third).[36]

In essence, the just person does not claim more than his share but recognizes that equal persons should receive equal things.

Justice is not one-dimensional, however. It is not determined solely by equality. Equal persons deserve equal things, but persons are not equal and the things that are used to equalize their inequality may not be the same. Justice is four-dimensional due to the presence of two parties and the two interests of those parties.[37] Proportional reciprocity equalizes these four dimensions. For example, consider the case of a physical confrontation between a ruler and a citizen. If a ruler strikes a citizen, the ruler should not be struck in return because of his station. Presumably, the ruler would make amends in some other way that did not diminish his dignity. By contrast, if a citizen strikes a ruler, the citizen "ought to be not only struck but also punished."[38] The example of a ruler and citizen throws into sharper contrast the distinction between the two parties and their matters of concern, but the four dimensions are present in transactions between any two people.

Aristotle's idea of self-sufficiency is related to his view of justice. Self-sufficiency is not autonomy. Indeed, as is noted above, it is the person standing outside of community that is suspect. Community is formed because of need (in the broadest sense, this would include for Aristotle the need for the pleasure of society). Because needs are different, community is formed by those who are unequal. "For no community comes into existence out of two doctors but rather out of a doctor and a farmer and, in general, out of those who are different and not equal. But these differences must be equalized," Aristotle writes.[39] People thus stay together through mutual exchange; they have to reciprocate good for good or there is no such exchange.[40] The nature of community thus leads people to consider what is in the interest of another, for the individual is not complete in himself but must have his own good to give to receive a good from another.

The summary above could be called Aristotle's ethic of self-sufficiency, and it is fundamentally communal in nature. It would find fault with individualism by arguing that a person's self-sufficiency is found within community. It would find fault with socialism by arguing that every member of community has some good to offer another, that is, to be capable of mutual exchange. As stated previously, Aristotle is opposed to indiscriminate public expenditure on behalf of the poor. Efforts to help the poor should give them the capacity to earn a living. A person thus contributes to the self-sufficient life of his city by having a view to the common good and by weighing his own claims in light of the good of others. Self-sufficiency and the common good thus go together rather than oppose one another.

It is no accident that money plays an integral role in Aristotle's discussion of justice. There must be reciprocal exchange between two parties, for "nothing prevents the work of one person from being superior to another."[41] The house-builder and the shoemaker, for example, make two vastly different products and cannot reasonably compensate each other by an exchange of their respective goods. Some common measure of need is required, and money fills this role.[42] The changing value of money itself also does not escape Aristotle's attention, although he does assume it to be more stable than commodities.[43] Implicit in his argument is a recognition that if the value of money itself changes, the terms reached in an earlier transaction are violated. Money is thus inherently tied to the concept of justice.

Aristotle discusses justice specifically in the context of regimes in the *Politics*. The three good regimes are kingship, aristocracy, and polity. All of these "look to the common advantage," although kingship and aristocracy are the only two "proficient with a view to virtue as a whole."[44] Corruptions of the three good regimes are tyranny, oligarchy, and democracy, respectively. These three deviations seek private interest, tyranny "for the advantage of the ruler," oligarchy "with a view to the advantage of the well off," and democracy "with a view to the advantage of those who are poor."[45] Most regimes are democratic or oligarchic due to the fundamental inequality present in most societies: the distinction between the people and the rich. Dividing lines between other social categories can be crossed, such as a warrior also being a farmer, but the poor cannot be rich, argues Aristotle.[46] Democracy and oligarchy are the corresponding forms of government for these two groups, and each regime has a "partial" view of justice, that is, the principal interest of its dominant constituency. What is esteemed in democracy is freedom and living as one wants. Oligarchy, by contrast, esteems wealth. The citizens of each regime are those who partake "in decision and office."[47]

Democracy and oligarchy can take different forms depending on the strength of the various societal elements that comprise them. The two regimes are stable to the extent that they incorporate aspects of the other. A democracy, for example, might fine the wealthy for not participating in the regime, while an oligarchy would not levy a fee on the free poor to do so.[48] Democracy, oligarchy, and tyranny are not defined by the number of people ruling but by the character of the regime. The distinction between democracy and oligarchy is not the many versus the few but between the poor and the rich, as noted above. Likewise, tyranny is not defined by the rule of one person, although this may customarily be the case. A regime is tyrannical

> if it rules in unchallenged fashion over persons who are all similar or better, and with a view to its own advantage and not that of the ruled. Hence it is rule over persons who are unwilling; for no free person would willingly tolerate this sort of rule.[49]

By contrast, political rule is rule over "free and equal persons" and is defined by ruling and being ruled in turn.[50]

Left to ever purer versions of themselves, both democracy and oligarchy tend toward tyranny. Regimes err in seeking to be ever more democratic or oligarchic, "tightening" the regime toward an extreme when it should be led toward the mean.[51] Democracy does so when the multitude overturns laws and institutions and rules with capricious, unrestrained power. When this happens, popular leaders play for the multitude the role a flatterer plays for the tyrant.[52] Laws and institutions also are discarded in oligarchy's path toward tyranny, as power is transferred or seized solely by force.[53]

Polity is the best possible answer to this fundamental divide between rich and poor. It is not based on virtue but integrates democratic and oligarchic elements for the common good, or justice. The "middling element" is the best building block for a polity because it is the mean between rich and poor. It finds common ground with rich and poor more easily, while rich and poor have greater difficulty bridging the chasm between themselves. The middle class is more capable of sharing the common duties of citizenship that promote justice. It is amenable to ruling and being ruled in turn, whereas the poor will not rule and the rich will not be ruled.[54] The institution of the middle class conditions a citizen to act virtuously toward other citizens, at least insofar as political life is concerned, for he tends to view others as equals and find commonality with them. Aristotle thus speaks of the value of the middle class in thoroughly modern terms but offers a better theoretical rationale for this institution than many of his modern successors.

Aristotle and Modern Political Thought

Aristotle fell well short of a modern view of equality, and the modern notion that equality inheres in human beings as human beings simply is a significant advance from the classical view. The difficulty with classical notions of equality partially can be resolved, however, by expanding the circle rather than cutting a new piece of philosophical cloth. Aristotle's placement of equality in the broader concept of justice and the practical application of justice in various political contexts arguably has no rival in political thought, ancient or modern.

Modernity's fundamental complaint with Aristotle and the classics is not that the deficiencies of classical thought, such as a limited view of equality, cannot be remedied or that classical thought is inapplicable. The brief overview above of the modern relevance of Aristotle's writings is evidence of their continued viability.

Modernity's fundamental complaint is that classical thought is grounded in a durable notion of community and human nature in community, that is, classical thought is grounded in the telos of nature. For the moderns, nature is not something that informs but becomes something to be left (Hobbes and Locke) or something that is lost (Rousseau). Whether it is left or lost and how it is left or lost thus become the corollary to Aristotle's four elements of justice. Aristotle's four elements of justice are integrative and aim for reciprocal equality and the common good. Whether nature is left or lost and how it is left or lost in modernity, however, become four points of departure from commonality, four avenues to what Aristotle would call partial views of justice. Order is esteemed in Machiavelli and Hobbes, property in Locke, reason in Kant, spirit in Hegel, production in Marx, and will in Nietzsche. Each of these thinkers speak to some aspect of justice but lack an integrating telos around which the whole of justice can be better approximated. And as Aristotle says, the whole of justice must be kept in view to see the whole of the city.

The classical sense of natural *right*, or what is right in light of human nature and man's nature in community, is different from modernity's view of natural *rights*. In Hobbes, modern thought shifts from nature and community to consent and the individual. Modern natural rights inhere in the individual person, however, and to the extent the nature of that person is durable, so will be his interest in justice. Modernity thus can discard the telos of nature much more easily than the justice of the common good, which continues to manifest itself in various forms of modern liberal thought, from Kant's categorical imperative to Rawls' original position. Aristotle has a view of justice that the moderns cannot escape but cannot reassemble.

Aristotle's telos of natural right does not have to be discarded to gain natural rights, however. The affinity between classical natural right and liberalism's natural rights is clear when they are viewed in the context of Aristotelian justice based on the premise that equal persons deserve equal things. Aristotle's telos of nature is discarded because of modernity's reevaluation of primary goods. Classical thought esteems the goods of the soul as primary; goods for the body and external goods are secondary and evaluated in light of the ultimate good of the soul.[55] There is an ordering in the soul of reason, spirit, and desire, not with reason as master but with reason guiding the other parts of the soul within limits for their good. When the integrated order of the soul breaks down, each part seeks alien pleasures.[56] In the *Republic*, Socrates illustrates the contortions of the soul with the contortions of political regimes, with the most deformed being tyranny. The pursuit of mastery, or tyranny, not only oppresses subjects but debases the tyrant. He is the most unfortunate of human beings for Socrates.[57] Aristotle does not discuss the tyrant's inward life so much as Socrates, but he does speak of the brutal nature of the tyrant's regime: he rules by suppressing anything that is good and strong in his domain.[58]

The pursuit of mastery thus debases the master, and this, in essence, is the classical indictment of modern political thought. Speaking of classical thinkers in general, Strauss writes, "Their implicit prophecy that the emancipation of technology, of the arts, from moral and political control would lead to disaster or to the dehumanization of man has not yet been refuted."[59] Modernity, in essence, elevates reason as master and unshackles the arts, or technology, from philosophy. Modern thinkers pursue discovery as an end in itself, leaving off the question of what new knowledge means for the ennoblement of humanity.

Modernity's milieu of mastery takes a strong and weak form. The strong form, as represented by Marx and Nietzsche, discards any notion of justice and morality as a construct of social power structures used for the benefit of those powers. The weak form of mastery, as represented by Kant and applied to contemporary democracy by Rawls, eschews force as legitimate in political affairs and affirms the inherent dignity of human beings. That dignity is derived from the capacity of human beings to make moral choices, however, and not from the choices they make. Man is an "unencumbered" agent, free from any obligations he does not choose for himself. "Freed from the sanctions of custom and tradition and inherited status, unbound by moral ties antecedent to choice, the liberal self is installed as sovereign, cast as the author of the only obligations that constrain," writes Sandel.[60]

To the extent that mastery advances, the ethic of self-sufficiency based on mutual exchange recedes. The strong form of mastery provides a pretext for tyrannies to treat their citizens as grist in the mill of vicious ideologies. The weak form of mastery results in a more neglected public square, generally unstained by political violence but also devoid of meaning that informs a sense of the common good.

Using classical philosophy to indict the tendency of modern political thought toward mastery should proceed with a recognition of classical philosophy's own shortcomings on the topic, especially in Aristotle's use of natural right as a justification for slavery. What is being argued here is not that Aristotle's view of natural right was complete or that the relationship between natural right and natural rights is always direct but that natural right provided a basis for beginning to understand the necessary elements for human flourishing in a political context. Consider the following sequence of Aristotelian premises: it is unnatural for equal persons to receive unequal things; free and equal persons are to be under political rule and not mastery; to be under political rule is to participate in decision and office, to rule and be ruled in turn. With these premises in mind, human nature in political community points toward durable requisites of citizenship, and natural rights are an effort to enunciate these. Rawls would steer clear of a concept like natural right but discusses basic liberties and primary goods with a related pretext: these are the things that extend the bounds of liberty based in part on historical tradition, or what the interminable trial of human nature before political tribunals has revealed about the enduring character of human nature and political tribunals.

Tocqueville

In the pantheon of modern thinkers, there is a classical witness. Tocqueville is doubly important for this argument because he not only brings classical instincts to bear on modernity but applies them in the American context in his great work, *Democracy in America.* Aristotle emphasizes the importance of equality in democracies, and Tocqueville sees equality as the "generative fact" of American democracy. Speaking of equality of conditions, he writes,

> Soon I recognized that this same fact extends its influence well beyond political mores and laws, and that it gains no less dominion over civil society than over government: it creates opinions, gives birth to sentiments, suggests usages, and modifies everything it does not produce.[61]

Tocqueville turns his eyes back to Europe and sees equality advancing in the Old World as well. He surveys the past seven centuries and concludes that every significant societal change has turned to equality's advantage. This onward advance of equality cannot be resisted but should be directed in the most favorable way. Glittering examples of excellence characteristic of aristocracy have been lost in the wake of democracy's advance, but a greater good for the mass of humanity has been realized.

Aristotle shows how tyranny can arise from both democracy and oligarchy. Aristocratic, or oligarchic, elements are negligible in the American society of Tocqueville's day. He sees the prospect of despotism in democracy, however, and bringing this danger to light is one of Tocqueville's central themes.

Equality, Political Freedom, and Centralization

Tocqueville makes an important distinction between equality and political freedom. Equality pertains to the political status of a person, not necessarily the quality of that status. Equality therefore can fortify or diminish personal liberty: fortify if conditions of equality empower personal and social advancement and diminish if such conditions are a pretext to eliminate distinctions of excellence. The benefits of equality are immediately and constantly felt, for self-regard is gratified by the evidence of equal station in many facets of daily life.

Political freedom, by contrast, involves all the civic labors that accompany self-government. It taxes body and mind with the charges not just of personal responsibility but personal responsibility in the context of community. It is the journey from self-interest to "self-interest well understood," Tocqueville's term for the placement of private interest in the context of the common good. The benefits of political freedom come with labor and are not as readily perceived as the benefits of equality.

For this reason, democratic citizens tend to prefer equality over freedom, but the pursuit of equality alone undermines their capacity for self-government. In the context of America's voracious desire for material well-being, a desire heightened by its middle-class composition, equality dulls the civic sense and intensifies a citizen's inward turn to his own small world of family and private interests. Citizens at once enjoy a sense of autonomy that they know is unrealistic. Their independence exposes their need, for in truth all are equally weak in a political sense, incapable of defending themselves due to their collective isolation. The need for social order persists, however, and is even more desired by a middle class that does not want to lose its private enjoyments. In a context of loosened social bonds, citizens find less security in their neighbors and more in their central government, most acutely in war but also in the normal maintenance of social order during times of peace. In the midst of a frantic pursuit of atomized private interests, the state is the "immense being" that rises above all, seems to have as its purpose the interests of all, and therefore accrues power over all by accession or seizure. The democratic citizen is thus one who will not tolerate a superior but may patiently endure the mastery of centralized power.[62]

There are two kinds of centralization that Tocqueville discusses: governmental centralization and administrative centralization. Governmental centralization is the capacity to address interests "common to all parts of the nation, such as the formation of general laws and the relations of the people with foreigners."[63] Administrative centralization pertains to centralized control of local interests that by nature vary depending on the locale.[64] In respect to these two forms of centralization, America was at opposite ends of the spectrum: it had almost no administrative centralization and a high degree of governmental centralization, more than any contemporary government in Europe.[65] Speaking of state governments in America, Tocqueville finds that they have almost no fetters on their scope of action. He writes,

> In America, the legislature of each state has before it no power capable of resisting it. Nothing can stop it on its way, neither privileges, nor local immunity, nor personal influence, not even the authority of reason, for it represents the majority that claims to be the unique organ of reason. It therefore has no other limits in its action than its own will.[66]

It is not, therefore, a lack of centralization that threatens state government but too much of it. "The social power, thus centralized, constantly changes hands because it is subordinate to popular power. Often it comes to lack wisdom and foresight because it can do everything," writes Tocqueville.[67] Tocqueville is echoing and offering additional theoretical support for Madison's earlier criticisms of state legislative majorities acting to the detriment of sound policy.

It is when governmental centralization is combined with administrative centralization that the danger of democratic despotism arises. This is because democracies naturally have a high degree of governmental centralization due to the power of majority opinion. If the power of majority opinion is actualized with the force of administrative control, personal liberty may be endangered. The kind of tyranny that emerges is dissimilar from the tyranny Aristotle had in mind. Ancient tyrannies such as Rome had nothing approaching the capacity of the modern state; much administrative control remained decentralized.[68] The kind of tyranny Tocqueville envisions is something new and only could be described by him rather than named. What he envisions, however, is a despotism of the administrative state: less harsh but more pervasive, less violent but less resistible. It extends its reach to manage ever larger sectors of social life while dulling the instinct for liberty among its citizens. Tocqueville describes it thus:

> Above these [citizens] an immense tutelary power is elevated, which alone takes charge of assuring their enjoyments and watching over their fate. It is absolute, detailed, regular, far-seeing, and mild. It would resemble paternal power if, like that, it had for its object to prepare men for manhood; but on the contrary, it seeks only to keep them fixed irrevocably in childhood … So it is that every day it renders the employment of free will less useful and more rare; it confines the action of the will in a smaller space and little by little steals the very use of it from each citizen. Equality has prepared men for all these things: it has disposed them to tolerate them and often even to regard them as a benefit.[69]

To the extent that equality has turned citizens toward private interests and away from the public square, it gradually reduces them to a state of unwitting servitude. The occasional election of public officials only preserves the illusion of sovereignty of the people, while in reality they have lost the capacity for self-government.[70]

Checks on Centralization

Democracy does not have to end in centralized despotism, however, and Tocqueville's purpose is to show how the errant tendencies of democratic government can be chastened. American democracy in particular has several features that protect the spirit of freedom. Township government is among the first of these. In European nations, political identity originated in the upper echelons of society. In America, by contrast, the township was the basic political building block, preceding the county, state, and national government.[71] America has a high degree of governmental centralization but almost no administrative centralization in large part due to the dominance of local government. "In America," Tocqueville writes, "you see written laws; you perceive their daily execution; everything moves around you and nowhere do you discover the motor. The hand that directs the social machine vanishes at each instance."[72] Tocqueville thinks that administrative decentralization has been carried too far in America, however. Some degree of administrative continuity can check erratic legislative behavior and the dominance of the majority.

Echoing one particular theme of decentralization in Aristotle, township government in America typically has many offices instead of just a few. Aristotle favors this because it facilitates ruling and being ruled in turn, precisely the reason that Tocqueville lauds township government. This explains in part why the courts in America play such an integral role in American democracy. Most public officials were elected, and elected officials typically only could be subject to the people or the courts for penalty. Between elections, the courts were the only means available to hold errant public officials accountable because there was no administrative hierarchy to which they were subject.

Rather than undermine national progress, decentralized township government is a principal strength of American democracy. In it is found the "spirit of freedom" that is lacking in Europe. Townships are to liberty what "primary schools are to science."[73] Because public administration occurs mainly at the local level, it is less regular and skillful but many times more powerful than in Europe. Decentralization facilitates rather than impedes works for the public good. It gives citizens a stake in and love for their country, consolidating social power through the "free concurrence of wills" rather than the dictates of tyranny.[74] It also promotes national stability by checking majority passion. Tocqueville writes, "Municipal bodies and the administrations of counties therefore form so many hidden shoals that delay or divide the flood of the popular will."[75]

Associations are a second bastion of political freedom. Aristocracies of old relied on the authority of nobles to ensure some degree of decentralization in governmental power. Nobles as a class had distinct interests from the monarchy, and each noble individually could speak for a larger sector of society due to feudal arrangements with his subjects. One great individual thus could advance a political purpose. In democracies where equality defines the social state, aristocratic means of checking central authority are not available. The association of many democratic citizens accomplishes the same purpose. Tocqueville discusses one example in particular: the temperance association in America. At first he wonders why these men are not content to simply drink water at home but then realizes that they are forming one great man from many to advance a social cause.[76] That such movements happen among citizens and do not proceed from the government is of great importance. Centralized advancement of social concerns tends to dictate and direct, while associations among citizens tend to educate and empower.[77]

Religion also is a support to American liberty. In contrast to Europe, where religion is seen as an impediment to freedom, the spirit of religion and the spirit of liberty work together in America.[78] "In Europe, Christianity has permitted itself to be intimately united with the powers of the earth. Today these powers are falling and it is almost buried under their debris," Tocqueville writes.[79] Religion is powerful in America because it is separated from government and not subject to political vicissitudes. It shapes culture and mores and thus has an influence that extends beyond political power.[80] Religion chastens the more harmful effects of equality: it tightens moral bonds that compensate for loosened social ties in the midst of equal conditions.[81] Religion restrains the destabilizing effects of America's headlong rush for material well-being, checking an inordinate desire for prosperity with moral conservatism.[82]

Commerce in general has negative and positive effects. Negatively, as discussed above, the pursuit of material well-being can lead citizens toward an insular focus on their own private affairs. Positively, material well-being enjoyed by the middle class gives them a stake in their country and a strong interest in order. In addition, and echoing a theme also present in Aristotle, commerce draws people into mutual exchange and thereby furthers the ends of society.[83] Finally, labor in America is defined by an unspecialized self-sufficiency that enlivens the soul. Tocqueville writes,

> In America, it sometimes happens that the same man plows his field, builds his dwelling, fashions his tools, makes his shoes, and weaves with his hands the coarse fabric that will cover him. This detracts from the perfection of industry, but serves powerfully to develop the intellect of the worker.[84]

Specialized industry, on the other hand, tends to undermine self-sufficiency and thereby dampen the spirit of liberty. Industrial specialization not only has a materializing effect on the worker but is a means by which a degraded form of aristocracy is introduced in democratic societies. As workers become more like cogs in a machine, focused on one aspect of the process of production, their intellect diminishes, while that of the captain of industry expands to ever broader circumferences. Anticipating Marx, Tocqueville writes,

> Master and worker here have nothing alike, and each day they differ more. They are joined only as two links at the extremes of a long chain. Each occupies a place that is made for him and that he cannot leave. The one is in a continual, strict, and necessary dependence on the other, and he seems born to obey as the latter is to command.[85]

The chasm of inequality in democracy is as real as in aristocracy but is not ameliorated by a sense of mutual obligation formerly present between noble and peasant. Captains of industry consume the usefulness of their workers and then entrust them to public charity.[86]

Finally, the centrality of marriage and the family in American life is a safeguard of liberty. Nowhere does Tocqueville find marriage more esteemed than in America.[87] The home is a place of order in America. The citizen is sustained by the joys of family life, and this sustenance moderates social and political behavior. The capacity for the common good in the home facilitates the ascertainment of common good in society. By contrast, the home in Europe is typically defined by turmoil. Its agitations inflame rather than moderate social and political disturbance.[88]

Integrating Aristotle and Tocqueville for Contemporary Analysis

Tocqueville's distinction between equality and political freedom adds theoretical depth and operational detail to Aristotle's premise that political rule is over free and equal persons and involves ruling and being ruled in turn. Equality alone cannot lead citizens to justice or the common good. It is a free, not just an equal, people that has the capacity for justice and the common good. Aristotle says that citizens must be educated toward the regime and that citizenship is defined by decision and participating in office. Tocqueville brings these two points together by saying that self-government is an inherently practical education. Citizens cultivate a spirit of liberty not by studying liberty but by practicing the civic disciplines of actual self-government.[89] Political freedom and centralization have an inverse relationship. Administrative centralization diminishes the capacity for justice or the common good by diminishing the capacity for self-government, by removing political life from the reach of its citizens.

Tocqueville's discussion of equality and political freedom lays bare a deficiency of political liberalism. Equality can lead people toward a tenuous isolation dominated by private interest. Equality can be atomizing and proceed apace as the capacity for self-government declines. In the life of the atomized citizen, the distant and faceless administrative state becomes more important than the neighbor next door. Political freedom necessarily involves placing private interest in the context of the common good, that is, it necessarily involves the citizen and his neighbor rather than just the citizen himself. The common good must involve more than just living as one wants. Justice in essence entails judgment about the things that nourish society on the one hand or diminish it on the other.

As with Aristotle, a theme of mastery is integral to Tocqueville's political thought. The implications of mastery have been discussed above for a despotism of the administrative state. When governmental centralization is combined with administrative centralization,

> it habituates men to make a complete and continual abstraction from their wills; to obey not once and on one point, but in everything and every day. It then not only subdues them by force, but it also captures them through their habits; it isolates them and afterwards fastens them one by one onto the common mass.[90]

Tocqueville also discusses mastery in the context of majority opinion in democracies. As long as a citizen moves within the confines of majority opinion, he enjoys the favor of society. If he ventures outside, he finds ostracism at every turn. The divided nature of European society afforded refuge for dissident thought, but the social power of the majority gives no quarter to contrary viewpoints in democracy. For this reason, Tocqueville concludes that there are no great writers in America. The Inquisition could not do as good a job as the tyranny of the democratic majority in restraining dissident opinion, and the effect on the citizen is just as degrading.[91]

Finally, the theme of mastery is present in the effects of American slavery. Slavery has degraded its captives not only to the point where they do not have a stake in their country but have no stake in themselves.[92] In classical thought, the mastery of the tyrant degraded both the tyrant and those subject to his rule. Socrates finds the tyrant to be the most miserable of human beings, required to sustain himself by sowing discord and terror in the heart of his subjects. The tyrant himself reaps the most bountiful harvest of his labors, however, with a soul darkened by faction and fear. In the American context, Tocqueville reiterates such themes by noting the fatal effects of slavery on the master. "So Christianity destroyed slavery only by asserting the rights of the slave; in our day one can attack it in the name of the master: on this point interest and morality are in accord," Tocqueville writes.[93] Slavery has weakened the mores of liberty in the South and suppressed economic development, Tocqueville finds. He sharply illustrates the disparity between the free and slave regions of the country by recounting his journey down the Ohio River. In the free territory of Ohio, on one bank of the river, work is esteemed and rewarded. In Kentucky, on the other side, labor is attached to the stigma of slavery. Slavery is less productive than free labor, and the master himself avoids work to avoid stigma. Ohio thus brims with social and economic activity while Kentucky is, for the most part, idle wilderness.[94]

The effects of mastery in each of these instances (the tyranny of the administrative state, the tyranny of the majority, and the tyranny of master over slave) have the same debilitating effects. In essence, force cannot sustain a society, a conclusion that supports Aristotle's distinction between mastery and the political rule of free and equal persons. Despotism in the presence of some other factor, such as religion, may appear to succeed, but despotism alone is not the basis for enduring progress. The Turk has been ruled despotically but still worked for a common purpose due to religious fervor. "Today religion is passing away; despotism alone remains to them: they fall," Tocqueville concludes.[95] Only in the uniting of their free wills do citizens find enduring political strength.[96]

A Socratic Diversion: Justice as the Advantage of the Strong

The first substantive definition advanced in the *Republic* for justice is "the advantage of the stronger."[97] Thrasymachus puts forward this view of justice, entering into the dialogue like a coiled beast, finally overcoming the restraining influence of his fellow interlocutors. Socrates says that he would have been speechless if he had not seen Thrasymachus coming, that is, seen Thrasymachus before he seized control of the argument. Socrates did see Thrasymachus coming, however, maintained his composure, and guided his hearers through an extended discussion of the types of human soul and their corresponding political regimes. Thrasymachus is eventually tamed and brought to see the corruption of the tyrant who rules under the banner of justice as the advantage of the stronger.

In seeing Thrasymachus coming, Socrates anticipates the approach of modernity. Thrasymachus' definition of justice is informed by a belief that there is no justice but only mastery. Nietzsche's abyss is not a modern problem but was present in Thrasymachus' understanding of justice and also present in Pilate's question to Jesus. For Nietzsche, morality is only a class construct designed to perpetuate the advantage of the strong. Tocqueville, building on Aristotle's distinction between natural and conventional justice, offers a more nuanced perspective that distinguishes between morality and honor. Morality is that general code that applies to people as human beings generally, whereas honor is a code formed by a more select group and may be used to perpetuate the domination of that group. European aristocracies, for example, advanced a concept of honor that esteemed the war-like virtues essential to their continued dominance in feudal society.

The distinction between natural and conventional justice, between morality and honor, applies to modernity itself. The "honor" of modernity sustains the mastery of reason, and like aristocrats of old, reason has done much for those in its service. Rational mastery of human nature and nature itself has come with a great price, however, as all mastery does. Scientific advancement has improved and destroyed the lives of many. The rational organization of the state has facilitated great social enterprises but has enervated a sense of what it means to be human. Technology facilitates access to and manipulation of a world of data but cannot determine value.

In the midst of modernity's milieu of mastery, however, enduring features of justice, or the common good, keep manifesting themselves. Human beings seek community for need and pleasure, and the same nature that leads them to community sustains them in that community as the prerequisites of justice are understood. Tocqueville spends much time on the dangers of equality because he wants to chasten democracy for its good. Among the many positive features of equality that he discusses, however, is that it allows people to see morality proper more clearly as constructs of honor are removed. Equality opens a vista to the common good but must be joined with political freedom, or the work of self-government, to realize justice.

To some extent, Thrasymachus speaks for each of Socrates' interlocutors, past and present, in challenging his pedantic and tiresome questioning, a questioning that always seems to overturn and never build up, a questioning that never leads to rest but only more labor. What holds Thrasymachus in the conversation? If Thrasymachus were to meet Socrates alone, it is doubtful he would do more than cast aspersions and be on his way. Certainly he would not endure the onslaught of Socrates' discourse on the right regime. What restrains Thrasymachus at first and sustains him in the dialogue is community, the presence of his companions in the dialogue, and so it is with every labor on behalf of justice.

An Aristotelian Reading of Rawls

Political liberalism can be seen as more dependent on Aristotelian concepts that it would care to admit, and elements of Rawls' "justice as fairness" can accompany Aristotle's justice as the common good in supporting an evaluation of public debt in light of considerations of justice.

Regarding proximity to Aristotle, Rawls relies on moral premises throughout *Justice as Fairness*, his restatement of *A Theory of Justice*. At the beginning of his argument, the distinction Rawls makes between "rational" and "reasonable" is a contemporary way to understand the classical distinction between partial views of justice that seek personal advantage and more complete views of justice that pursue personal interest with a view to the common good. Rawls states,

> [R]easonable persons are ready to propose, or to acknowledge when proposed by others, the principles needed to specify what can be seen by all as fair terms of cooperation. Reasonable persons also understand that they are to honor these principles, even at the expense of their own interests as circumstances may require, provided others likewise may be expected to honor them.[98]

The purely rational person, however, may see an opportunity for uncooperative advantage and take it. "Common sense views the reasonable but not, in general, the rational as a moral idea involving moral sensibility," Rawls writes.[99] The reasonable person in Rawls may be compared to the just person in Aristotle that takes only his share, and the rational person in Rawls may be like the unjust person that takes more than what is due him.

The basis for equality in Rawls is the two moral powers possessed by human beings: "the capacity for a sense of justice" and "the capacity for a conception of the good."[100] The conception of the person that Rawls is deriving is not based on "metaphysics or the philosophy of mind, or from psychology" but, rather, is "normative and political."[101]

> [T]he conception of the person is worked up from the way citizens are regarded in the public political culture of a democratic society, in its basic political texts (constitutions and declarations of human rights), and in the historical tradition of the interpretation of those texts,

writes Rawls.[102] Several comments are in order following this statement by Rawls. First, the great texts of classical philosophy certainly are part of the corpus to which Rawls is referring and have enduring relevance to contemporary political discourse. Second, terms like "culture" and "norms" are important ones for Rawls in deriving his concept of the person. Rawls does not mention the telos of nature, but what he is describing here approaches it: enduring characteristics of human beings in political community.

The veil of ignorance in the original position plays in part the role of virtue in Aristotle's development of justice. Behind the veil, people deliberating in the original position do not know who they will be in the society they are organizing and thus are relieved, to use Aristotelian terminology, of partial views of justice that obscure what is held in common as free and equal human beings. Justice, or virtue entire, accomplishes a similar feat for Aristotle. Virtue leads a citizen to consider his interests in light of the interests of others. It leads him to take only his share given particular circumstances.

The difficulty for Rawls is that the veil of ignorance is removed, bringing to the fore the pivotal question of whether the basic structure fashioned in the artificially just setting of the original position can endure the vicissitudes of actual politics. This is a question of great importance for several reasons. First, the basic structure that speaks to fundamental constitutional organization has the benefit of being fashioned in the original position but does not remain there; it must be regulated to ensure that the cumulative effect of just actions over time, such as those that result in the accumulation of wealth, do not undermine the background justice established by the original basic structure. In addition to the regulation of the basic structure, the fact that the basic structure only covers constitutional fundamentals poses a second critical challenge to the durability of justice as fairness. Ordinary legislation on the full range of political issues does not occur behind the veil in the original position but in the full light of self-interested day where citizens act on all the parochial elements of their identity. Public reason might restrain self-interested legislation but applies primarily to constitutional issues and less to matters of ordinary policy.[103]

Moreover, the distinction between constitutional and legislative issues is problematic in itself. Legislation may impinge on individual liberty just as much as the underlying constitutional structure and perhaps more so. The capacity for justice or the common good is just as necessary in a legislature as in a constitutional convention. Furthermore, courts are no guarantee that liberties will be preserved, or remain non-negotiable, to use Rawls' language. Indeed, that certain rights are non-negotiable is why Rawls prefers justice as fairness to the political principle of utility that has no fixed points of value but leaves all political questions open to reevaluation in light of evolving political circumstances.[104] And that Rawls does defend certain values or liberties as non-negotiable is an indication that justice as fairness is a comprehensive doctrine in itself.

Finally, in concluding *Justice as Fairness*, Rawls argues that his framework leads to a "moral psychology" where reasonable and rational persons are able to forego self-interest (to the extent that "reasonable" implies), cooperate fairly, and build trust that reinforces such behavior.[105] But what is moral psychology other than the trust-building behavior of virtue? Virtue by any other name still results in sustainable relationships built on a sense of the common good.

Moral themes therefore undergird the general framework of justice as fairness, and Rawls also endorses specific moral judgments, perhaps most emphatically when he references Lincoln's contention that nothing is wrong if slavery is not wrong.[106] Lincoln's view of justice was informed by more than just equality, however. His desire to preserve the principle of equality as the "sheet anchor"[107] of republicanism was driven by a more fundamental concern with what ennobles man as man. He was committed to the Union but wanted to make the Union worthy of saving. The Civil War thus was not only a contest over slavery, per se, or just between two regions of the country, but for the fate of self-government itself. This was the thesis of the Gettysburg Address: "testing whether … any nation so conceived and so dedicated, can long endure."[108] Lincoln grasped what Tocqueville before him and Martin Luther King did after: that racial injustice is not only cruel for the oppressed but corrupts the oppressor. He was a practical politician and would have been content with stopping slavery's spread. War came because the South would not abide that restriction. Lincoln's comment that the country would become wholly slave or wholly free was an empirical overstatement but a theoretical truth: the country would wholly lose or wholly preserve an understanding of human liberty. For all his brilliance and political skill, Douglas' failure as a statesman was essentially a miscarriage of justice. He temporized procedurally with enduring demands of human liberty. As Jaffa eloquently chronicles, Douglas obscured politically the character of the choice confronting the nation over slavery. He would have maintained through popular sovereignty (the nineteenth-century version of the procedural republic) the trappings of justice without its essence, the letter of the law without its spirit. The essence of sovereignty in Lincoln's mind was not based on a popular vote, however, but on the contention that all men are created equal and that unalienable rights come with unalienable encumbrances of self-government, that liberty does not sustain itself but must be chosen and defended, and that the choice and the defense at once reveals and strengthens what is noble and good in humanity.

The American Civil War and other epic chapters in western civilization inform the values that political liberalism seems at times to take for granted. Justice as fairness is thus not a "freestanding" political concept but is sustained by a set of hard-won principles that undergird free government. Seeking to place a patina of proceduralism on a set of enduring and costly value judgments in the past obscures judgments that must be made to preserve self-government in the present. Such judgments certainly pertain to public debt and with themes akin to those that informed Lincoln, for debt can be a type of bondage and a way, to paraphrase Lincoln, for one generation to wring its bread from the sweat of another's brow.

Rawls is thus close to Aristotle in many ways but lacks Aristotle's consistency through a frank acknowledgment of justice's relationship with virtue. The distinction Rawls makes between democratic society and community underscores the contemporary dilemma of having a public conception of justice severed from private considerations of virtue. Aristotle's recognition of different degrees of unity is a better way to express the distinction Rawls wants to make, however. A human being is the highest expression of unity. A family (one example of community) is less unified, obviously, but more unified than a city. Seeking to make the city into a family is to make the city something other than a city. Socrates' proposal to this effect in the *Republic* is errant in that it seeks to impose excessive unity on a broader political setting that is by its nature more diverse.[109] Varying degrees of unity do not transmute justice into something different depending on context, however. The wellspring of virtue in an individual life may take the course of a thousand tributaries flowing through the varied terrain of social context, but the tributaries are still dependent on the source. Aristotelian justice or the common good or virtue entire is flexible enough to account for different contexts and be at work in all of them.

Furthermore, it is not virtue that results in an oppressive comprehensive doctrine but the lack of it. As mentioned above, Aristotle makes an explicit distinction between mastery and political rule and discerns that mastery by nature degrades those human beings that enforce it or are subject to it. Political rule is over free and equal persons (phrasing, incidentally, that Rawls uses as well) and is defined by ruling and being ruled in turn, a theme that informs Rawls' second principle of justice.[110] Political rule recognizes there are different claimants on the regime, and the whole of justice keeps these claims in view. Justice or the common good or virtue entire seeks to incorporate the claims of the lesser parties to ensure political stability, precisely what Rawls is trying to do indirectly through the veil of ignorance and directly through the difference principle. Rawls thus is not breaking entirely new ground with justice as fairness but crossing back and forth across a path already charted by Aristotle that more explicitly acknowledges enduring human characteristics in community and thereby arrives more directly at its destination of justice as the common good.

Aside from this general comparison of Aristotle and Rawls, there are several additional points in Rawls' argument worth mentioning in regard to public debt. First, generational concerns must be an integral consideration of just constitutional government, Rawls argues, and he deals with such concerns in a more theoretically coherent way than Aristotle and Tocqueville. Both Tocqueville and Rawls discuss how generational financial arrangements can impinge on liberty. Tocqueville sees in the division of physical property in family estates a feature of democracy that tends to weaken generational bonds forged around enduring and particular social settings.[111] Political freedom is thereby undermined to the extent that a sense of community is enervated. Rawls likewise uses estates as an example but makes a more explicit and nuanced theoretical case that finances can undermine just political arrangements. As mentioned above, wealth accumulation over time is an instance of incrementally just steps that end in a condition of such unequal means that background justice is compromised.[112] Incidentally, Rawls' line of reasoning here can be applied easily to the issue of public debt, albeit in an opposite direction: debt is the disinheritance of the young at the hands of the old, of succeeding by former generations.

There is also a sense in Rawls that centralization is antipathetic to political liberalism. He distinguishes between a constitutional and a procedural democracy, with the former having limits defined to protect certain liberties and the latter capable of doing anything supported by a majority (this distinction may qualify but does not necessarily invalidate Sandel's general description of Rawlsian liberalism as a "procedural republic"). Should the distinction matter for a democratic people? Rawls concludes that it should and argues that a constitutional form of democracy affords more opportunity for deliberation on the character of human liberty in political society. Rawls writes,

> It would seem, then, that the political sociology of a constitutional regime will differ from that of a procedural democracy. The conceptions of person and society are more fully articulated in the public charter of the

> constitution and more clearly connected with the basic rights and liberties it guarantees. Citizens acquire an understanding of the public political culture and its traditions of interpreting basic constitutional values.[113]

A constitutional democracy thus has educative value that helps its citizens understand their role in preserving the liberties they enjoy, a theme that shares an affinity with Aristotle's notion of self-sufficiency and Tocqueville's idea of political freedom.

Conclusion

From Aristotle's treatises on ethics and politics in antiquity to Tocqueville's measured protest against modernity, the theme of justice, or the common good, is one of the most enduring and foundational to sustainable human relationships. Justice arises in community, and the whole of justice must be kept in view for a society to be well-ordered, Aristotle argues. Partial views of justice undermine community by skewing for personal advantage the balance of obligations to and benefits from society. Political issues turn in some form or fashion on these central questions of justice, and public indebtedness is one of these.

Injustice is defined by an incapacity for community. Aristotle's four dimensions of justice (the two parties and the two interests) are warped with a view to private gain at the expense of others, or what Aristotle would call seeking more than one's share. Public debt can be seen in this light and certainly has been seen in this light by American leaders of a more classical persuasion. Among the Founders, Thomas Jefferson was one of the most ardent foes of public indebtedness (even though his zeal against debt did not seem to extend to his private affairs). He specifically was concerned with the generational hazards of public debt, of those now living taking credit that others would have to pay later. This was "swindling futurity," in Jefferson's words.[114] More generally, public debt could be a means to actively corrode the bonds of community, to use government to recreate a hostile state of nature rather than leave it. In discussing government's departure from sound principles, Jefferson writes,

> Then begins, indeed, the *bellum omnium in omnia* [the war of all against all], which some philosophers observing to be so general in the world, have mistaken it for the natural, instead of the abusive state of man. And the fore horse of this frightful team is public debt. Taxation follows that, and in its train wretchedness and oppression.[115]

Democracies have features that incline them toward partial views of justice that undermine the common good. Equality can be empowering or it can be isolating. To the extent that it turns citizens inordinately toward their private affairs and away from the exertions of self-government, equality may direct democracy toward the soft tyranny of the administrative state. Added to this is the character of democratic society that is constantly in flux. Tocqueville writes,

> In democratic centuries, on the contrary, when the duties of each individual toward the species are much clearer, devotion toward one man becomes rarer: the bond of human affections is extended and loosened. In democratic peoples, new families constantly issue from nothing, others constantly fall into it, and all those who stay on change face; the fabric of time is torn at every moment and the trace of generations is effaced. You easily forget those who have preceded you, and you have no idea of those who will follow you. Only those nearest have interest.[116]

In essence, the rapid pace of social change in democracy may give it an inherent bias toward dismissing the generational aspect of the common good, of discounting the future effect of current policies.

These empirical tendencies of democracy that tend to enervate community are reinforced by the milieu of mastery in modern political thought. Justice can be declared an illusion, as the strong form of mastery represented by Marx and Nietzsche does, or justice can be given only public connotations of equality and severed from private notions of virtue, as in the weak form of mastery represented by Kant and Rawls. Both outcomes of diminished justice weaken the impetus for and lessen the rewards of self-government. Both outcomes also influence the scope, tenor, and purposes of the modern administrative state and bear on the issue of public debt. For Aristotle, by contrast, justice is virtue entire because it is virtue practiced in relation to another human being. The *Ethics* precedes the *Politics* for a reason: the application of justice in the life of the individual person provides the basis for understanding the organization of political life. Lincoln had a view of justice that integrated private and public concerns, and the question of ennoblement that he squarely addressed is perennial, applying with equal force to changing political contexts.

Empirical democracy and contemporary political thought on democracy can be chastened for their own benefit, however. As to the actual functioning of democracy, justice is possible to the extent that social mores and governmental institutions can direct self-interest toward the common good, what Tocqueville called self-interest well-understood. Some of those mores and institutions include decentralized government, religion, associations of private citizens, the positive effects of commerce, and the well-being of the family. Statistical modeling in Chapter 4 will seek to incorporate aspects of these to assess their effect on public debt. With regard to modern political thought, the strong form of mastery stands resolutely at odds with any existential validation of justice as a normative guide to politics. The soft form of mastery as exemplified by Rawlsian liberalism draws nourishment from classical sources, however, and delineating this philosophical affinity can bring forward a more substantive and consistent view of justice even as modernity's superior grasp of human equality is highlighted. Aristotle has a firmer grasp of justice than Rawls; Rawls has a firmer grasp of equality than Aristotle. Western civilization has advanced through trials such as the American Civil War to the extent that both perspectives have been allowed to speak to each other, and America was fortunate to have a leader in Lincoln who listened to both.

Justice manifests itself in the sustainable relationships of community that ennoble human beings. By contrast, faction follows in the train of injustice. If public debt has become a way for earlier generations to defraud those that follow, for the older to defraud the younger, it should be more pronounced in jurisdictions with greater communal discord, with less of a sense of the common good. To reiterate Jefferson's refrain, the common good has a distinctly generational aspect: it is not just between extant citizens but between the older and the younger, between the living and those yet to be born that the common good must be found concerning questions of public debt. This is particularly true in a country that holds unalienable rights as a birthright of freedom. The birthright of freedom is not the same, however, for generations that inherit the fiscal excesses of their forebears. In Aristotle's words, equal persons are not receiving equal things. Someone has claimed more than their share.

Notes

1 John Rawls, *Justice as Fairness: A Restatement*, ed. Erin Kelly (Cambridge, MA: Belknap Press, 2001), 18–19.
2 Richard Kraut, "Aristotle and Rawls on the Common Good," in *The Cambridge Companion to Aristotle's Politics*, ed. Marguerite Deslauriers and Pierre Destreé (New York: Cambridge University Press, 2012), 356–357.
3 Michael J. Sandel, *Democracy's Discontent: America in Search of a Public Philosophy* (Cambridge, MA: Belknap Press, 1996), 4.
4 Niccolo Machiavelli, *The Prince*, trans. Harvey C. Mansfield (Chicago: University of Chicago Press, 1998), 61.
5 Niccolo Machiavelli, *Discourses on Livy*, trans. Harvey C. Mansfield and Nathan Tarcov (Chicago: University of Chicago Press, 1996), 129–130.
6 Aristotle, *Politics*, trans. Carnes Lord (Chicago: University of Chicago Press, 2013), 1283a25.
7 Ibid., 1323a15–1324a4.
8 Ibid., 1284a20.
9 Ibid., 1284a20–1284b3.
10 Ibid., 1287a26.
11 Ibid., 1281b1–8.
12 Ibid., 1287b8.
13 Ibid., 1296a9.
14 Ibid., 1295b1–25.
15 Ibid., 1301b26–29.
16 Ibid., 1317b3–17.
17 Ibid., 1281b1–9.
18 Aristotle, *Nicomachean Ethics*, trans. Robert C. Bartlett and Susan D. Collins (Chicago: University of Chicago Press, 2011), 1134b18–22.
19 Ibid., 1308a4–24.
20 Ibid., 1309a34–1309b14.
21 Ibid., 1320a29–1320b17.
22 Ibid., 1309b19–34.
23 Ibid., 1317a10–39.
24 Ibid., 1320a12–16.
25 Ibid., 1320b4–7.
26 Ibid., 1269a9–28.
27 Ibid., 1312b39–1313a17.

28 Ibid., 1313b1–3.
29 Ibid., 1275a23–24.
30 Ibid., 1310a13–15, 1296b14–17.
31 Ibid., 1262b37–1263a40.
32 Ibid., 1280a26–31.
33 Ibid., 1280a31–1280b34.
34 Ibid., 1253a1–8.
35 Ibid., 1282b17–22.
36 Aristotle, *Ethics*, 1134a2–7.
37 Ibid., 1131a18–21.
38 Ibid., 1132b30–31.
39 Ibid., 1133a17–19.
40 Ibid., 1132b35–1133a2.
41 Ibid., 1133a12.
42 Ibid., 1133a20.
43 Ibid., 1133b13–14.
44 Aristotle, *Politics*, 1279a18, 1279b1.
45 Ibid., 1279b6–10.
46 Ibid., 1291b2–12.
47 Ibid., 1275a23.
48 Ibid., 1297a15–1297b1.
49 Ibid., 1295a20–23.
50 Ibid., 1255b19.
51 Ibid., 1309b19–34.
52 Ibid., 1292a23.
53 Ibid., 1292b5–10.
54 Ibid., 1295a35–1296b13.
55 Aristotle, *Ethics*, 1098b12–20.
56 Plato, *The Republic*, trans. Allan Bloom (New York: Basic Books, 1968), 586d–587a.
57 Ibid., 578b–c.
58 Aristotle, *Politics*, 1313a35–1313b33.
59 Leo Strauss, "What is Political Philosophy?" *Journal of Politics* Vol. 19 No. 3 (August 1957): 366.
60 Sandel, *Democracy's Discontent*, 12.
61 Alexis de Tocqueville, *Democracy in America*, trans. Harvey C. Mansfield and Delba Winthrop (Chicago: University of Chicago Press, 2000), 3.
62 Ibid., 644.
63 Ibid., 82.
64 Ibid.
65 Ibid., 84.
66 Ibid.
67 Ibid., 85.
68 Ibid., 662.
69 Ibid., 663.
70 Ibid., 664–665.
71 Ibid., 40.
72 Ibid., 67.
73 Ibid., 57.
74 Ibid., 87–89.
75 Ibid., 250.
76 Ibid., 492.
77 Ibid., 491–492.
78 Ibid., 43.
79 Ibid., 288.

80 Ibid., 279.
81 Ibid., 282.
82 Ibid., 279–280.
83 Ibid., 369–370.
84 Ibid., 387.
85 Ibid., 531.
86 Ibid., 532.
87 Ibid., 279.
88 Ibid.
89 Ibid., 291.
90 Ibid., 83.
91 Ibid., 245.
92 Ibid., 304.
93 Ibid., 334.
94 Ibid., 332.
95 Ibid., 89.
96 Ibid.
97 Plato, *Republic*, 338c.
98 Rawls, *Justice as Fairness*, 7.
99 Ibid.
100 Ibid., 18–19.
101 Ibid., 19.
102 Ibid.
103 Ibid., 91.
104 Ibid., 115–117.
105 Ibid., 196.
106 Ibid., 29.
107 Harry V. Jaffa, *Crisis of the House Divided: An Interpretation of the Issues in the Lincoln-Douglas Debates* (Seattle: University of Washington Press, 1973), 348.
108 Abraham Lincoln, "Gettysburg Address," The Avalon Project, Yale Law School. Accessed November 7, 2016 at http://avalon.law.yale.edu/19th_century/gettyb.asp.
109 Aristotle, *Politics*, 1261a10–1262a25.
110 Ibid., 42.
111 Tocqueville, *Democracy in America*, 46–53.
112 Rawls, *Justice as Fairness*, 52–53.
113 Ibid., 146.
114 Thomas Jefferson, Letter to John Taylor, May 28, 1816, in *The Writings of Thomas Jefferson*, Library Edition, Volume 15, ed. Andrew A. Lipscomb (Washington, D.C.: Thomas Jefferson Memorial Association, 1903), 23.
115 Thomas Jefferson, Letter to Samuel Kercheval, July 12, 1816, in *The Writings of Thomas Jefferson*, Library Edition, Volume 15, ed. Andrew A. Lipscomb (Washington, D.C.: Thomas Jefferson Memorial Association, 1903), 40.
116 Tocqueville, *Democracy in America*, 483.

Bibliography

Aristotle. *Nicomachean Ethics*. Translated by Robert C. Bartlett and Susan D. Collins. Chicago: University of Chicago Press, 2011.

Aristotle. *Politics*. Translated by Carnes Lord. Chicago: University of Chicago Press, 2013.

De Tocqueville, Alexis. *Democracy in America*. Translated by Harvey C. Mansfield and Delba Winthrop. Chicago: University of Chicago Press, 2000.

Jaffa, Harry V. *Crisis of the House Divided: An Interpretation of the Issues in the Lincoln-Douglas Debates*. Seattle: University of Washington Press, 1973.

Jefferson, Thomas. Letter to John Taylor, May 28, 1816. In *The Writings of Thomas Jefferson*, Library Edition, Volume 15, edited by Andrew A. Lipscomb, 17–23. Washington, D.C.: Thomas Jefferson Memorial Association, 1903.

Jefferson, Thomas. Letter to Samuel Kercheval, July 12, 1816. In *The Writings of Thomas Jefferson*, Library Edition, Volume 15, edited by Andrew A. Lipscomb, 32–44. Washington, D.C.: Thomas Jefferson Memorial Association, 1903.

Kraut, Richard. "Aristotle and Rawls on the Common Good." In *The Cambridge Companion to Aristotle's Politics*, edited by Marguerite Deslauriers and Pierre Destreé, 350–374. New York: Cambridge University Press, 2012.

Lincoln, Abraham. "Gettysburg Address." The Avalon Project, Yale Law School. Accessed November 7, 2016 at http://avalon.law.yale.edu/19th_century/gettyb.asp.

Machiavelli, Niccolo. *Discourses on Livy*. Translated by Harvey C. Mansfield and Nathan Tarcov. Chicago: University of Chicago Press, 1996.

Machiavelli, Niccolo, *The Prince*. Translated by Harvey C. Mansfield. Chicago: University of Chicago Press, 1998.

Plato. *The Republic*. Translated by Allan Bloom. New York: Basic Books, 1968.

Rawls, John. *Justice as Fairness: A Restatement*. Edited by Erin Kelly. Cambridge, MA: Belknap Press, 2001.

Sandel, Michael J. *Democracy's Discontent: America in Search of a Public Philosophy*. Cambridge, MA: Belknap Press, 1996.

Strauss, Leo. "What is Political Philosophy?" *Journal of Politics* Vol. 19 No. 3 (August 1957): 343–368.

3 Of Keynes, Crisis, and Credit

An Overview of American Fiscal Trends in the Twentieth Century

> What belongs in common to the most people is accorded the least care: they take thought for their own things above all, and less about things common, or only so much as falls to each individually.
>
> —Aristotle, *Politics*

William Breit begins his discussion of the balanced-budget norm in American fiscal history by referencing primitive superstitions that had practical benefit, but for reasons other than those supposed. One example in particular is the burning of an animal skeleton and using the remains as a magical guide for the next day's hunt. Of course, magic had nothing to do with the success or failure of the next day's hunt, but burning the remains randomized as well as any modern statistical computation the areas hunted and thus helped balance the demand for and supply of food.

Likewise, Breit describes the norm of budget balance that prevailed in American fiscal affairs from the Founding to the New Deal as a helpful "mythology." The real benefit of budget balance was to limit the size of government, for "the size of the state in a democracy is inextricably linked to the possibility of deficit financing."[1] Balanced budgets were part of the Constitution, not in the written text but as what Aristotle and Machiavelli would call a custom or Amar would later describe as part of America's "unwritten constitution."[2] Other unwritten norms to which Breit compares budget balance are political parties, judicial review, and a president's cabinet.[3]

But is the norm of budget balance a mythology? And why is an expansive state (what Breit refers to in Hobbesian terms as "Leviathan") dangerous? Why is state expansion dependent on deficits and not simply on increasing revenues and expenditures in tandem? Breit spends most of his time reviewing the norm of budget balance and its early challengers and does not answer these questions. He is concerned with deficits and with an expansive state, but his description of budget balance as mythology removes from him the very ground on which to restrain fiscal tendencies he views as threatening. Indeed, describing the norm of budget balance in this way is more akin to the general tendency of economic thought after the 1930s: that the principles governing public and private debt are different and that public debt should be a fiscal tool in the hands of government to achieve socially desirable goals, namely satisfactory levels of employment.

If justice has to do with the assessment of value, and Aristotle has shown that it does (the ascertainment of the common good between different parties with distinct interests), then government finance and its attendant norms are not mythical, if justice itself is more than myth. Government deficits that lead to unsustainable government debt impinge on justiciable (not necessarily in court but in general terms) valuation in two principal ways: by undermining the government's ability to pay its creditors and by transferring costs incurred by former and present generations to future taxpayers whose interest is not considered in the initial transaction. Debt, whether public or private, involves valuation and the obligation of both parties to fulfill their commitments related to that determined value.

Breit does not intend to deal with the implications of his description of budget balance as myth, but one of his interlocutors at the same conference carries Breit's description to its logical conclusion. Armen Alchian sees in government the equivalent of the Mafioso. Watching a political convention is like "watching gangsters selecting their leader who will then extort and steal your wealth."[4] Government fiscal responsibility is as mythical as corporate social responsibility. What defines a government is the control and use of force. Alchian adds his voice to the modern chorus of Thrasymachus: justice is the advantage of the strong. The Mafioso of Sicily perform governmental functions similar to the government of the United States. Moral philosophers may indulge in romantic notions of social contract, but the hard science of economics should study the acquisition and use of power.

Alchian's cynicism causes him to miss some fairly obvious features of American democracy, perhaps the first of which, given his view of political conventions, is that affiliations with organized crime usually are a disqualifier for public office. More generally, that there is a difference between the Mafioso and the American government illustrates the difference between mastery and political rule. The Mafioso would not be concerned with a balanced budget, Alchian argues, and such matters should not occupy the time of scholars. The Mafioso need not be concerned with a balanced budget or any other sense of obligation arising from justice because their regime is based on force. For regimes not so organized, however, for those based on political rule over free and equal persons, there must be a sense of the common good, or justice. Budget balance need not concern tyrants, but it must concern any society that believes justice to be more than the advantage of the strong.

Alchian is a useful foil because of the extremity of his views. The economists of the twentieth century most responsible for theoretically undermining the norm of budget balance certainly do not compare free government to the Mafioso. Indeed, they would use government deficits to sustain democracy with social goods only government can procure.[5] To the extent that such theory and its practical application undermine sustainable budgeting, however, these economists have an empirical affinity with Alchian and the chorus of Thrasymachus.

Their theory achieves in practice what it does not espouse in intent: the movement of a governing regime away from political rule of free and equal persons and toward the mastery of a government that transfers an unjust debt burden to future generations.

Review of Debt and Revenue for Local, State, and National Government

Before considering the main theoretical strands of thought on government deficits and debt, it would be helpful to review fiscal trends over the time period of this book. For purposes of accurate comparison, all numbers below are in real 2010 dollars, and, unless otherwise noted, all figures and tables are derived from the author's statistical analysis. As discussed in the next chapter, data is not always available for each variable precisely at decennial years. When this occurs, the data point closest to the decennial year is used. For example, the 1913 Census report *Wealth, Debt, and Taxation* provides a standardized, comprehensive review of local, state, and federal finances closest to 1910 and is used to fill many of the data points for that decennial measurement.

Table 3.1 shows local, state, and federal debt levels in billions of dollars from 1870 to 1990. In 1910, local debt ($84.7 billion) was over twice as large as state and federal debt combined ($37.2 billion). Local debt grew significantly over the course of the century, rising by 1,067 percent to just under $1 trillion by 1990. States held $9.3 billion in debt in 1910, or roughly a tenth of the local total, but experienced a more dramatic increase in subsequent decades. State indebtedness rose to $605.7 billion by 1990, an increase of over 6,400 percent. Federal indebtedness experienced the most dramatic rise during this time period, rising from

Table 3.1 Local,* State, and Federal Debt, 1870–1990 (Billions of 2010 Dollars)

Year	*Local Debt*	*State Debt*	*Federal Debt*
1870		6.1	42.8
1880		6.9	47.9
1890		6.3	37.7
1900		6.9	56.0
1910	84.7	9.3	27.9
1920		12.7	250.0
1930	217.8	37.9	254.4
1940	250.3	55.0	668.8
1950		47.9	2,332.6
1960	433.0	160.6	2,110.6
1970	669.9	299.5	2,082.8
1980	662.0	389.0	2,419.8
1990	988.6	605.7	5,451.5

Source: Author's analysis of U.S. Census data.

Note

* Census data is not available on local debt in 1920 and 1950.

$27.9 billion in 1910 to $5.45 trillion in 1990, an increase of almost 20,000 percent. Overall, local, state, and federal debt grew from $121.9 billion in 1910 to $7.05 trillion in 1990, an increase of almost 5,700 percent.

Revenue figures for the three levels of government (Table 3.2) follow similar trends. Local revenue in 1910 of $30.5 billion roughly matched state and federal revenue combined. This rough proportion held true through 1930 but changed markedly during the Depression, with state and federal revenue growing to $192.1 billion by 1940 compared to $80.3 billion at the local level. Between 1910 and 1990, local revenue rose to $719.6 billion (an increase of 2,259 percent), but state and federal revenue increased much more rapidly, from $8 to $941.2 billion (11,665 percent) and $22.5 billion to $1.92 trillion (8,443 percent), respectively. Overall local, state, and federal revenue grew from $61 billion in 1910 to $3.58 trillion in 1990, an increase of 5,774 percent.

Local debt and revenue figures indicate the relative importance of local government at the beginning of the century, and fiscal trends in local, state, and federal government illustrate the decline of local government as the principal forum for democratic government in the U.S. Another observation that can be made from Table 3.1 is the greater responsiveness (or, alternatively, constraints) of local government when faced with economic hardship, both in terms of debt and revenue. Between 1930 and 1940, a decade dominated by economic depression, local government debt increased 14.9 percent, from $217.8 to $250.3 billion. State government debt increased during this decade by 45 percent, from $37.9 to $55 billion. Finally, federal debt increased most dramatically, by 162.9 percent, from $254.4 to $668.8 billion. A similar pattern is seen in revenue levels. Local revenue increased by 2.9 percent between 1930 and 1940, from $78 to $80.3 billion. State revenue increased by 224 percent during the same time period, from $25.6 to $83.1 billion. Federal revenue increased from $34.4 to $109 billion, or 216.9 percent. Although not as pronounced as during the Depression, local government responsiveness is apparent on a few data points during

Table 3.2 Local,* State, and Federal Revenue, 1910–1990 (Billions of 2010 Dollars)

Year	*Local Revenue*	*State Revenue*	*Federal Revenue*
1910	30.5	8.0	22.5
1920			46.4
1930	78.0	25.6	34.4
1940	80.3	83.1	109.0
1950	137.5	136.8	394.5
1960	230.0	220.1	735.6
1970	417.5	469.2	1,154.3
1980	522.6	683.3	1,491.9
1990	719.6	941.2	1,922.3

Source: Author's analysis of U.S. Census data.

Note

* Census data is not available on local revenue in 1920.

the economically difficult decade of the 1970s. Local debt actually declines during this decade by 1.2 percent while state and federal debt increase by 29.9 and 16.2 percent, respectively. Local revenue increases 25.2 percent but less than state revenue (45.6 percent) or federal revenue (29.2 percent). In terms of revenue, the states expanded over the course of the century more rapidly than the federal government (in percentage terms), belying the notion that the states have been indolent in the face of federal assertiveness. The federal government distinguishes itself most readily in terms of debt growth. As mentioned above, federal debt grew by 20,000 percent from 1910 to 1990, compared to a 1,067 percent increase in local debt and a 6,400 percent increase in state indebtedness.

The 1930s and 1940s are interesting decades in which to compare state and federal levels of government. State debt rises in the 1930s but falls during the 1940s, while federal debt rises significantly in both decades. State revenue rises as quickly in the 1930s as federal revenue (in percentage terms) but not nearly as fast in the 1940s. As will be illustrated in Figure 3.5 below, these numbers give insight into the types of crises that lead to governmental centralization and which level of government gains fiscal share relative to the others depending on the type of crisis.

If the analysis of federal debt begins at 1950, it appears that the federal government made slight progress toward budget balance through 1970, reducing the federal debt from $2.33 trillion to $2.08 trillion in that time period. Obviously, this is not the view that economists concerned with the national debt take when reviewing postwar fiscal trends. Federal debt was inordinately high after World War II (WWII), and that it was not reduced further in subsequent decades represents a significant break from historical practice of peacetime reduction of debts incurred in war.

The aggregate debt and revenue numbers discussed above are presented in Tables 3.3 and 3.4 in per capita amounts. Again, all amounts are in real 2010 dollars. Figures 3.1 and 3.2 provide a visual illustration of the data in Table 3.1. Because federal debt rises to such high levels by 1990, Figure 3.1 shows only state and local debt for trends in these series to be seen more clearly. Figure 3.2 then adds federal debt numbers for all three (local, state, and federal) to be seen in comparison.

Figure 3.3 provides a graphical representation of data in Table 3.2 and does so in a way to underscore two principal observations: the growth of government at all levels and the growing centralization of government at the state and federal levels relative to local. Total revenue at the local, state, and federal level grew from $61 billion in 1910 to $3.58 trillion in 1990, an increase of over 5,700 percent. Within those levels of government, local revenue's share of the total declined from 50 to 20 percent.

Figure 3.4 shows how formative the Depression and WWII were for setting fiscal trends at the local, state, and national level for the latter half of the twentieth century. As might be expected, local government lost revenue share relative to the federal government in the 1930s as national councils were better able to respond to national economic crisis. What may not be as intuitive, however, is

Table 3.3 Local,* State, and Federal Debt Per Capita, 1870–1990 (Billions of 2010 Dollars)

Year	*Local Debt*	*State Debt*	*Federal Debt*
1870		160	1,122
1880		140	970
1890		101	608
1900		92	751
1910	924	102	305
1920		120	2,374
1930	1,781	310	2,080
1940	1,910	420	5,105
1950		320	15,561
1960	2,437	904	11,877
1970	3,326	1,487	10,342
1980	2,948	1,733	10,777
1990	4,012	2,458	22,121

Source: Author's analysis of U.S. Census data.

Note

* Census data is not available on local debt in 1920 and 1950.

Table 3.4 Local,* State, and Federal Revenue Per Capita, 1910–1990 (Billions of 2010 Dollars)

Year	*Local Revenue*	*State Revenue*	*Federal Revenue*
1910	333	88	246
1920			441
1930	638	209	281
1940	613	634	832
1950	917	913	2,632
1960	1,294	1,238	4,140
1970	2,073	2,330	5,732
1980	2,328	3,043	6,644
1990	2,920	3,819	7,800

Source: Author's analysis of U.S. Census data.

Note

* Census data is not available on local revenue in 1920.

that government within states also centralized during the Depression, showing that the national government is not the only level to expand its relative size during crisis. To underscore the activity of state governments during the Depression, they did not lose revenue share relative to the federal government during the 1930s. The federal government centralized relative to the states only during WWII, a crisis to which only the national government could respond. State government centralization relative to local government was facilitated by one crisis, the Depression, and state revenue as a percent of state and local revenue stayed fairly fixed through 1990. Federal government centralization was facilitated by

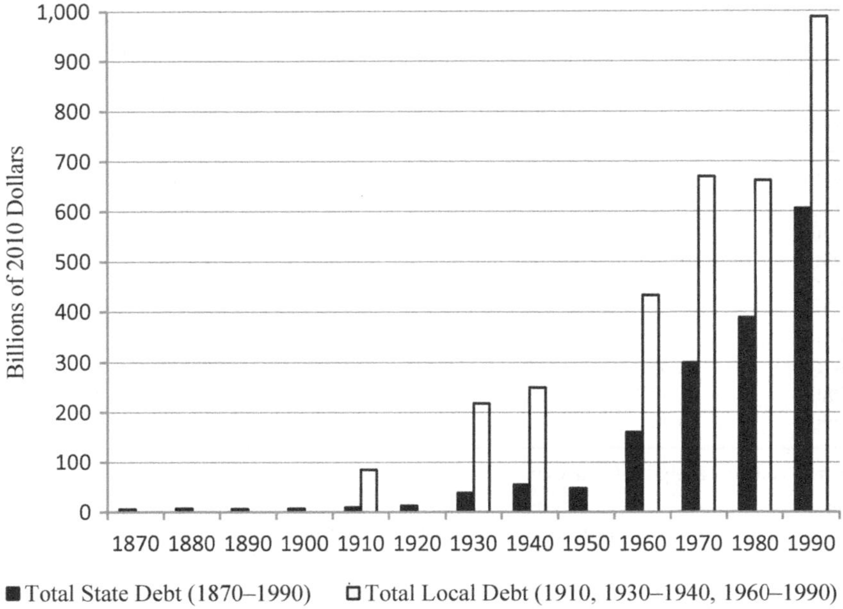

Figure 3.1 Total Local and State Debt.

Source: Author's analysis of U.S. Census Data.

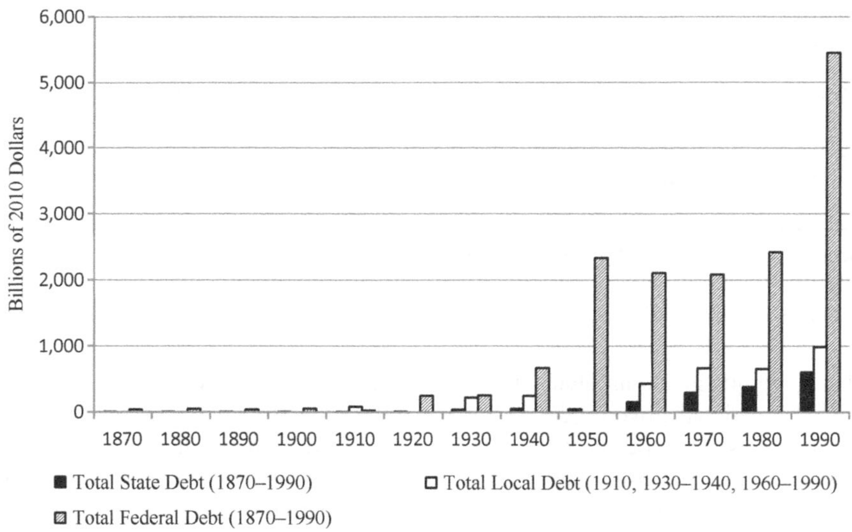

Figure 3.2 Total Local, State, and Federal Debt.

Source: Author's analysis of U.S. Census Data.

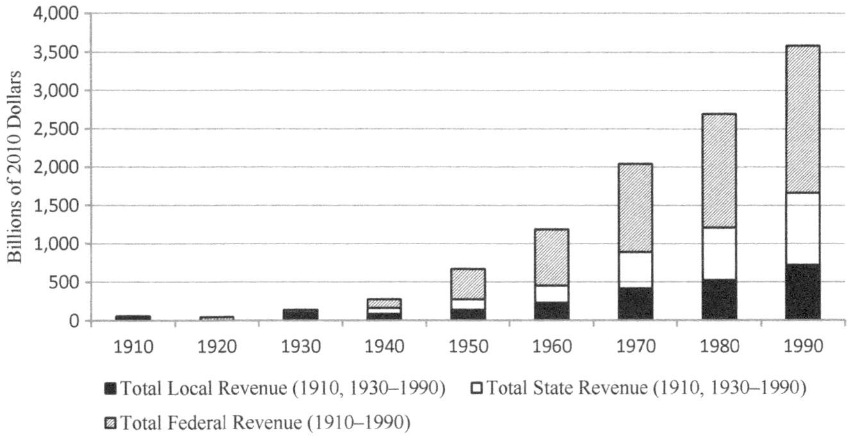

Figure 3.3 Total Local, State, and Federal Revenue.

Source: Author's analysis of U.S. Census Data.

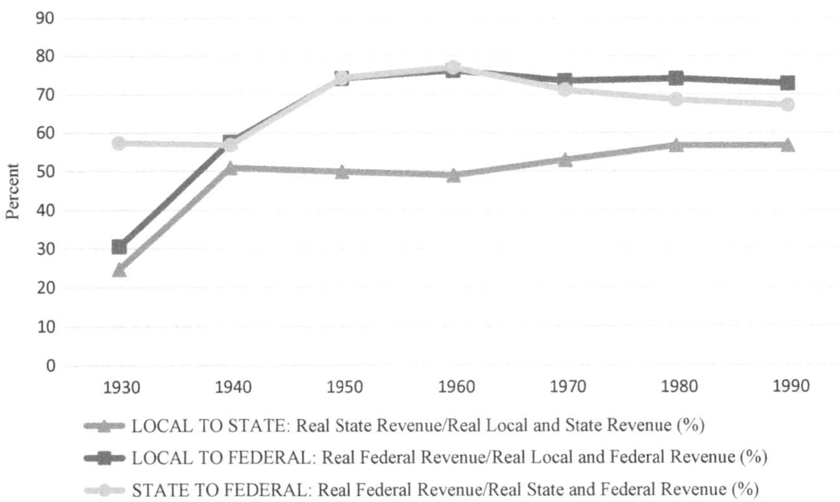

Figure 3.4 Measures of Centralization.

two crises, the Depression and WWII. It gained revenue share relative to state government only during WWII because state revenue also increased during the Depression. The federal government gained revenue share relative to the local government in both crises because local government was not prepared to respond to either. Thus, federal centralization relative to local government increased more than federal centralization relative to the states. This graphic supports the notion that not only federal but state government centralizes in crisis. The type of crisis matters, however, depending on the capacity of the governmental level to respond. Echoing Tocqueville, the importance of crisis in centralization is underscored by the relatively stable revenue shares of local, state, and federal government after the tumultuous years of economic depression and war.

Figure 3.4 above only measures centralization between governmental levels. Centralization of government also pertains to the growing share of the economy that government comprises. Federal net outlays as a percent of gross domestic product rose from approximately 3 percent in 1930 to just over 20 percent in 1990.[6]

Several Theoretical Perspectives on Debt

Postwar economic theory on the national debt has been described as a three-ring circus: Keynesians occupy one ring and are represented by scholars such as Lerner; the classical view, represented best by Buchanan, occupies another; and the neoclassical thought of Barro fills the third.[7]

The publication of Keynes' *General Theory* in 1936 led to what is typically described as a "fiscal revolution" in government affairs. Prominent Keynesian economist Lerner articulates the core principle of Keynes' teaching: that government is responsible through expansionary policies to correct market deficiencies to ensure satisfactory levels of employment.[8] Government must do this because markets are not self-clearing: prices do not adjust efficiently to return markets to equilibrium and a state of full-employment. Say's Law, which embodied the classical view that markets do correct themselves, does not hold. Keynes argued that supply is not determinative but rather demand. In an economic downturn, much less a depression, consumers are more risk averse and spend less to conserve their liquidity. During recessionary periods, workers may not be willing to accept reduced wages, and if they are, unemployment still may rise due to diminished consumption. Reduced demand thus must be offset by expansionary government policies. Such policies necessarily entail budget deficits (as more spending is needed at the time tax revenue is falling due to economic contraction), but this growth in national debt is desirable from a macroeconomic standpoint because such indebtedness is "internal" (at least that which is held by citizens of the nation itself). Repaying the nation's internal debt only represents payments from one part of society to another. National wealth overall is not changed, and the nation benefits by having government stimulus in times of economic need. Furthermore, national debt does not impose a burden on future taxpayers from the standpoint of the collective. The funds paid to buy government debt, such as when a citizen buys a treasury bond, represent the immediate sacrifice to sustain government borrowing. The repayment of that debt over time is simply the right hand placing something in the left, or to use the oft-quoted Keynesian phrase, "we owe it to ourselves."

Indeed, the Keynesians seem to mean "we owe it to ourselves" in several ways: we owe it to ourselves to take on public debt to help ourselves out of recession, and we owe the debt itself to ourselves. Public debt is thus different from private debt, and it is a "false analogy" to compare the two.[9] Maxims of thrift that apply to private credit do not apply to public accounts. When one person owes a particular sum to another, the repayment of the debt represents a transfer of wealth from one individual to another and therefore brings into play principles of budgeting to match income and expenditure. For the reasons stated above, such considerations do not apply to public finance.

Principles of private debt do apply to external debt, however. If debt held internally to a country is not harmful and even beneficial, it follows that debt held by foreigners is harmful, for repayment of this debt represents a reduction in national wealth. External debt is therefore to be avoided.

A view of markets as not self-correcting and of debt as a public good to correct such market deficiencies laid the theoretical groundwork for government empirically to take the role of *paterfamilias*, the principal agent entrusted with the fundamental issues of livelihood for its citizens.[10] While it took several years for Keynes' views to become widely known after publication of the *General Theory*, Keynesianism could be described as ascendant from the latter 1940s to the early 1970s, when it began to suffer theoretical setbacks for an inability to account for the simultaneous presence of high unemployment and inflation (which together constituted stagflation) in the American economy.

An outline of the classical view that Keynes and his followers were seeking to dislodge begins to take shape as these central assumptions of Keynesianism are discussed. Espoused by the likes of David Hume, Adam Smith, and David Ricardo, classical thinking understood debt as transferring burdens to future generations. Hume saw a fundamental conflict between public credit and national survival.[11] Smith described as a mercantilist fraud the argument that public debt imposes no burden on future generations.[12] He also discussed the concept that would later be called "fiscal illusion," or the tendency of public officials to conceal the true cost of their policies by raising debt instead of taxes.[13] Smith had observed debt being used to fund a century of war between European powers and believed hostilities could be avoided or of shorter duration if policymakers and their constituents bore the true financial costs of those campaigns.[14] Writing several generations after Smith, Ricardo was a classical thinker who developed an equivalence theorem for debt and taxes that could (and would) be used to justify public debt. He did not embrace the theorem as a guide for sound debt policy, however, acknowledging along with Smith the tendency of debt to obscure fiscal reality.[15]

Barro contemporized Ricardo's equivalence theorem in the 1970s to argue that the entire debate over debt and taxes is misguided.

> [He] rejected the subjectivist [Buchanan's] proposition that public debt enables the present generation of taxpayers to enrich itself at the expense of future generations. He also rejected the Keynesian proposition that the substitution of bond finance for tax finance would increase aggregate spending,

write Vaughn and Wagner.[16] Both of these suppositions could be defended on the grounds that public debt and taxes are regarded as commensurate by the rational taxpayer. Consider a specific example of the theorem at work. The government issues public debt in the amount of $1,000,000 that matures in 50 years. If an individual citizen's share or the share of his heirs in repaying that debt is $100, the equivalence theorem holds that this citizen would have no preference between the cost of a bequest to have that $100 available in 50 years or a current tax of $100. Hence, the rational taxpayer has no preference between public debt repaid in the future and taxes paid in the present.

The concept works with mathematical certainty but has serious limitations in reality. If government can raise debt easier than taxes or if citizens do not structure their present finances to account for future debt payments, then Ricardo's theorem is empirically unworkable. Even a cursory review of fiscal finances in the twentieth century appears to confirm the first deficiency of the equivalence theorem. Figures 3.5 and 3.6 below illustrate that federal debt is much less rationalized to the tax base (personal income) than federal revenue. Decentralization restrains this tendency, with state and local debt staying in better proportion to personal income levels. Ricardo's theorem thus may be more applicable to decentralized government settings, at least from the standpoint of decentralized government keeping debt in better proportion to the capacity to repay.

As for the second fundamental assumption supporting the equivalence theorem, many families undoubtedly make financial bequests to their heirs. Barro is not miserly in claiming all such bequests as support for his theory, even the cost of raising a child.[17] But wills from a parent do not begin with an assessment of the national debt and future tax burden for the child. Bequests are driven by all the complex considerations of family life but must start with available resources. Many families would have the means to more than compensate for any future tax burden of their heirs. Whether they do so or not depends in part on the closeness of family relationships and the soundness of investments made.

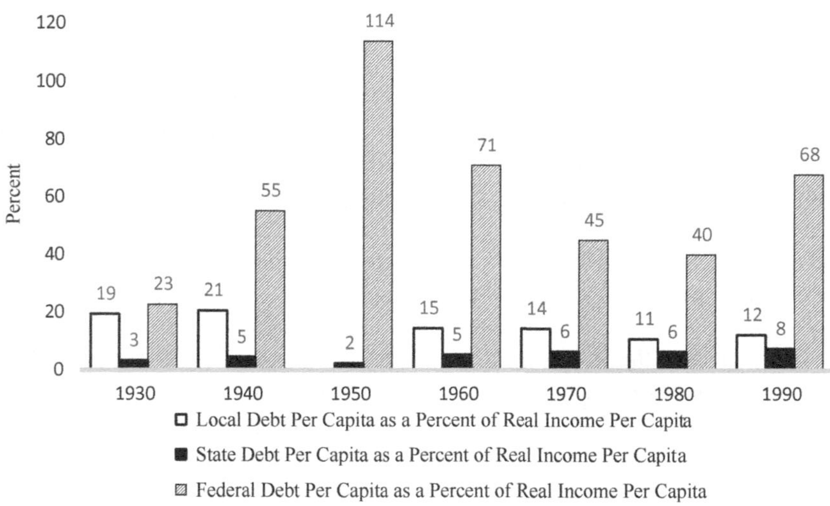

Figure 3.5 Local, State, and Federal Debt Per Capita Relative to Tax Base.

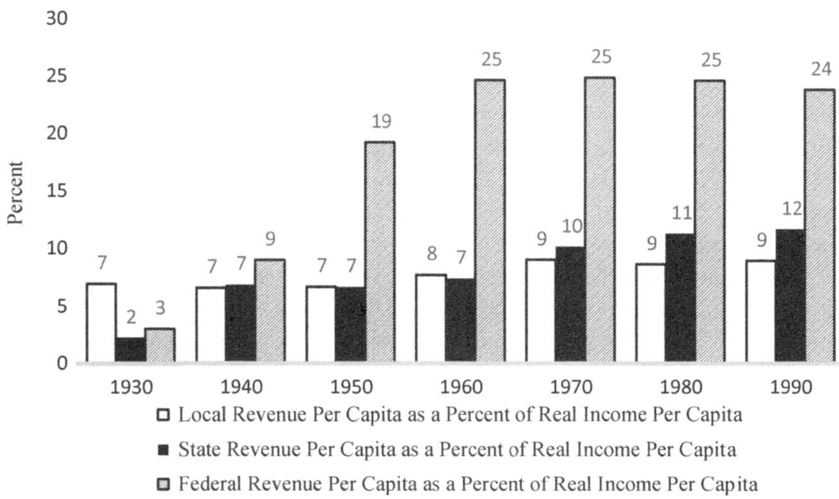

Figure 3.6 Local, State, and Federal Revenue Per Capita Relative to Tax Base.

Many more families simply would not have the means to sustain their heirs, whether they want to or not.

If all families could leave bequests and if all families were inclined to do so with perfectly executed investment decisions, simply knowing the future tax bill would prove to be an insurmountable hurdle. Ricardo himself recognized this particular challenge.[18] As discussed above, this study deals with official debt figures only. The most informed public officials, those who have advanced degrees related to some aspect of public policy and who work on such issues for their livelihood, disagree about the extent of the government's off-balance sheet liabilities. The typical citizen is much less likely to have a clear view of this future tax burden. By contrast, the average citizen knows his current taxes. Perhaps with the help of an accountant, he calculates them each year and pays the Internal Revenue Service by April 15. He has the proper information to assess the effect of taxes on his livelihood and the motivation to resist tax increases that burden his livelihood more. By contrast, national indebtedness is an invisibility to him. He hears talk of its growth and may have a foreboding that it is unsustainable but feels that he has as much influence over it as his single vote has over the presidential election. At the local level, however, to the extent that increases in debt translate into an increase in taxes, this same citizen sees the two burdens in a similar light. The cost of the bond to build a new school begins to show up immediately on his property tax bill. He may have the same inclination to resist the tax at the local level as he does the federal, but also has the means, due to his proximity to the issues at hand, to lend informed support if the need for the new school is apparent. Considerations such as these may explain in part why local and state debt levels are much better rationalized to the tax base and why federal revenue is much better rationalized to the tax base than federal debt.

Barro's theoretical affinity is with classical thought, but the empirical effect of the equivalence theorem is Keynesian. Theoretically, Barro is saying that the debt bill must be paid and that debt issued in the present is only a future tax. Furthermore, Keynesian expansionary policies do not create national wealth because debt necessarily involves these future tax liabilities.[19] Buchanan, discussed below, would find much to like in both of these points. Also, in describing debt and taxes as equivalent, Barro does not seem to be ignoring the preference voters and policymakers may have for debt over taxes, at least in the short run. This is the message of his second major article (1979) on the equivalence theorem: the equivalence of debt and taxes is valid as a "first-order proposition," but second-order effects related to taxation must be considered in the timing of debt issuance, namely that debt is used in a way to keep tax rates stable.[20] Debt will be issued to cover temporary increases in government spending so that taxes do not rise. Likewise, debt will have a "countercyclical" relationship with income; debt use will decline as income and, presumably, tax revenue rises.[21] The difficulty, however, is that the "countercyclical" never comes. In the context of the twentieth-century administrative state, a rise in income does not translate into a cessation of debt issue, much less debt repayment as it did through much of the nineteenth century. A classical theoretical beginning has a Keynesian empirical end: equating debt and taxes in the real world where debt issuance is easier than raising taxes engenders a higher tolerance for debt.

While Barro brought forward one element of classical thought in a way that practically aided a flagging Keynesianism, Buchanan sought to contemporize the essential corpus of classical thought to undermine Keynesianism in general. One of his important works, *Public Principles of Public Debt*, is organized to rebut several of the principal assumptions of Keynesianism discussed above, namely that public debt does not burden future generations of taxpayers and that public and private debt are not analogous.

Buchanan's significant contributions to the debate over public debt revolve in part around his grasp of the history of economic thought on government finance. He understands the strengths and weaknesses of the early classical thinkers (Hume, Smith, and Ricardo, among others) and documents how early classical deficiencies were corrected by the end of the nineteenth century, most completely in the work of a French scholar, Leroy-Beaulieu (that Buchanan is the first to translate into English). Drawing on mature classical thought, Buchanan addresses the first Keynesian assumption by arguing that the sacrifice of capital to fund public debt is not made at the time of purchasing the government security, for the purchaser is acting freely to maximize his own utility with the investment.[22] He has assayed the market and concluded that a Treasury bond enhances his financial position more than other possible investments. He anticipates an income stream, and his expectations are met if he is repaid. He has sacrificed nothing. The burden of repaying the debt lies with the citizen who will be taxed in the future.

He also reinforces Leroy-Beaulieu's moderation of the early classical tendency to see all government spending as wasteful.[23] For classical thinkers such as Hume and Smith, public debt drew capital out of the market where it would be used efficiently. Government expenditure was inherently profligate and always represented a diminished return on such assets. Buchanan recognizes that government expenditure may be wasteful or beneficial and that it is possible for public debt to profit taxpayers if used prudently.

Buchanan also aids his cause by placing classical thought in its historical context. Classical thinkers were not making their arguments in a vacuum, and what they were arguing against, at least in part, were elements of mercantilism that Keynesianism would later revive. Mercantilists such as Voltaire and Melon believed that public debts "are the debts which the right hand owes to the left hand … [The taxpayer who repays] may be pitied, but the nation will not be impoverished," states Leroy-Beaulieu in describing mercantilist thought.[24] Or, as Vaughn and Wagner would characterize the Keynesian view, "changes in individual utilities are 'mere' distribution problems and do not count importantly in policy debates."[25]

Buchanan's coverage of mercantilism at once diminishes the novelty of Keynesianism and places historical constraints on Keynesian thought by requiring it to answer for mercantilist deficiencies. As Buchanan convincingly argues, the sacrifice to fund public debt is not borne by the creditor who buys the government security but by the taxpayer in the future who will repay the debt. Public debt is not something "we owe to ourselves." It is owed by one part of society to another, and a Keynesian collectivist view blurs the distinction between the interests of these two groups. The bondholder has an interest in his investment. His expectations are met if he is repaid. The taxpayer in the future may or may not have an interest in repaying the debt. If the funds were used for government expenditures that benefit him, he has an interest. If they were not, he does not and has been assigned unjustly a bill that he did not agree to pay. Appeals to collective well-being fall on the deaf ears of citizens who have been fleeced by earlier generations to pay for public debt they did not incur to fund government expenditures for which they have seen no benefit. Generations who inherit the burden of government profligacy have not been treated as free and equal but subject to the fiscal mastery of generations before them. Injustice between generations contributes to the loss of the common good among the living as the bill comes due. Fiscal crisis helped bring about the French Revolution.[26] The right hand of the French state had not been transferring undiminished national wealth to the left but seizing the assets of the left through public debt that was put to ill use. Resulting civil war between the two appendages was the ultimate rebuke to the mercantilist vision of collective good.

Buchanan's strength in the history of economic theory is not matched by a grasp of several historical empirical limits to his argument. He is so focused on doing battle with Keynes that he overstates the classical norm of budget balance in America and Keynes' role in overturning that norm. A customary storyline of the New Deal is that the excesses of laissez-faire economics in America reached a climax with the stock market crash of 1929, confronting an out of touch and inept Hoover administration with a crisis beyond its ken, a crisis that Roosevelt's enlightened leadership forcefully addressed by using fiscal tools with Keynesian theoretical support. The reality is different, however.

Hoover was a liberal Republican who entered Harding's cabinet over the objections of conservative members of the Senate.[27] As Commerce Secretary, he represented the U.S. in efforts to aid Europe after World War I (WWI) and won the praise of Keynes himself while doing so.[28] If Hoover's leadership had been matched in other circles, Keynes believed an enduring peace could have been achieved. Hoover took economic planning seriously and ran a deficit in 1932 (his last year in office) not out of step with those of the New Deal.[29] Indeed, Roosevelt attacked Hoover in the 1932 campaign for not balancing the federal budget.

As for Keynes' influence during the decade of depression, his *General Theory* was not published until 1936, as stated above, and his views did not gain prominence until some years later. Stein, whose focus is not on the theory of the Keynesian revolution but its history, has a more accurate assessment of the norm of budget balance and Keynes' role in undermining it. He finds the norm of budget balance not that resilient in the late 1920s, and Keynes had little influence in undermining it further through the 1930s.[30] In the face of depression, the government was running deficits at the behest of necessity rather than Keynesian theory. "The New Deal and Keynes were developing along parallel tracks, but no substantial influence from Keynes on the New Deal has been found," Stein writes.[31]

There is no doubt after reading the accounts of Savage, Breit, and Stein that the norm of budget balance was much more dominant in the nineteenth and early twentieth centuries than during the New Deal and afterward. This norm is reflected in budget trends, with federal balance sheets more often than not showing surpluses in peacetime that were used to pay down debt incurred in times of war or economic hardship.

That the norm was not as dominant as Buchanan implies, however, can be seen most clearly in state fiscal affairs. If the norm of budget balance were pervasive in American politics, it should be present in state as well as federal budgets, and the performance of the states in restraining debt did not match that of the federal government at certain points in the nation's history. As Ratchford recounts, the states have experienced periods of severe financial hardship due to fiscal mismanagement.[32] To use contemporary budget terminology in describing the national government of the nineteenth century, the federal government was until the New Deal subject to fairly severe tax and expenditure limits. Its scope of action was narrow enough that it had to "engage in unprecedented spending" to reduce budgetary surpluses.[33] Until the first half of the twentieth century, the federal government would have had difficulty being expansionary even if it had wanted to. As the tables and figures discussed above show, most government occurred at the local level and secondarily at the state. Debt and revenue numbers were higher at these lower levels of government. Incorporating the fiscal history of the states in the discussion of American debt thus adds empirical insight and the benefit of comparative statistical analysis.

The merits of Keynesianism in mitigating recession have been debated extensively for three-quarters of a century. Reviewing those arguments here would not be productive or necessarily relevant to the question at hand. The primary point to make from this cursory review of Keynesian thought and U.S. fiscal history in the twentieth century is that the federal government was using deficit finance to support the economy before Keynes published the *General Theory* and has used deficit finance even more vociferously after Keynesianism has waned theoretically. Once understood, Keynesianism only held sway theoretically and empirically for a quarter of a century, until simultaneous unemployment and inflation during the 1970s undermined its theoretical coherence. While its theoretical validity has been called into question, the empirical use of Keynesianism has continued unabated, most recently in the expansionary policies of the U.S. and other governments to mitigate the effects of the Great Recession during the last decade. This divergence in the theoretical and practical validity of Keynesianism reveals its true strength and the source of its enduring appeal: Keynesianism fits the government of the age that seeks to be responsible for fundamental issues of livelihood for its citizens, that seeks to be *paterfamilias*.

Toward an Explanation of Public Debt in Terms of Justice or the Common Good

The three modes of thinking about public debt outlined above afford different insights into fiscal policy but do not explain the proclivity to use debt. Keynesianism posits an explanation for when debt should be used. Barro contemporizes the Ricardian theory of equivalence between debt and taxes but does not answer why a citizen would want either one. The classical view acknowledges that debt may be beneficial for public goods that could not otherwise be attained and harmful if used to transfer current fiscal burdens to future generations. Concerns with justice infuse Buchanan's argument and methodology but as yet have not been operationalized in modeling. This book seeks to offer an explanation for how a theoretical sense of justice or the common good can have an empirical effect on debt levels.

Drawing on Aristotle and Tocqueville and empirical evidence presented in the next chapter, an explanation for the proclivity to use debt (which is related to but not the same as the actual level of debt) is given in terms of the capacity for political freedom that follows from the interaction of political institutions and cultural mores. Debt is particularly prone to injustice because uncertainty in the future hinders questions of valuation tied to a just accommodation of the interests of the two parties, creditor and debtor, involved in the exchange.

When government is added as an intermediary, which is necessarily true in all matters pertaining to public debt, the parties are no longer two and the interests are no longer two. The multiplicity of interests at work in the government come into play, and the type of government involved influences the interests. To the extent that a centralized administrative state is issuing the debt, the likelihood declines of the debt being used in a way that benefits the future taxpayer, for as will be discussed in Chapter 6, this form of government is defined more by the rent-seeking activity of interest groups than the pursuit of commonly held national interests.

The multiplicity of interests is complicated by their invisibility. The interests of the government (the intended use of the funds) are not presented to the bond purchaser before he buys the bond. He cares only for a sound investment that will yield the stated return. He enters into the bond purchase freely for his own gain and does not care what the government does with his capital, so long as he is repaid. What the government uses the money for is important to the taxpayer who later foots the bill, but an administrative state less capable of ascertaining enduring national interests at the time the money is borrowed will be even less capable of explaining that interest at some point in the future. The party that provides the funds and the party that repays them thus never meet and may not even be contemporaries. The government deals with the creditor at one point in time when the security is sold and the taxpayer at another when the bill is paid. The creditor does not know the taxpayer's interests and the taxpayer does not know the creditor's terms. The third party, the government as intermediary, binds one person without his knowledge to terms with a person who does not care how the money is used, a sequence of events susceptible to abuse to say the least. The whole arrangement rests on government serving as a faithful representative of both parties: to ensure the creditor is repaid and the taxpayer is benefited through the productive use of the funds borrowed.

During times of relative normalcy (excluding wars and other disasters), the size of the debt itself becomes an indication of the extent to which government has acted as a faithful agent. The larger the debt, the more justice has been undermined. This is so because the larger the debt the more time required to pay and the more difficult it is to predict what the interests of taxpayers that far into the future will be. The larger the debt, the more evident it is that government has pursued its own interests at the expense of the taxpayer who occupies an increasingly distant time horizon of repayment. He has become only a source of liquidity and not one to whom government must give an account. Debt thus is prone to undermine political rule of free and equal persons in favor of a mastery that allows the present to benefit at the expense of the future.

With these thoughts in mind, the capacity for political freedom is explained in terms of the two primary factors of mores and institutions, with the theme of justice or the common good influencing the interpretation of each. Mores speak to the general cultural capacity of a people to ascertain justice or the common good. In terms of debt, the capacity of the living to find justice or the common good among themselves is indicative of their capacity to find justice or the common good between themselves and future generations. Negatively, the inclination of citizens to be unjust to posterity can be measured by their inclination to be unjust to each other. The capacity for political freedom thus offers an explanation for aversion to debt, and the incapacity for political freedom may explain society's proclivity for debt.

With a view to political freedom, institutions speak to the governing arrangements that seek to ensure the political rule of free and equal persons as opposed to mastery. Centralization may run the gamut from the state of nature, or no centralized political authority at all, to the highest degree of centralized power found in tyranny. Centralization is needed to constitute society but can reach levels where political rule is undermined in favor of mastery. Tyranny can result in extreme democracy and extreme oligarchy, Aristotle argues, and Tocqueville invests considerable energy in offering a modern rationale for how democratic tyranny comes to be. Integrating both thinkers, it is thus the incorporation of democratic and oligarchic elements in government that best approximate justice or the common good from an institutional standpoint. A republican form of limited constitutional government serves as an example of this. The Founders thus could establish a government based on the proposition that all men are created equal, with the principal purpose of that government being to protect the natural inequalities that result from the diverse faculties of citizens.[34]

Durkheim discusses in his book, *Suicide*, the concept of "anomie," or the breakdown of norms and social bonds that lead people to isolation and despair.[35] Mencken's illustration of the effects of anomie and its opposite, what he calls "conformity," on suicide rates is seen in Figure 3.7.[36] Suicide rises at the

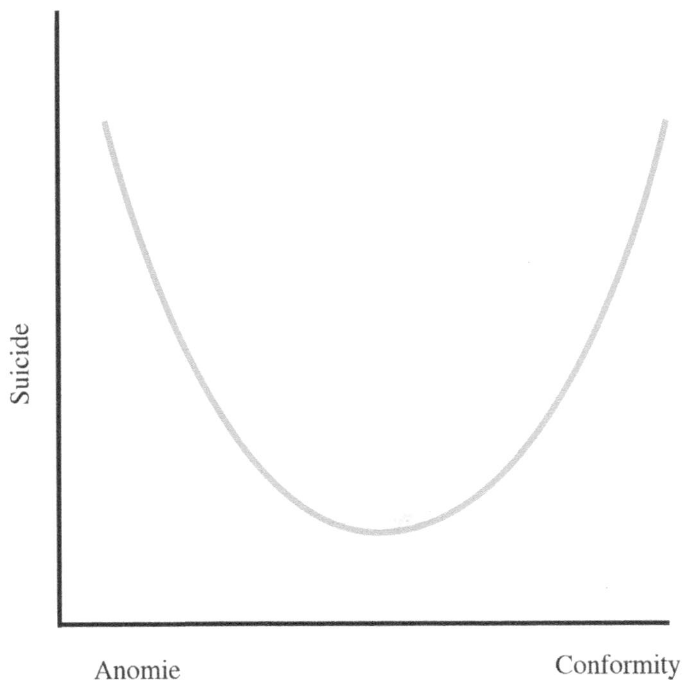

Figure 3.7 Mencken's Illustration of Durkheim.

extremes of anomie and conformity. An example of extreme conformity might be the mass suicide in Jonestown, Guyana in 1978.

Mencken's illustration of Durkheim illustrates the health of an individual person, and a corollary to Durkheim is posited for the institutional health of a political regime. Curve AB in Figure 3.8 illustrates Aristotle's argument on the relationship of democracy and oligarchy to centralized political power. The integration of democratic and oligarchic elements into a governing arrangement gives both of these principal factions a stake in the regime and prevents either from centralizing power in a way that leads to tyranny. As a regime moves toward extreme democracy or extreme oligarchy, the use of force undermines the rule of law. The democratic mob and the oligarchic tyrant both govern through a mastery that supplants the political rule of free and equal persons. In the context of modern democracy, Tocqueville shows how the centralized administrative state removes items of political concern from the cognizance of local government, thereby undermining political freedom while preserving a degraded form of equality.

Curve CD in Figure 3.9 adds the second principal factor of mores in explaining the proclivity to use debt. Please note that curve AB and curve CD correspond to two different measurements on both the X and Y axes. Whereas curve AB measures centralization (Y axis) in terms of the integration of democracy and oligarchy (X axis), curve CD measures justice or the common good (Y axis) in terms of the capacity of a people to integrate considerations of equality and

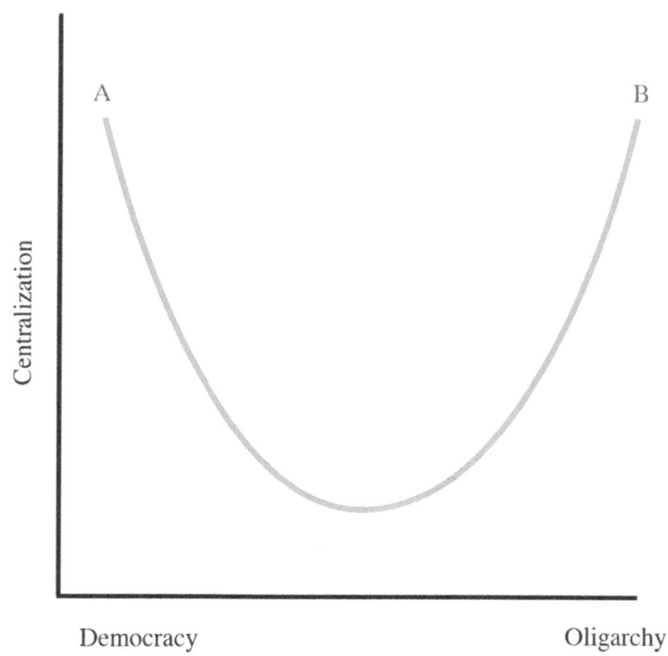

Figure 3.8 An Aristotelian View of Centralization.

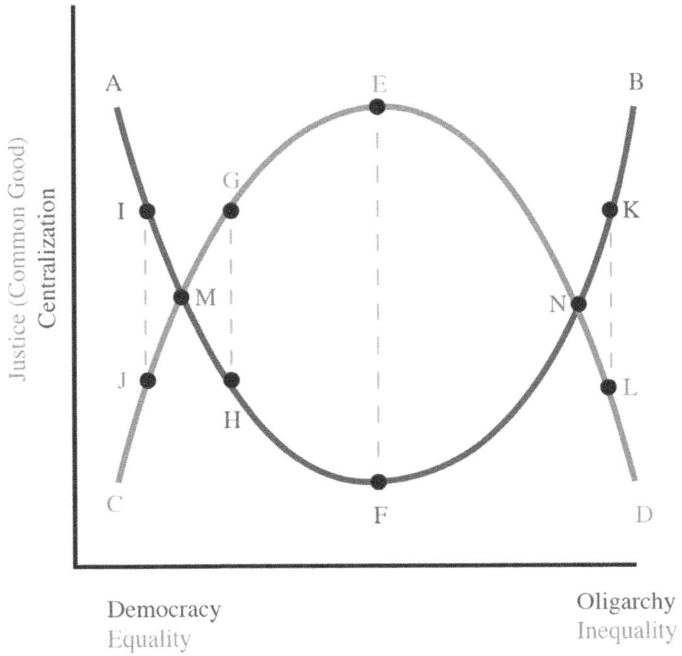

Figure 3.9 The Capacity For Political Freedom.

inequality (X axis). Point F on curve AB represents the ideal arrangement of shared power achieved through the incorporation of democracy and oligarchy. Likewise, point E on curve CD represents the highest capacity of a people to ascertain justice or the common good by integrating considerations of equality and inequality. The distance between points E and F represents the longest possible distance between curves AB and CD, the greatest institutional and cultural capacity for political freedom, and the strongest inclination against using debt that may transfer present obligations to future generations. Points G and H reflect a society that has moved toward a greater emphasis on democracy. Its political institutions have more centralized authority, and its mores are less inclined to integrate considerations of equality and inequality. The distance between points G and H is shorter than between points E and F. The society defined by points G and H has less institutional and cultural capacity for political freedom and less aversion to using public debt to transfer present obligations to future generations.

Points M and N represent the beginning of the primacy of mastery over political freedom in democracy and oligarchy, respectively. At these points, the rule of law is no longer a reliable matrix by which to calculate public debt, for the rule of law has been undermined by the use of force. With regard to debt, this means that private resources may be seized by public authorities to repay the debt or that the debt may be abnegated by those authorities. Between points M and N, there is a measure of the institutional and cultural capacity for political freedom. Beyond points M and N is a measure of a regime's mastery (points I and J in democracy and points K and L in oligarchy), where institutional restraints on political authority give way to ever more repressive forms of tyranny and the cultural capacity to integrate considerations of equality and inequality becomes increasingly enervated.

An assumption in the foregoing discussion is that institutions and mores mirror each other when viewed through the prism of political freedom, such that point E is the precise analog to point F and point G to point H. This need not be so, however. There may be a society defined by point G on the mores curve CD and point F on the institutions curve AB. Within points M and N, such an arrangement could still serve as a measure of a society's capacity for political freedom, as the distance between points E and F is still greatest and represents the greatest capacity. Over an expanse of time, however, it is a fairly reliable assumption that a point on the mores curve CD will be the rough analog of a point on the institutions curve AB. This is seen in the relative persistence of political and cultural institutions. Free regimes do not succumb to tyranny overnight, and peoples emerging from more repressive forms of government have difficulty in acquiring the institutions and mores based on individual liberty and the rule of law. Finally, this illustration of political freedom is applied to indebtedness in the present study but can serve as a matrix by which to evaluate other threats to the capacity for self-government.

Conclusion

The norm of budget balance cannot be a myth if justice itself is more than mythical. In a democratic society where sovereignty ultimately resides in the people, the beneficial use of public debt is based on several critical assumptions: first, that citizens will consider their own interests in light of the interests of future generations; and, second, that government will be so organized institutionally to serve as a faithful intermediary between the interests of present and future generations.

Important strands of economic theory in the last century have been used as a pretext to justify more public debt. Keynesians advocate deficit spending to ward off recession and maintain satisfactory levels of employment. Their emphasis on the collective leads to the conclusion that public debt (internally held) represents no loss in wealth to a society, as the right hand simply is transferring money to the left. "We owe it to ourselves" is the Keynesian mantra. Barro draws on classical reservoirs to argue that debt and taxes are equivalent. His argument is theoretically aligned with the classical emphasis on the individual and recognizes, in a way that may be supportive of budget balance, that debt is really a future tax, that the bill will have to be paid. In an empirical context where it is much easier to raise money through debt than taxes, however, the empirical effect of Barro is Keynesian: less aversion to the use of public debt. In addition, when it comes to debt repayment, Barro's assumption that bequests will be made for this purpose is subject to many shortcomings. Barro's thesis is theoretically impregnable—the mathematical equivalence of a present tax and a bequest to repay debt in the future is beyond refutation—but subject to the dual unreality of debt and taxes being equivalent policy options and bequests covering repayment of public credit.

The classical view as contemporized by Buchanan recognizes that public debt may be used to secure public goods that otherwise would not be available and thus leave society better off than if the debt had not been issued. The default position for Buchanan, however, particularly in light of the theoretical and empirical weaknesses of Keynesianism and rising debt levels in the latter half of the twentieth century, is that public debt is not being used for good but as a vehicle to transfer present obligations to the future.

These three lines of thought provide different vantage points from which to view debt but do not explain the proclivity to issue debt. Keynesianism says when debt should be used. Barro shows that debt and taxes are equivalent but does not say why a taxpayer would want either one. Buchanan makes sound fiscal arguments to show that debt is a means to enrich the present at the expense of the future. The moral implications of public debt are thus taken seriously but not operationalized.

Drawing on Aristotle and Tocqueville, the institutional and cultural capacity for justice or the common good can begin to explain a society's penchant for debt. The capacity for justice or the common good in the present is reflective of a capacity for justice or the common good between the present and the future. Likewise, an incapacity for justice or the common good in the present is reflective of an incapacity for justice or the common good between the present and the future, which in terms of fiscal policy choices, means a stronger proclivity to use public debt for present benefit at the expense of future taxpayers.

Notes

1 William Breit, "Starving the Leviathan," in *Fiscal Responsibility in Constitutional Democracy*, eds. James M. Buchanan and Richard E. Wagner (Boston: Leiden, 1978), 10.
2 Akhil Reed Amar, *American's Unwritten Constitution: The Precedents and Principles We Live By* (New York: Basic Books, 2012).
3 Breit, "Starving the Leviathan," 10.
4 Armen A. Alchian, "Comments," in *Fiscal Responsibility in Constitutional Democracy*, eds. James M. Buchanan and Richard E. Wagner (Boston: Leiden, 1978), 54.
5 Richard A. Musgrave and Peggy B. Musgrave, *Public Finance in Theory and Practice*, Second Edition (New York: McGraw-Hill, 1976), 7.
6 Federal Reserve Bank of St. Louis and U.S. Office of Management and Budget, "Federal Net Outlays as Percent of Gross Domestic Product [FYONGDA188S]." Accessed October 7, 2016 at https://fred.stlouisfed.org/series/FYONGDA188S.
7 Karen I. Vaughn and Richard E. Wagner, "Public Debt Controversies: An Essay in Reconciliation," *Kyklos* Vol. 45 (1992): 37.
8 Abba P. Lerner, "Keynesianism: Alive, If Not So Well, At Forty," in *Fiscal Responsibility in Constitutional Democracy*, eds. James M. Buchanan and Richard E. Wagner (Boston: Leiden, 1978), 59.

9 James M. Buchanan, *Public Principles of Public Debt* (Homewood, IL: Richard D. Irwin, 1958), 48.
10 Vaughn and Wagner, "Public Debt Controversies," 39.
11 Breit, "Starving the Leviathan," 15.
12 Buchanan, *Public Principles of Public Debt*, 103.
13 Daniel Shaviro, *Do Deficits Matter?* (Chicago: University of Chicago Press, 1997), 29.
14 Ibid.
15 Breit, "Starving the Leviathan," 16.
16 Vaughn and Wagner, "Public Debt Controversies," 37.
17 Shaviro, *Do Deficits Matter?*, 69.
18 Ibid., 30.
19 Robert J. Barro, "Are Government Bonds Net Wealth?" *Journal of Political Economy* Vol. 82 No. 6 (November–December 1974): 1095–1117.
20 Robert J. Barro, "On the Determination of the Public Debt," *Journal of Political Economy* Vol. 87 No. 5 Part 1 (October 1979): 940–971.
21 Ibid., 940.
22 Buchanan, *Public Principles of Public Debt*, 39.
23 Ibid., 42, 111.
24 Ibid., 109–110.
25 Vaughn and Wagner, "Public Debt Controversies," 40.
26 Shaviro, *Do Deficits Matter?*, 15.
27 Herbert Stein, *The Fiscal Revolution in America* (Chicago: University of Chicago Press, 1969), 7.
28 Ibid., 134.
29 James D. Savage, *Balanced Budgets and American Politics* (Ithaca, NY: Cornell University Press, 1988), 169.
30 Herbert Stein, "The Decline of the Budget-Balancing Doctrine or How the Good Guys Finally Lost," in *Fiscal Responsibility in Constitutional Democracy*, eds. James M. Buchanan and Richard E. Wagner (Boston: Leiden, 1978), 50.
31 Stein, *Fiscal Revolution*, 148.
32 B.U. Ratchford, *American State Debts* (Durham, NC: Duke University Press, 1941).
33 Savage, *Balanced Budgets*, 136.
34 Alexander Hamilton, James Madison, and John Jay, *The Federalist* (New York: Barnes & Noble, 2006), 53.
35 Emile Durkheim, *Suicide* (London: Routledge, 1952).
36 Carson Mencken, Class Lecture in Multivariate Statistical Analysis, Baylor University, Waco, Texas, March 1, 2012.

Bibliography

Alchian, Armen A. "Comments." In *Fiscal Responsibility in Constitutional Democracy*, edited by James M. Buchanan and Richard E. Wagner, 53–55. Boston: Leiden, 1978.

Amar, Akhil Reed. *American's Unwritten Constitution: The Precedents and Principles We Live By*. New York: Basic Books, 2012.

Barro, Robert J. "Are Government Bonds Net Wealth?" *Journal of Political Economy* Vol. 82 No. 6 (November–December 1974): 1095–1117.

Barro, Robert J. "On the Determination of the Public Debt." *Journal of Political Economy* Vol. 87 No. 5 Part 1 (October 1979): 940–971.

Breit, William. "Starving the Leviathan." In *Fiscal Responsibility in Constitutional Democracy*, edited by James M. Buchanan and Richard E. Wagner, 9–24. Boston: Leiden, 1978.

Buchanan, James M. *Public Principles of Public Debt*. Homewood, IL: Richard D. Irwin, 1958.

Durkheim, Emile. *Suicide*. London: Routledge, 1952.

Federal Reserve Bank of St. Louis and U.S. Office of Management and Budget. "Federal Net Outlays as Percent of Gross Domestic Product [FYONGDA188S]." Accessed October 7, 2016 at https://fred.stlouisfed.org/series/FYONGDA188S.

Hamilton, Alexander, James Madison, and John Jay. *The Federalist*. New York: Barnes & Noble, 2006.

Lerner, Abba P. "Keynesianism: Alive, If Not So Well, At Forty." In *Fiscal Responsibility in Constitutional Democracy*, edited by James M. Buchanan and Richard E. Wagner, 59–69. Boston: Leiden, 1978.

Mencken, Carson. Class Lecture in Multivariate Statistical Analysis, Baylor University, Waco, Texas, March 1, 2012.

Musgrave, Richard A. and Peggy B. Musgrave. *Public Finance in Theory and Practice*, Second Edition. New York: McGraw-Hill, 1976.

Ratchford, B.U. *American State Debts*. Durham, NC: Duke University Press, 1941.

Savage, James D. *Balanced Budgets and American Politics*. Ithaca, NY: Cornell University Press, 1988.

Shaviro, Daniel. *Do Deficits Matter?* Chicago: University of Chicago Press, 1997.

Stein, Herbert. "The Decline of the Budget-Balancing Doctrine or How the Good Guys Finally Lost." In *Fiscal Responsibility in Constitutional Democracy*, edited by James M. Buchanan and Richard E. Wagner, 35–53. Boston: Leiden, 1978.

Stein, Herbert. *The Fiscal Revolution in America*. Chicago: University of Chicago Press, 1969.

Vaughn, Karen I. and Richard E. Wagner. "Public Debt Controversies: An Essay in Reconciliation." *Kyklos* Vol. 45 (1992): 37–49.

4 Modeling Injustice

SOCRATES: When licentiousness and illness multiply in a city, aren't many courts and hospitals opened, and aren't the arts of the law court and medicine full of pride when even many free men take them very seriously?

GLAUCON: How could it turn out differently?

SOCRATES: Will you be able to produce a greater sign of a bad and base education in a city than its needing eminent doctors and judges not only for the common folk and the manual artisans but also for those who pretend to have been reared in a free fashion? Or doesn't it seem base, and a great sign of lack of education, to be compelled—because of a shortage at home—to use a justice imported from others who are thus masters and umpires?

GLAUCON: Certainly, basest of all.

—Plato's *Republic*

A review of fiscal trends at the local, state, and federal level shows that the usage of public debt is driven more by empirical politics than economic theory. The norm of budget balance that held at the federal level until the New Deal was supported by what scholars would call today significant tax and expenditure limits. Such limits did not apply at the state level, at least in the same way and over the same time period, and the states experienced periods of severe economic hardship exacerbated by fiscal mismanagement, of which unsustainable debt was a part. As such, the norm of budget balance, while certainly more prevalent in the nineteenth than in the twentieth century, was not as pervasive as scholars like Buchanan argue. An effort to demonstrate how justice or the common good influences the use of debt cannot proceed, therefore, by comparing the present to an earlier "golden age" of budget balance. The hypothesis concerning the relationship between justice and debt is, therefore, ceteris paribus, that a society more capable of ascertaining justice or the common good is less likely to shift its own fiscal burden to future taxpayers through public debt. Conversely, a society characterized by injustice or the loss of the common good is more likely to do so.

A rigorous test of the hypothesis stated above faces several challenges, the most important of which is proper specification of a historically valid variable for "injustice." Second, the injustice variable must be placed in a robust longitudinal model incorporating some version of the socioeconomic, demographic, political, and institutional variables developed by the literature. To accomplish both of these challenging tasks, historical data was mined to derive the dependent and independent variables of interest for the time period 1920–1990. The resulting model, discussed below, yields significant results for the selected injustice variable and other variables with some theoretical bearing on debt. No other model in the literature reviews state debt over such an extended time period or incorporates important cultural measures such as voter turnout and religious affiliation. Annual data on variables of interest is not available for much of the time period in question, but data points for most variables are available roughly every ten years, or on a decennial basis. As discussed below, the institutional part of the model could be better specified to include constitutional debt limits in addition to or in place of balanced-budget rules (which are included). In general, however, the strength of the model is that customs underlying institutions can be brought into sharper relief as the longevity of analysis increases. This is so because institutions, while they certainly retain some degree of independent force, see that independent force diminish in the longer run as they are shaped by custom.

Literature Review

The literature on fiscal federalism is vast and not clearly delineated, incorporating several disciplines and conceivably relating to most studies of governmental structure. For the sake of coherence, a basic overview of the initial discussion between Musgrave, Tiebout, and Oates will be provided, followed by the juxtaposition of two helpful review essays that frame developments in federalism research and point to the central challenges faced by the literature. Finally, a more targeted assessment of important federalism studies touching on themes of indebtedness will be conducted.

Inquiries related to federalism should be made with an awareness of secular budgeting trends and major political developments. As Poterba discusses, public budgeting in the U.S. has been defined by the often-incompatible paradigms of budget balance and social planning.[1] The former has longer historical antecedents in American government and is concerned with matching revenues and expenditures. The latter has been ascendant in much of the post-New Deal era and is focused on using public funds for economic and social purposes, namely smoothing economic cycles and redistribution of income. Social planning's advance was slowed in the 1970s as persistent peacetime deficits undermined theoretical and political support for unrestrained spending and opened the door to closer scrutiny of budgetary processes and institutions. The "Tax Revolt" initiated by Proposition 13 in California led to the adoption of tax and expenditure limits (TELs) in various states. Debate over federal budget rules intensified with rapidly growing deficits during the Reagan administration, and political momentum for such measures as a balanced-budget amendment accelerated with the Republican takeover of Congress following the 1994 election.

As budgetary procedures and institutions were taken more seriously, the states offered a context for comparative analysis. American states are especially well-suited for such analysis because they share a common national society but exercise a high degree of independence from the federal government, making their fiscal policies more diverse and independent.[2]

Returning to federalism specifically, Oates begins his foundational text *Fiscal Federalism* with a brief overview of three principal ways, as identified by Musgrave in *The Theory of Public Finance*, in which a purely market-based society may fail to achieve important public policy goals in the modern welfare state: the market may fail to distribute income equitably; the market may fail to ensure stable economic growth (the central concern of Keynesian theory); and the market may fail to efficiently allocate resources either due to imperfections within the market itself or by its neglect of public goods that fall outside of the typical scope of market-oriented activities.[3] Correcting these deficiencies is the primary task of the public sector, an assignment that Oates accepts and considers within the confines of fiscal federalism.

Is a centralized or decentralized system of government the most capable at addressing these issues? The centralized government is better equipped to address all three of these fundamental challenges because it possesses the requisite authority relative to the jurisdiction: it can set policy binding all members of society, whereas local governments only have limited jurisdictions subject to the inflow and outflow of human and material resources. If a local government sought to raise taxes for income redistribution purposes, the wealthy would be inclined to move. If a local government sought to stimulate its economy with expansionary fiscal policy, the costs would be borne inordinately by its own citizens but dissipated across the porous jurisdictional lines of the locality. If all local governments had the power to print money for economic expansion or debt service, the likely outcome would be rampant inflation. Finally, a local government would have no incentive to pay for public goods that other localities would equally enjoy. Oates uses a missile system as an example: a purely decentralized system would not have the proper organizational mechanisms to contemplate and construct such a defense, beneficial as it might be.[4]

A centralized system capable of setting policy for a national jurisdiction with less porous borders is thus better equipped to address the public policy challenges identified by Musgrave. Nevertheless, as Oates points out, decentralization offers advantages that centralization does not. For one, a centralized system of distributing public goods tends to result in uniformity across jurisdictions. A decentralized system, by contrast, is better tailored to meet the interests specific to local communities. Second, decentralization affords the opportunity for greater policy innovation. In economic terms, a centralized system represents the stagnancy of monopoly, while a decentralized system of numerous localities more closely approximates the dynamism of numerous, competitive market actors. Lastly, decentralized systems "may lead to more efficient levels of public output, because expenditure decisions are tied more closely to real resource costs."[5] The provision of revenue from the center reverses the incentives of localities in the matter of public goods: they will not want to contribute toward a public good that others enjoy, but they will want to take from a public good that others provide. Tiebout's earlier article informs much of Oates' analysis on these benefits from decentralization. Musgrave's critique of market limitations in providing for public goods does not apply at the local level, Tiebout argues, because of market-oriented dynamics between local jurisdictions (Tiebout does not address the other two goals of equitable income distribution and economic stabilization).[6]

Oates concludes that the benefits from centralized and decentralized systems point to the desirability of federal governmental structures. "What is clearly desirable is a form of government that combines the advantages of these two polar forms and avoids the most serious shortcomings of each; a federal organization of government meets this need."[7] His "Decentralization Theorem" follows from this conclusion and affirms that

> in the absence of cost-savings from the centralized provision of a good and of interjurisdictional external effects, the level of welfare will always be at least as high (and typically higher) if Pareto-efficient levels of consumption of the good are provided in each jurisdiction than if any single, uniform level of consumption is maintained across all jurisdictions.[8]

The theorem thus establishes a "presumption in favor of decentralized finance."[9]

Oates' framework for considering federalism pointed subsequent research in a more holistic direction. Earlier political science analysis had taken a rule-bound approach to federalism, defining federal structures in too rigid a manner. Approaching federalism from an economic perspective allowed the topic to be viewed in less dichotomous terms and as being practiced more along a continuum. This more flexible approach pointed researchers toward consideration of an array of social, economic, and cultural factors in understanding federal systems. Oates also covered themes that would remain central to federalism scholarship, such as the function and scope of intergovernmental aid, the tax and debt structures of federal systems, the effect of federal systems on the size of government, and definitional issues related to important terms like decentralization.

Oates[10] and Faguet[11] provide helpful overviews of federalism research after the contemporary parameters of the scholarship were established. Oates tends to focus on market-oriented themes, in keeping with the organizing principle of his foundational framework. He mentions new research on tax policy, for example, to inform how taxes should be structured for localities to avoid driving away people and resources. Scholarship has shown that local government is responsive to macroeconomic concerns and engages in income redistribution, two areas that his federalism theory would allocate to central authority. The argument for decentralization has benefited from the insight that the benefits from local specialization of public goods are larger than previously understood due to the relative inelasticity of demand for such goods. Thus, if Tiebout's model based on the mobility of citizens between jurisdictions is qualified by less mobility, there is still great advantage to tailoring public services at the local level. Various purposes of intergovernmental grants are discussed with the "qualification … that such a system of grants must not be too large in the sense of undermining fiscal discipline at the lower level of government."[12] Wariness is warranted when it comes to intergovernmental aid. Such aid theoretically should act like an increase in personal income in the jurisdiction that receives it and should produce, therefore, a similar budgetary response as an increase in such income. Research indicates that this is not the case, however, and that intergovernmental aid results in much greater public spending by the recipient government than is occasioned by an increase in income within that jurisdiction. Oates does not draw this conclusion explicitly, but the implication is that the "flypaper effect" of intergovernmental aid from the center to decentralized governmental entities obscures a potential benefit of decentralization: a more direct linkage between expenditures and taxes that leads to fiscal accountability. Research affirming the role of states as policy laboratories is mentioned, and an important challenge to that assumption is reviewed. Rather than innovate on policy for the public good, the states can be seen as engaged in a "race to the bottom." Oates concludes that the benefits from local government competition are real, that distortions are also present, and that research needs to be done to sort out the significance of both. Inman and Rubinfeld[13] show that there is reason to believe a decentralized system encourages citizen engagement, and Weingast[14] argues that federal structures limiting the confiscatory powers of central government were essential to economic development in England and the U.S. Devolution of important powers to local jurisdictions underlies rapid economic growth in China, Weingast also concludes. McKinnon spends more time on one of the conditions Weingast specifies for his federal structure: the presence of hard budget constraints on subnational governments.[15] Local government reliance on its own sources of revenue are essential to a healthy federal system: money creation must be off limits and intergovernmental transfers from the center restricted.[16] Institutional arrangements that give policymakers the right incentives also must be considered alongside the assignment of various powers to different levels of government. Referencing Shah's[17] work, "These rules or procedures must make the costs of public programs as fully visible as their benefits in ways that make public officials accountable for their decisions," Oates writes.[18] Brennan and Buchanan make the argument that competition between localities obliges them to follow fiscally frugal policies, thereby keeping the size of government smaller.[19] The evidence for this thesis appears mixed, Oates concludes. The effect of federalism on economic development must be interpreted in light of the setting of each country and that country's familiarity or lack thereof with federal systems. Of critical importance in federal structures in developing countries is the role of intergovernmental aid. Countries that decentralize some degree of policy control without giving localities the means to raise and be responsible for their own revenue are prone to economic and fiscal mismanagement.

An undercurrent in Oates' review essay becomes the central theme in Faguet's later assessment of the literature: the conflicting results of federalism research on the relative benefits of decentralization. Faguet does not go out of his way to attack Oates' original paradigm but shows more clearly how research is calling into question the market-oriented assumptions at the heart of Oates' framework. In short, the literature simply does not point clearly toward the benefits of centralization or decentralization but remains conflicted in almost every area of inquiry. For one, different theoretical assumptions concerning federal structures can lead to different preferences for centralized or decentralized systems. As one part of their argument, for example, Besley and Coate show that if central authority can tailor goods to local needs or if there are spillover effects from local expenditures that make them Pareto inefficient, then Oates' Decentralization Theorem does not hold.[20] Government accountability is the best argument for decentralization, Faguet argues, and this is achieved through the only direct effect of decentralization: changing the incentives of government officials and local citizens. When local officials are elected from below rather than appointed from above, their focus shifts to the needs of the local citizenry, and the local citizenry, sensing this shift, responds by greater engagement in civic affairs.

> Surprisingly often, both enthusiasts and critics of reform omit this basic point in favor of second- and third-order arguments about whether decentralization can increase growth or reduce ethnic conflicts ... Many of these things, such as inflation, the fiscal deficit, and ethnic conflicts and political stability in a nation more broadly, are important, and decentralization may indeed affect them. But it does so via incentives and accountability; there is no direct effect.[21]

Faguet divides federalism research into the three areas of quality of governance, economic performance, and government accountability.[22] After reviewing the conflicting results of research in each of these areas, Faguet poses the question that follows from his thesis: why is federalism research so conflicted in its outcomes? He replies by arguing that scholars have been plagued with sloppy definitions of decentralization and wrong methodological assumptions. Asking whether decentralization improves this or that aspect of governance misses the contextual point that should inform all research on federalism. Decentralization will both improve and harm indices of good government depending on the incentives it gives to officials and citizens. Rather than ask if decentralization improved or harmed a particular measure of good government, it would be better to ask why the good or the bad resulted as it did.

Rodden underscores the definitional issue more forcefully than Faguet, pointing to blunt, dichotomous measures of federalism in most previous studies and the difficulty of finding good data for cross-national analysis. "The most clearly discernible *Leitmotiv* in these studies is a growing disappointment with decentralization and federalism, especially among developing countries," Rodden writes.[23] Decentralization and federalism are not the same. Decentralization is the "shift of authority towards local governments and away from central governments, with total government authority over society and economy imagined as fixed," and can be measured in terms of fiscal affairs, policy development, and political function.[24] With regard to fiscal decentralization, for example, the extent of intergovernmental aid is critical to determining the degree to which the federal structure is in fact decentralized. Good data on this particular point is hard to come by, however, Rodden states. Federalism, by contrast, is "not a particular distribution of authority between governments, but rather a process—structured by a set of institutions—through which authority is distributed and redistributed."[25] Deficiencies in considering the relevant features of federalism and the use of inappropriate independent variables to interpret the effects of decentralization have contributed to confusion in the literature. "The links between theory and empirical analysis have been quite tenuous in the first generation of empirical studies," Rodden states,[26] a conclusion echoed by Rodden and Eskeland.[27]

Consider the results of several important studies that implicate aspects of indebtedness. One early study by Roubini and Sachs reviews deficits in developed (OECD) countries and finds that the structure of political institutions is significant in explaining such deficits.[28] They do not focus on federalism per se, but find that more diffuse arrangements of political power (such as more diverse coalitions or more partisan change in governance) tend to increase deficits. Castles reviews 21 developed countries and finds that centralization has had a negative influence on economic growth and inflation.[29] Also taking a negative view, Wibbels concludes that the macroeconomic performance of developing nations has suffered due to federal structures that allow local governments to avoid difficult fiscal decisions.[30] Deficits, debt, and inflation all fared more poorly under federal systems.

A strong defense of the benefits of decentralization is provided by Qian and Roland.[31] Focusing on the interesting case of privatization, they find that China's transfer of economic authority to local governments resulted in a much more efficient management of the privatization effort. In their mutual competition for the policies and inputs of economic growth, local officials had much less incentive to bail out privatizing firms (what Qian and Roland call the soft budget constraint) than if such privatization had been handled by a central authority, as it had been in Russia and Eastern Europe. Leachman et al. review budget performance in 15 developed countries and find that federalism improves fiscal balance in the presence of strong fiscal institutions that encourage spending discipline.[32] Rodden and Eskeland lend support to the conclusions of Qian and Roland: central governments with a firm commitment against soft budget constraints and lacking ambitions to redistribute income between localities are best suited to encourage local fiscal discipline.[33] On the other hand, Ong (2012) takes exception to Weingast directly and indirectly challenges Qian and Roland. Local governments in China are incurring excessive amounts of debt due to the lack of hard budget constraints. A closed political system does not afford the checks on such behavior assumed by the Oates framework, and China's macroeconomic stability is in jeopardy as a result.[34]

Rodden and Wibbels employ nuanced measures of federalism and variables to measure political and economic context to conclude that, in contrast to other studies, decentralization has the fiscal benefit of reduced deficits (overall national and local) and the macroeconomic benefit of restrained inflation.[35] Deficits and inflation are likewise influenced in a similar fashion by shared party affiliation between national and local officials. These fiscal and macroeconomic outcomes are conditioned on local fiscal autonomy that is not undermined by intergovernmental aid, however, a finding consistent with federalism theory and empirical research overall. Rodden amplifies on this finding by showing that fiscal decentralization in developed countries tends to restrain the size of the public sector when lines of fiscal autonomy are clear and expand it otherwise.[36]

Rodden and Eskeland build on Inman's[37] analysis to show that market assets have a historical aspect to them and can act as restraints in the absence of hard budget rules from central authority. The refusal of the U.S. government to rescue states from default in the 1830s and 1840s set important norms of fiscal accountability at the local level and led to a variety of self-imposed, as opposed to hierarchical, budget constraints. In part due to this history of American federalism, states have among the highest degree of fiscal autonomy in the world.[38]

Hallerberg and Marier's review of budget discipline in Latin American and Caribbean countries permits a broader discussion of an important topic in the debate over decentralization.[39] The common pool resource problem is the central challenge posed to fiscal stringency. To take this point and depart from their article for a moment, there are characteristics inherent in the decentralized political structures of democracy, such as diffuse decision making and multiple veto players, that may incline such governments toward greater indebtedness. Of course, the political benefit of liberty is seen as a political good worthy of this risk. This leads to two observations related to interpreting the inconsistencies in the literature over the effects of centralization on public debt. First, comparative studies of developed democracies that seek to measure the effects of centralization on fiscal outcomes are essentially defining the margins of a political system that is fundamentally decentralized, that is, a political system that has chosen liberty as its primary good. Second, comparative studies that incorporate developed democracies and developing countries with varying degrees of democratic governance should be conducted and interpreted with the greatest of care in light of the difference in their fundamental political orientation: developed democracies are fundamentally decentralized, having liberty as their organizing principle, while developing countries share in that principle to varying degrees and, on balance, have a much higher degree of centralization, as Oates recounts.[40] To the extent that developing countries share in the ordering principle of liberty, decentralization may result in improved indices of good government or it may foster multiple fiefdoms of autocracy in the place of a central tyranny. The question that follows is not whether decentralized, developed democracy results in less debt than autocracy, for the political good of liberty is worth the risk of fiscal imbalance, but what centralizing and decentralizing features in democracy help it overcome the common pool resource problem, and these may be characterized as centralizing or decentralizing, depending on the context. Returning to Hallerberg and Marier, they find that a strong finance minister in cabinet and a strong president help check fiscal excesses under certain political conditions.

Freitag and Vatter study the level of decentralization in Swiss cantons and determine that decentralization helps limit debt in time of economic hardship (but not during economic prosperity), in part due to the presence of a large number of small local administrative units.[41] Contrary to the balance of the literature, however, they find that intergovernmental aid is associated with improved levels of fiscal balance.

Hallerberg and Ylaoutinen offer another example of the kind of fine-grained analysis that assesses public debt in the context of a country's political institutions.[42] They review fiscal policy outcomes of Central and Eastern European countries, identify fiscal practices best suited to the political institutions of those countries, and show that debt levels increase to the extent that those countries depart from particularized fiscal management practices. These conclusions build on an earlier argument by Porter and Olsen: centralization and decentralization must be considered in light of the values and tasks within a political context.[43] Inman likewise emphasizes broader cultural assets that influence the effect of decentralization. Speaking of the U.S., Inman writes, "The economy's mature banking system, ... a nationally integrated capital market, and in more recent years local bankruptcy standards protecting creditors' interests have helped minimize the financial spillovers from a local government default."[44] A lack of strength in the executive and relatively weak political parties have allowed local governments to secure inefficient intergovernmental aid, however.

An Aristotelian Contribution to Federalism Theory

As an economic perspective with Oates helped political science begin to break out of a rule-bound approach to federalism, so political theory may return the favor and come to the aid of a federalism literature whose organizing principles have been undermined by conflicting results. Drawing on Chapters 2 and 3, Aristotle and Tocqueville can help place the debate over centralization in the context of the primary good of political freedom. As discussed in Chapter 3 (please see Figure 3.8), both democracy and oligarchy can centralize. The democratic mob (point A) and the oligarchic tyrant (point B) both undermine the political rule of free and equal people. Centralizing tendencies should not be seen as oligarchic, and decentralizing tendencies should not be seen as democratic. What is "decentralizing" is that which restrains mastery and enhances political freedom and may entail oligarchic elements in democracy (such as a strong finance minister or president (Hallerberg and Marier 2004) or democratic elements in oligarchy.

Figure 3.9 incorporates the institutional curve AB with the mores curve CD to show that different societies have different capacities to mitigate harmful institutional policies or accentuate beneficial ones. For example, when an institutional shift from optimum point F to suboptimum point H occurs, a society at point E (with the greatest capacity in terms of mores for justice or the common good) suffers less of a decline in political freedom than a society at point G.

With regard to debt, the society at point E will have a greater capacity to sustain fiscal balance in the face of institutional changes that encourage indebtedness. This is precisely the kind of textured analysis that fiscal federalism research is calling for. It helps explains, for example, why federalism supports private property and sound economic management in the U.S. but undermines those very same things in Argentina and Russia.[45] Moreover, political freedom as an organizing theoretical framework appears to be more durable than the economic focus of the original Oates framework. Faguet points in this direction, too, arguing that good governance is the most important source of legitimacy for decentralization.

Studies of State Debt

Studies on state indebtedness can be divided into general assessments of overall trends and more targeted analysis of a political or institutional variable in influencing debt levels. Studies with the broader methodology can have specific variables of interest but seek to incorporate a wider mix of socioeconomic, political, and institutional variables to develop a more comprehensive view of factors influencing debt levels. This book uses the broader methodological framework with emphasis on explaining the relationship of justice or the common good to indebtedness. In this category of research on state debt, Bahl and Duncombe,[46] Clingermayer and Wood,[47] and Greer and Denison[48] are the three best representatives.

A strength of Bahl and Duncombe is their disaggregation of state debt into various categories: "full-faith and credit" and "non-guaranteed debt." As the name implies, full-faith and credit debt obligates the fiscal powers of the state for repayment. Public non-guaranteed debt does not obligate the state in this way and typically is backed by a revenue source affiliated with the project financed by the debt or by appropriation from the legislature. Because legislative appropriation may be required to pay the debt, public non-guaranteed debt can be referred to as "moral obligation" bonds. Finally, private non-guaranteed debt may be used to support projects such as industrial development or hospital bonds.[49] Bahl and Duncombe's analysis brings into sharper relief the increasing reliance of state governments on non-guaranteed debt. Limited to 1988–1990, they find that demographic measures such as population change and population density have a positive impact on debt levels, that per capita income does not impact debt, that the size of the public sector (revenue per capita) has a positive relationship with indebtedness, and that debt limits do constrain debt. Speaking of the last finding, Bahl and Duncombe state, "There may be a general antidebt climate in some states that discourages all forms of debt."[50]

Closest in spirit to the present study, Clingermayer and Wood review total state indebtedness from 1961 to 1989 with a view to inform various features of fiscal federalism. They begin by alluding to the reputation of the states as being more frugal than the federal government. Various forms of debt limitation have been tried by the states, and the states thus can be used in comparative analysis to assess the influence of these and other variables on public debt levels.

Clingermayer and Wood overstate the incidence of state default in the nineteenth century and the role of Keynes in encouraging deficit financing, but their modeling is well-conceived and applied. Like Bahl and Duncombe, they find that the size of the public sector measured in revenue per capita has a positive influence on debt. Unlike Bahl and Duncombe, they find that personal income does, too. The amount of federal intergovernmental aid to the state increases debt, but Clingermayer and Wood do not draw conclusions related to centralization from this. They also include a series of helpful lagged variables assessing the impact on debt of the change (rather than the level) in personal income, state revenue per capita, and intergovernmental aid per capita. Declines in each of these encourage debt issues, a finding that is supportive of Barro's (1979) tax smoothing argument. State ideology is significant in explaining debt, with more liberal states incurring more debt. Centralization within a state, measured by state revenue as a percent of state and local revenue, was not significant, nor was divided government. They found weak support for the "political business cycle" hypothesis. Debt increases in years before an election with high electoral competition. Tax and expenditure limits also had a weak influence on debt levels but in the opposite direction intended by the voters, indicating that public officials had found ways to circumvent such restraints and continue to incur debt. After presenting their findings, Clingermayer and Wood shift the focus back to fiscal federalism to inform the national policy debate over public debt. They conclude that factors driving state debt are similar to those at the federal level and that mechanisms employed by the states to limit debt will not be effective in restraining national indebtedness.

Greer and Denison are not focused on state debt per se but the factors that contribute to the concentration of debt at the state, as opposed to the local, level. They discuss the three arguments developed by Inman and Rubinfeld[51] in favor of the decentralization afforded by fiscal federalism: efficient resource allocation, political participation, and preservation of personal liberties. Variables in the model are organized around these three categories, and several demographic and socioeconomic variables also are included (income, unemployment, population density, education, race, and a young and elderly age cohort). The influence of these factors is considered for both total debt stock and new debt issues. Greer and Denison find that debt concentrates at the state level with both increases in income and unemployment. Ideology is significant in explaining debt concentration, with liberal states having greater concentration of indebtedness at the state level. The number of municipalities per 1,000 population also has a positive relationship with debt concentration at the state level.

With regard to all three studies, the use of longitudinal data in Clingermayer and Wood and Greer and Denison produces findings that are more robust than the cross-sectional analysis of Bahl and Duncombe. To address issues of non-stationarity, Clingermayer and Wood use the change from year to year in per capita debt. The other two studies account for both the stock and flow of debt, or the amount in a given year and the new debt issue. State debt cannot be studied without considering fiscal federalism, but only Clingermayer and Wood frame their research questions and modeling to use state debt patterns to inform analysis of public debt in the nation overall. As such, their review is the closest approximation to the present study in method and intent.

Two separate studies are worth mentioning for their treatment of state debt in a way that brings considerations of justice more clearly to the surface, although the authors do not go so far as to discuss their analysis in that light. Clingermayer[52] and Ellis and Schansberg[53] test an argument by Cukierman and Meltzer[54] that the percent elderly in a population has a positive influence on the level of public debt, as elderly individuals near the end of life have a greater incentive to support debt rather than taxes. Their findings are the opposite of those hypothesized, however: the size of the elderly population has a negative relationship with various measures of debt. While this modeling outcome should not be dismissed, it does not appear that the initial hypothesis of these studies is well-conceived. The most important government programs for the elderly are at the federal level, and it would seem that their incentive to increase public indebtedness would apply, if at all, to questions of federal debt. Second, it is not clear why the elderly would prefer debt to taxes more than other age cohorts. A middle-aged couple raising a family may have more incentive to prefer debt to higher taxes. Other mitigating factors might include different preferences for elderly with children as opposed to those without.

Methodology and Variable Selection

Table 4.1 provides descriptive statistics for the dependent and independent variables used in the principal regression models. A decennial measurement for the dependent and independent variables is taken for each of the 48 contiguous states from 1920 to 1990, yielding a total of 384 observations for most time series. Census records are used to construct the time series for the bulk of the variables. When data is not always available for each variable precisely at decennial years, the data point closest to the decennial year is used. For example, a balanced-budget rule (BBR) enacted in 1912 is assigned to census year 1910, while a BBR enactment in 1915 is assigned to 1920. A full listing of data sources used is included in the statistical appendix. Unless otherwise noted, all figures and tables below are derived from the author's statistical analysis.

Two iterations of real state debt per capita are used as dependent variables: real state debt per capita and a right-censored version of real state debt per capita. Real state debt per capita would be the preferred dependent variable, but its skewness and kurtosis are high at 2.6 and 8.35, respectively. A right-censored version of real state debt per capita omits 5 percent of the highest observations (19 out of 384) to reduce skewness and kurtosis to more acceptable levels (1.52 and 1.8, respectively). Both models produce similar results.

Select independent variables seek to determine the effect of social and fiscal characteristics on state indebtedness. The models incorporate several population measures: population density (incorporating both population and area) and various measures of urbanization (percent of the population in cities less than

Table 4.1 Descriptive Statistics

	N	*Mean*	*Median*	*SD*	*Min*	*Max*	*Skewness*	*Kurtosis*
Dependent Variables								
Real State Debt Per Capita	384	1,026.36	504.38	1,356.41	0.00	8,876.84	2.60	8.35
Real State Debt Per Capita (Censored)	365	792.09	474.17	844.55	0.00	3,895.90	1.52	1.80
Independent Variables								
Population Density	384	124.05	54.83	189.26	0.70	1,041.95	2.70	7.37
Population Density (log)	384	3.93	4.00	1.42	–0.35	6.95	–0.23	–0.07
Population (%) in Cities < 100,000	384	81.68	81.18	15.26	33.23	100.00	–0.50	–0.21
Population (%) in Cities > 100,000	384	18.32	18.82	15.26	0.00	66.77	0.50	–0.21
Age of State	384	120.27	125.00	47.44	8.00	203.00	–0.22	–0.81
Voter Turnout	384	57.17	61.35	15.95	7.45	83.27	–1.13	0.81
Vote For Democrat President (%)	384	47.20	45.48	12.55	19.17	97.50	1.12	2.59
Protestant/Catholic Population	334	7.22	1.74	16.69	0.16	212.30	6.96	72.04
Protestant/Catholic Population (log)	334	0.80	0.55	1.43	–1.82	5.36	0.65	–0.23
Real Income Per Capita (2010 Dollars)	336	17,531.18	16,236.11	8,739.10	3,349.70	44,609.00	0.42	–0.62
Real Income Per Capita/1000 (2010 Dollars)	336	17.53	16.24	8.74	3.35	44.61	0.42	–0.62
Real IG Aid to the State Per Capita (2010 Dollars)	336	514.01	346.25	441.81	7.94	2,455.73	0.87	0.49
State Revenue as % of State Plus Local Revenue	336	52.42	54.57	12.72	15.00	79.70	–0.66	0.15
Total Balanced Budget Rules	384	3.10	3.00	2.27	0.00	8.00	0.26	–0.82
Lawyers/1,000 Population	336	1.54	1.36	0.69	0.57	4.54	1.27	1.77

Source: Author's analysis of select datasets included in Appendix.

100,000, between 100,000 and 300,000, and greater than 300,000). Age of the state measures whether fiscal sclerosis has any explanatory power regarding state debt.

Voter turnout and racial composition should be mentioned together. As an intuitive and frequently used measure of civic health, voter turnout is an important independent variable. Racial makeup of a state could be included as well but would have limited explanatory power from 1920 to 1990 due to voting restrictions on most non-whites for much of that time period. This historical feature is evident statistically in the high correlation (0.82) between the percentage of the white population and voter turnout. Voter turnout thus offers much greater insight than racial composition into a state's proclivity for debt but is a measure of the civic involvement of only white voters for much of the century.

A measure of ideology would be valuable for a study of this kind. Party affiliation is one option. In the early twenty-first century, public debt is an issue that tends to differentiate Democrat from Republican, at least rhetorically, with Republicans generally more in favor of fiscal stringency. This has not been the case in earlier periods of American history, and evaluating the relationship between debt and party affiliation statistically is one way to measure whether debt has been a defining issue between Republicans and Democrats during the time period in question. Several studies have relied on the party affiliation of the governor or the party in control of the legislature to measure a state's political ideology. While not without merit, using such indices can distort the true political leaning of a state. Ideology may be the dominant factor in elections, but they also are shaped by other important variables such as candidate quality. A Republican may win the governorship in a predominantly Democratic state (Christie in New Jersey) and vice versa (Henry in Oklahoma). In this case, the governor's party affiliation would skew his state's measure of political ideology. Second, this particular research question needs a variable that is comparable across states. With these issues in mind, the vote for president has advantages over other variables. Instead of a variable subject to the vagaries of intrastate politics, the vote for president is measuring the ideological response of all states to one candidate at one time. The percent vote received by the candidate is not the key factor for modeling purposes but how the vote percentage for that candidate varies among the states. The percent vote for the Democratic presidential candidate by decade is thus used as one possible measure of state ideology, keeping in mind the limitations on its explanatory power due to significant ideological shifts within the two major parties over the course of the twentieth century and regional factors complicating the national posture of both parties.

The effects of a state's religious composition on public budgeting are measured by including the Protestant/Catholic population ratio. The Census Bureau surveyed religious life in America until 1936, with reviews in that year and in previous years (1890, 1906, 1916, and 1926). Surveys of similar scope were conducted by privately funded denominational interests in 1952, 1971, 1980, and routinely every ten years from 1980 forward. All of these databases (through 1990) were accessed at the Association of Religious Data Archives (ARDA) and used to derive summary totals for Protestants and Catholics in a given year. As with other variables, religion surveys occurring mid-decade were placed in the closest decennial census year (1906 in 1910; 1916 in 1920; 1926 in 1930; 1952 in 1950; and 1971 in 1970). There is no adequate survey of religious composition by state near 1960, however, and this variable has a slightly smaller sample size as a result (334). As the two largest religious groups, the percentage of Protestants and the percentage of Catholics are negatively correlated. The Protestant to Catholic ratio is the best way to capture the relationship of both variables with state debt and avoid correlation issues between the two when modeled separately.

The model incorporates several economic and fiscal variables. Per capita income is included as a measure of a state's economic health. The Census began measuring income by state in 1929, and this data point thus has a slightly smaller sample size (336). Intergovernmental aid to the state (almost all of which is from the federal government) is intended as a measure of a state's tendency toward centralization. Census records do not have this variable for 1920, thus leaving a slightly smaller sample size (336). State revenue own source as a percent of state and local revenue own source is included as a measure of centralization within a state. This variable also has a slightly smaller sample size (336) due to data unavailable for a particular decade. Balanced-budget rule stringency may serve as a measure of general state norms on debt, although such rules do not pertain directly to debt levels themselves due to the distinction between current and capital account spending in state finances. Balanced-budget rules typically apply to the former and are designed to restrain deficits, while debt is a capital account item not typically subject to balanced-budget rules. Data on state balanced-budget rules is taken from the extensive work on the topic by Hou and Smith[55] and Smith and Hou.[56] Constitutional debt limits that apply directly to capital account items would be a more appropriate institutional variable than balanced-budget rules, but a detailed taxonomy for debt limits on the order of the Hou and Smith taxonomy of balanced-budget rules has not been developed. Still, balanced-budget rules may signify a culture of budget balance.

Finally, and most importantly for this model, is the development of a variable to measure societal injustice. State crime data could be used, but this approach has the empirical limitation of a lack of reliable, consistent data for the time period in question and the theoretical limitation of injustice being broader than crime. Injustice measures the incapacity for the common good, the breakdown of relationships that make society function. It is associated with faction, both criminal and civil. One possible way to measure the extent of not only criminal but civil faction is the number of proceedings at law in both categories. The extent of a society's criminal and civil litigation incorporates formal violations of the law and informal judgments between citizens that they have been wronged, and wronged to a degree that relational means of resolution are inadequate and relief under law must be sought. As with much social science data, statistics on litigiousness by state are available only for recent decades. One variable that may serve as a substitute and is available through the time period in question, however, is the size of the bar in the various states. The number of lawyers by state is assumed to be an adequate representation of state injustice, not that lawyers are unjust or create injustice, but that they are the handlers of injustice. It is a blunt instrument, to be sure, but the other modeled variables are as well. Models are at best general approximations of reality, and the meaning of each significant variable is open to some degree of speculation. After the models are discussed, more time will be spent in the next chapter on the possible meaning of the injustice variable.

The pooled time series used for analysis involves repeated measurements from the same set of 48 lower American states from 1920 to 1990. Modeling techniques must account, therefore, for correlated data. Generalized Estimating Equations (GEE) are a sufficient means to model correlated data, and this technique is used in all models through PROC GENMOD in SAS.[57]

Preliminary Modeling

As discussed above, two iterations of real state debt per capita are used as dependent variables: real state debt per capita with a skewness of 2.6 and a kurtosis of 8.35 and a right-censored version of real state debt per capita with a skewness of 1.52 and a kurtosis of 1.80 (omitting 5 percent or 19 out of 384 observations). The models for both dependent variables had approximately similar results. The censored version of real state debt per capita is used in final modeling due to more acceptable levels of skewness and kurtosis.

In addition, the independent variables of real income per capita and real intergovernmental aid per capita have a strong positive correlation and are modeled separately to address potential issues with multicollinearity. Of course, the limitation of modeling these two variables in this manner is that the significance of both cannot be assessed controlling for the other. Preliminary modeling also showed that the size of a state's urban population is significant in explaining real state debt per capita. Modeled variables include the percent of a state's total population living in cities less than 100,000, in cities between 100,000 and 300,000, and in cities greater than 300,000. The percent of a state's population in cities less than 100,000 had a significant and positive relationship with state debt, and the percent of a state's population in cities over 100,000 had a significant and negative relationship with state debt. The two variables (percent population in cities less than 100,000 and percent population over 100,000) are inverse percentages and cannot be modeled together. They also are modeled separately.

To summarize, there are three final models using real state debt per capita (censored) as the dependent variable: (1) real income per capita without real intergovernmental aid to a state per capita; (2) real intergovernmental aid to a state per capita without real income per capita; and (3) percent of a state's population in cities greater than 100,000 (percent of a state's population in cities less than 100,000 is used in the first two models.

Final Models

Model 1: Real Income Per Capita Without Real Intergovernmental Aid to a State Per Capita

A generalized estimating equation (GEE) through PROC GENMOD in SAS is used to regress covariates of interest on real state debt per capita (censored) in the following form:

$$y_{it} = \alpha + \beta_{it} + \gamma_{it} + \mu_{it} + \delta_{it} + \theta_{it} + \vartheta_{it} + \rho_{it} + \psi_{it} + \chi_{it} + \tau_{it}$$

Where y_{it} is real state debt per capita in a given state *i* at time *t*; α is the constant; β_{it} is the log of the population density of a given state *i* at time *t*; γ_{it} is the percent population in cities less than 100,000 of a given state *i* at time *t*; μ_{it} is the age of a given state *i* at time *t*; δ_{it} is the percent voter turnout of a given state *i* at time *t*; θ_{it} is the percent vote for Democratic presidential candidate in a given state *i* at time *t*; ϑ_{it} is the log of the Protestant/Catholic population ratio in a given state *i* at time *t*; ρ_{it} is \$1,000 increments of real income per capita in a given state *i* at time *t*; ψ is state revenue own source as a percent of total local and state revenue own source in a given state *i* at time *t*; χ is the number of balanced-budget rules in force in a given state *i* at time *t*; and τ is the number of lawyers per 1,000 population in a given state *i* at time *t*.

As Table 4.2 indicates, population density, percent population in cities less than 100,000, voter turnout, the Protestant/Catholic population ratio, real income per capita, state revenue as a percent of local and state revenue, and the numbers of lawyers per 1,000 population are significant in Model 1. The error term for

Table 4.2 Regression of Real State Debt Right Censored* on Select Variables (1920–1990), Real Income Per Capita Without Real IG Aid to State Per Capita

Parameter	*Estimate*	*Standard Error*	*Pr>|Z|*
Intercept	–2,155.15	476.81	<0.0001
Population Density (log)	144.21	62.52	0.0211
Population in Cities < 100,000 (%)	17.48	3.36	<0.0001
Age of State	–0.30	2.07	0.8844
Voter Turnout	–7.39	3.65	0.0430
Vote for Democrat President (%)	–3.92	2.83	0.1661
Protestant/Catholic Population (log)	–75.16	38.09	0.0484
Real Income Per Capita/1,000	48.09	10.87	<0.0001
State Revenue as % of State Plus Local Revenue	10.65	2.70	<0.0001
Total Balanced Budget Rules	–17.09	16.41	0.2978
Lawyers/1,000 Population	320.20	145.89	0.0282

Source: Author's analysis of select datasets included in Appendix.

Note

* 5 percent of the highest observations (or 19 out of 384).

Model 1 is well-behaved, with a skewness of 0.82 and a kurtosis of 0.99. The QIC is 286.81.

The model above uses a natural log for the independent variables population density and Protestant/Catholic population ratio. The dependent variable real state debt per capita and the other independent variables are in linear form. As such, the parameter estimates for each significant variable have the following interpretation: population density (log) has a significant and positive relationship, with every unit increase in population density (log) increasing real state debt per capita by 144.21; the percent population in cities less than 100,000 has a significant and positive relationship, with every unit increase in the percent population in cities less than 100,000 increasing real state debt per capita by 17.48; voter turnout has a significant and negative relationship, with every unit increase in voter turnout decreasing real state debt per capita by 7.39; the Protestant to Catholic population ratio (log) has a significant and negative relationship, with every unit increase in the Protestant to Catholic population ratio (log) decreasing real state debt per capita by 75.16; real income per capita has a significant and positive relationship, with every unit increase ($1,000) in real income per capita increasing real state debt per capita by 48.09; state revenue as a percent of local and state revenue has a significant and positive relationship, with every unit increase in state revenue as a percent of local and state revenue increasing real state debt per capita by 10.65; and the number of lawyers per 1,000 population has a significant and positive relationship, with every unit increase in the number of lawyers per 1,000 population increasing real state debt per capita by 320.20. Age of the state, Democratic vote for president, and total balanced-budget rules are not significant.

Model 2: Real Intergovernmental Aid to a State Per Capita Without Real Income Per Capita

A generalized estimating equation (GEE) through PROC GENMOD in SAS is used to regress covariates of interest on real state debt per capita (censored) in the following form:

$$y_{it} = \alpha + \beta_{it} + \gamma_{it} + \mu_{it} + \delta_{it} + \theta_{it} + \vartheta_{it} + \rho_{it} + \psi_{it} + \chi_{it} + \tau_{it}$$

Where y_{it} is real state debt per capita in a given state i at time t; α is the constant; β_{it} is the log of the population density of a given state i at time t; γ_{it} is the percent population in cities less than 100,000 of a given state i at time t; μ_{it} is the age of a given state i at time t; δ_{it} is the percent voter turnout of a given state i at time t; θ_{it} is the percent vote for Democratic presidential candidate in a given state i at time t; ϑ_{it} is the log of the Protestant/Catholic population ratio in a given state i at time t; ρ_{it} is the real intergovernmental aid per capita in a given state i at time t; ψ is state revenue own source as a percent of total local and state revenue own source in a given state i at time t; χ is the number of balanced-budget rules in force in a given state i at time t; and τ is the number of lawyers per 1,000 population in a given state i at time t.

As Table 4.3 indicates, population density, percent population in cities less than 100,000, voter turnout, the Protestant/Catholic population ratio, real intergovernmental aid to the state per capita, state revenue as a percent of local and state revenue, and the numbers of lawyers per 1,000 population are significant in Model 2. The error term for Model 2 is well-behaved, with a skewness of 0.92 and a kurtosis of 1.34. The QIC is 284.41.

The parameter estimates for each significant variable have the following interpretation: population density (log) has a significant and positive relationship, with every unit increase in population density (log) increasing real state debt per capita by 240.98; the percent population in cities less than 100,000 has a significant and positive relationship, with every unit increase in the percent population in cities less than 100,000 increasing real state debt per capita by 14.10; voter turnout has a significant and negative relationship, with every unit increase in voter turnout decreasing real state debt per capita by 9.08; the Protestant/Catholic population ratio (log) has a significant and negative relationship, with every unit increase in the Protestant/Catholic population ratio (log) decreasing real state debt per capita by 117.79; real intergovernmental aid to the state per capita has a significant and positive relationship, with every unit increase in real intergovernmental aid to the state per capita increasing real state debt per capita by 1.10; state revenue as a percent of local and state revenue has a significant and positive relationship, with every unit increase in state revenue as a percent of local and state revenue increasing real state debt per capita by 6.93; and the number of lawyers per 1,000 population has a significant and positive relationship, with every unit increase in the number of lawyers per 1,000 population increasing real state debt per capita by 327.53. Age of the state, Democratic vote for president, and total balanced-budget rules are not significant.

Table 4.3 Regression of Real State Debt Right Censored* on Select Variables (1920–1990), Real IG Aid Per Capita Without Real Income Per Capita

Parameter	*Estimate*	*Standard Error*	*Pr>|Z|*
Intercept	–1,552.02	544.79	0.0044
Population Density (log)	240.98	46.35	<0.0001
Population in Cities < 100,000 (%)	14.10	3.62	0.0001
Age of State	–1.47	1.45	0.3114
Voter Turnout	–9.08	3.79	0.0167
Vote for Democrat President (%)	–3.52	3.44	0.3067
Protestant/Catholic Population (log)	–117.79	36.39	0.0012
Real IG Aid to the State Per Capita	1.10	0.12	<0.0001
State Revenue as % of State Plus Local Revenue	6.93	3.40	0.0417
Total Balanced Budget Rules	–15.30	13.80	0.2677
Lawyers/1,000 Population	327.53	94.62	0.0005

Source: Author's analysis of select datasets included in Appendix.

Note

* 5 percent of the highest observations (or 19 out of 384).

Model 3: Percent of a State's Population in Cities Greater Than 100,000

A generalized estimating equation (GEE) through PROC GENMOD in SAS is used to regress covariates of interest on real state debt per capita (censored) in the following form:

$$y_{it} = \alpha + \beta_{it} + \gamma_{it} + \mu_{it} + \delta_{it} + \theta_{it} + \vartheta_{it} + \rho_{it} + \psi_{it} + \chi_{it} + \tau_{it}$$

Where y_{it} is real state debt per capita in a given state i at time t; α is the constant; β_{it} is the log of the population density of a given state i at time t; γ_{it} is the percent population in cities greater than 100,000 of a given state i at time t; μ_{it} is the age of a given state i at time t; δ_{it} is the percent voter turnout of a given state i at time t; θ_{it} is the percent vote for Democratic presidential candidate in a given state i at time t; ϑ_{it} is the log of the Protestant/Catholic population ratio in a given state i at time t; ρ_{it} is the real intergovernmental aid per capita in a given state i at time t; ψ is state revenue own source as a percent of total local and state revenue own source in a given state i at time t; χ is the number of balanced-budget rules in force in a given state i at time t; and τ is the number of lawyers per 1,000 population in a given state i at time t.

As Table 4.4 indicates, population density, percent population in cities greater than 100,000, voter turnout, the Protestant/Catholic population ratio, real intergovernmental aid to the state per capita, state revenue as a percent of local and state revenue, and the numbers of lawyers per 1,000 population are significant in Model 1. The error term for Model 3 is well-behaved, with a skewness of 0.92 and a kurtosis of 1.34. The QIC is 284.41.

Table 4.4 Regression of Real State Debt Right Censored* on Select Variables (1920–1990), Population in Cities Greater than 100,000

Parameter	*Estimate*	*Standard Error*	*Pr > |Z|*
Intercept	–142.21	280.40	0.6120
Population Density (log)	240.98	46.35	<0.0001
Population in Cities > 100,000 (%)	–14.10	3.62	0.0001
Age of State	–1.47	1.45	0.3114
Voter Turnout	–9.08	3.79	0.0167
Vote for Democrat President (%)	–3.52	3.44	0.3067
Protestant/Catholic Population (log)	–117.79	36.39	0.0012
Real IG Aid to the State Per Capita	1.10	0.12	<0.0001
State Revenue as % of State Plus Local Revenue	6.93	3.40	0.0417
Total Balanced Budget Rules	–15.30	13.80	0.2677
Lawyers/1,000 Population	327.53	94.62	0.0005

Source: Author's analysis of select datasets included in Appendix.

Note

* 5 percent of the highest observations (or 19 out of 384).

The parameter estimates for each significant variable have the following interpretation: population density (log) has a significant and positive relationship, with every unit increase in population density (log) increasing real state debt per capita by 240.98; the percent population in cities greater than 100,000 has a significant and negative relationship, with every unit increase in the percent population in cities greater than 100,000 decreasing real state debt per capita by 14.10; voter turnout has a significant and negative relationship, with every unit increase in voter turnout decreasing real state debt per capita by 9.08; the Protestant/Catholic population ratio (log) has a significant and negative relationship, with every unit increase in the Protestant to Catholic population ratio decreasing real state debt per capita by 117.79; real intergovernmental aid to the state per capita has a significant and positive relationship, with every unit increase in real intergovernmental aid to the state per capita increasing real state debt per capita by 1.10; state revenue as a percent of local and state revenue has a significant and positive relationship, with every unit increase in state revenue as a percent of local and state revenue increasing real state debt per capita by 6.93; and the number of lawyers per 1,000 population has a significant and positive relationship, with every unit increase in the number of lawyers per 1,000 population increasing real state debt per capita by 327.53. Age of the state, Democratic vote for president, and total balanced-budget rules are not significant.

Discussion of Dependent Variable Real State Debt Per Capita and Significant Independent Variables, with Charts on Historical Trends and State Rank

Real State Debt Per Capita

To provide a general overview in the trend of real state debt per capita, please see Figure 4.1 below. Although 1920–1990 is the time period under review, earlier decades are included for comparison's sake. Real state debt per capita actually declined from $160 in 1870 to $120 in 1920. It did not trend upward that significantly until the 1950s, rising to $904 by 1960 and $2,458 by 1990. From 1920 to 1990, real state debt per capita increased by 1,948 percent. Table 4.5 ranks the states by the mean of their decennial measurements of real state debt per capita from 1920 to 1990.

Population Density

Population density is significant in all three models above and has a positive relationship with state debt. This supports the findings in Bahl and Duncombe and Clingermayer and Wood. Greer and Denison do not find population density significant, but they also are asking a different research question. Instead of focusing on state debt, as with Clingermayer and Wood and Bahl and Duncombe, Greer and Denison are assessing the ratio of state to local debt, or the concentration of debt at the state level. Their finding that population density is

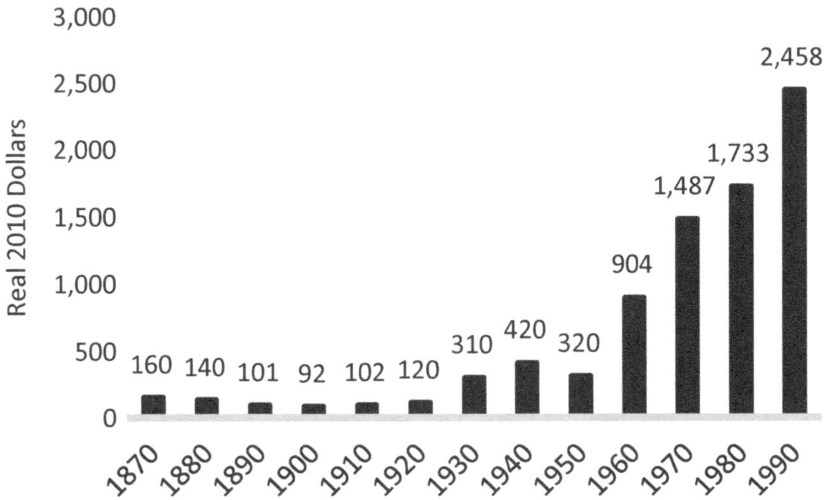

Figure 4.1 Real State Debt Per Capita.

Table 4.5 State Rank: Real State Debt Per Capita (1920–1990)

Rank	*State*	*RSDP*	*Rank*	*State*	*RSDP*
1	DE	3,298	25	MN	799
2	RI	2,441	26	OK	797
3	CT	2,338	27	NV	779
4	OR	2,032	28	AL	760
5	NY	2,010	29	AR	722
6	MA	1,982	30	MI	712
7	NH	1,794	31	WI	658
8	VT	1,780	32	OH	653
9	MD	1,741	33	MS	646
10	LA	1,480	34	UT	611
11	NJ	1,479	35	NC	591
12	SD	1,394	36	VA	574
13	WV	1,259	37	MO	544
14	KY	1,208	38	TN	543
15	ME	1,204	39	ID	532
16	SC	1,048	40	GA	525
17	WY	1,019	41	FL	502
18	CA	990	42	CO	440
19	MT	965	43	IN	438
20	WA	962	44	NE	351
21	PA	942	45	TX	304
22	IL	899	46	AZ	296
23	ND	859	47	KS	293
24	NM	803	48	IA	271

Source: Author's analysis of select datasets included in Appendix.

not significant in explaining a higher state to local debt ratio adds context to the significance of population density in this book and in Clingermayer and Wood and Bahl and Duncombe: as population density places more demand on state borrowing, for infrastructure and other needs, the increased borrowing is not borne inordinately by the state but seems to be shared by state and local governments. Figure 4.2 illustrates the national trend in population density for 1920–1990. Table 4.6 ranks the states by the mean of their decennial measurements of population density for the same time period.

Centralization Variables: City Size, State to Local Revenue Ratio, and Real Intergovernmental Aid to the State Per Capita

Three variables in the model can be interpreted as pertaining to centralization, and all three manifest a significant and positive relationship with state debt. City size is discussed first because it lays the theoretical groundwork for dealing with the other two variables.

Municipal population may not be among the first factors in the study of political centralization, but the centralization of population is an empirical corollary to the centralization of a political system, and for this reason can be used to inform a theoretical framework for understanding the principles and outcomes of centralization.

Statistical analysis in these three models indicates that city size influences state debt levels. The percent of a state's population living in cities less than 100,000 has a significant and positive effect on state debt, and the percent of a state's population living in cities greater than 100,000 has a significant and negative effect on state debt. This is a new finding in the literature but one that has a close affinity with

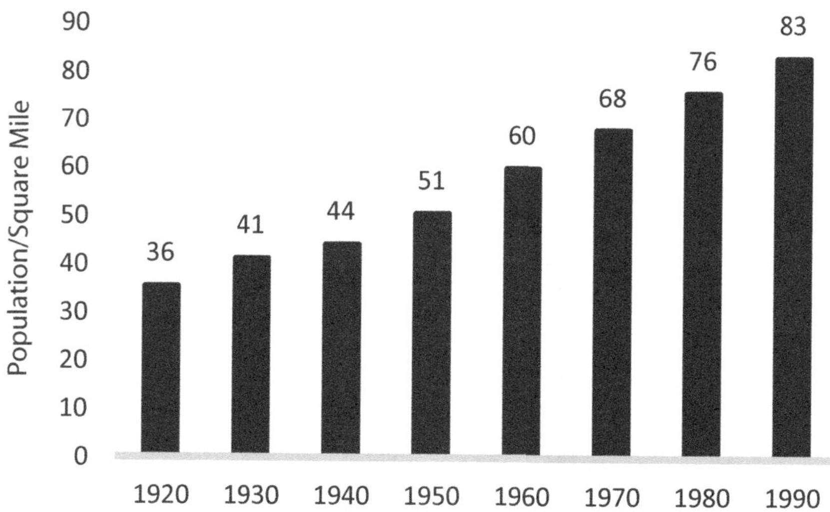

Figure 4.2 Population Density.

Table 4.6 State Rank: Population Density (1920–1990)

Rank	*State*	*POPD*	*Rank*	*State*	*POPD*
1	RI	784.0	25	AL	62.9
2	NJ	750.1	26	MO	61.3
3	MA	633.1	27	IA	47.7
4	CT	481.6	28	MS	47.0
5	NY	322.5	29	VT	45.4
6	MD	297.5	30	WA	41.9
7	PA	238.8	31	MN	41.4
8	OH	211.4	32	AR	38.0
9	DE	211.1	33	TX	36.6
10	IL	168.1	34	OK	36.5
11	MI	121.9	35	ME	30.9
12	IN	120.0	36	KS	25.4
13	VA	97.5	37	NE	18.5
14	FL	96.1	38	OR	17.8
15	CA	92.7	39	CO	17.6
16	NC	91.1	40	AZ	12.6
17	TN	85.3	41	UT	11.2
18	SC	79.0	42	ND	9.3
19	KY	76.8	43	SD	8.8
20	WV	75.0	44	ID	8.0
21	NH	74.0	45	NM	7.0
22	GA	70.9	46	MT	4.5
23	LA	69.6	47	NV	3.7
24	WI	69.3	48	WY	3.3

Source: Author's analysis of select datasets included in Appendix.

Greer and Denison's conclusion that the number of local governments has a positive effect on the state to local debt ratio, or the concentration of debt at the state level. Essentially, as the number of local governments rises (reducing the average city size), they find that debt concentrates at the state level. Greer and Denison speculate that this concentration occurs to reduce interest costs and enhance transparency, as Trautman would suggest.[58] But Trautman is talking about public authorities for which the state may be able to borrow and not municipalities responsible for incurring their own indebtedness. In addition, the use of public authorities by a state government often is not to enhance transparency but to obscure it by pursuing fiscal goals in venues not subject to various limits on taxes, expenditures, and debt.

Another explanation is warranted and may pertain to the interaction of community size and fiscal affairs. Skidmore has shown that states tend to expand their assistance to local governments when those governments are subject to tax and expenditure limits.[59] Just as Skidmore has shown that revenue tends to concentrate at the state level in the presence of local tax and expenditure limits, so Greer and Denison have shown that state debt increases as the number of municipalities rises (and the average municipality size necessarily falls). An explanation integrating both of these findings is that community size itself acts as a limit on taxes, expenditure, and debt.

Consider Table 4.7 comprised of data from the 2002 Census of Governments on various fiscal measures according to municipal size. As municipal size increases, so do per capita levels of revenue, expenditure, intergovernmental aid, and debt. A table of this kind does not prove that city size in itself influences fiscal outcomes; such a hypothesis would require more rigorous statistical evaluation. Different institutional and infrastructure characteristics no doubt influence higher levels of revenue, expense, and debt as city population increases. A theoretical case for the relevance of city size to fiscal policy can be made, however.

Aristotle argued that a city should be large enough for self-sufficiency but not so large that its citizens would not be able to judge each other's qualities.[60] His comments on city size can be interpreted in light of his broader argument on justice. Knowledge of others, or some degree of personal accountability, is integral to questions of justice based on valuation of parties and interests. Decentralization increases an Aristotelian ethic of self-sufficiency based on the accountability that comes with mutual exchange. In fiscal affairs, expenditures at the local level are made for things about which citizens have more direct knowledge and are able to make personal judgments on the merit of the expense. Likewise, debt issues proceed with a greater awareness of their expense, as property and other forms of taxation may be adjusted immediately to begin paying the bond. As discussed previously, this is why Barro's case for a Ricardian equivalence between debt and taxes may be more valid at the local rather than the national level of government. Local government obliges citizens to see taxes and debt in a more similar light.

Tocqueville does not approach jurisdiction size in the same way that Aristotle does but combines a classical sense of community with a modern understanding of the hazards of centralization. It is in the township where the spirit of freedom resides, where citizens develop the capacity for self-government that only comes from the successful formation of community. Lassen and Serritzlew's[61] analysis of jurisdiction size and political efficacy does not deal directly with fiscal affairs, but their conclusion that smaller jurisdiction size increases the political efficacy of citizens provides contemporary support to Tocqueville's argument on local government.

Table 4.7 Per Capita Fiscal Amounts by City Size

City Size	*G Rev*	*IG Rev*	*G Exp*	*Total Debt*
Less than 10,000	908	223	891	1,005
10,000–24,999	1,084	228	1,085	1,233
25,000–49,999	1,158	279	1,151	1,358
50,000–74,999	1,268	313	1,254	1,454
75,000–99,999	1,344	359	1,325	1,678
100,000–199,999	1,471	421	1,463	1,911
200,000–299,999	1,572	553	1,587	2,079
300,000 or more	2,808	966	2,884	4,554

Source: 2002 Census of Governments (pp. 28–29).

The last two variables pertaining to centralization are the centralization of government at the state level and federal intergovernmental aid to the state. Of the two, the first is more typically used as a measure of centralization, with intergovernmental aid alternatively being seen as a measure of dependence on central authority or cooperation with central authority. Clingermayer and Wood evaluate centralization of government within a state by using the ratio of state to local revenue own source, the same variable included in this study. They do not approach the variable with broader philosophical arguments pertaining to centralization but merely assume that state debt will be higher if the state takes on more policy responsibility relative to local government.[62] Likewise, they evaluate intergovernmental aid to the state in terms of such aid substituting for or stimulating the use of state resources, and presumably less or more debt, respectively.[63] In their model, state centralization is not significant in explaining state indebtedness, but intergovernmental aid does have a positive influence on state debt.

There is a theoretical thread that can tie together the significance of both of these variables. To the extent that an expansive administrative state obscures the elements of valuation essential to justice or the common good, to the extent that the benefit is perceived but the cost is obscured, such a government is likely to rely on debt more than taxes to achieve its fiscal goals. The diminished ethic of self-sufficiency that defines the state's internal fiscal structure, evidenced by the relative withering of local government relative to central power, also characterizes the state's external dealings. Its tendency to centralize internally reflects its tendency toward external centralization, or its tendency to look to the federal government for aid. It is not outside the theoretical realm of reason that state governments inclined to rely on outside assistance to achieve their policy goals also will be a government inclined to indebt the future for the benefit of the present.

The circle can be closed by applying this line of reasoning to a state's dealings with its own cities. The findings presented herein begin to illustrate the contours of intergovernmental relations within a state. Larger municipalities incur more debt and receive more intergovernmental aid from the state than smaller cities (the figures for intergovernmental aid in Table 4.7 include federal and state intergovernmental aid to cities, but the bulk of this aid comes from the state). In a positive light, larger municipalities are better "partners" for the state. In a negative light, an ethic of self-sufficiency is less at work as the jurisdiction size increases. Larger cities are at once more willing to transfer fiscal burdens to the future and look to the state for assistance.

If there is one near-constant in the varied fiscal federalism literature reviewed above, it is the tendency of uncircumspect intergovernmental aid to enervate fiscal responsibility by blurring lines of accountability. As the studies cited above demonstrate, this occurs in a variety of political contexts and in both developed and developing nations. This book affirms this perspective in federalism research and shows how increased levels of such aid can explain partially levels of state debt.

Figure 4.3 illustrates the national trend in percent population living in cities less than 100,000 for 1920–1990 (with the percent population living in cities greater than 100,000 being derived by subtracting this percent from 100). The most striking thing to note about this illustration is the durability of this percentage over the course of the century. Table 4.8 ranks the states by the mean of their decennial measurements of percent population living in cities less than 100,000.

Figure 4.4 illustrates the national trend in state revenue as a percent of local and state revenue (state centralization) for 1930–1990. Table 4.9 ranks the states by the mean of their decennial measurements of state centralization for the same time period.

Figure 4.5 illustrates the national trend in intergovernmental aid to the state per capita for 1930–1990. Table 4.10 ranks the states by the mean of their decennial measurements of intergovernmental aid to the state per capita.

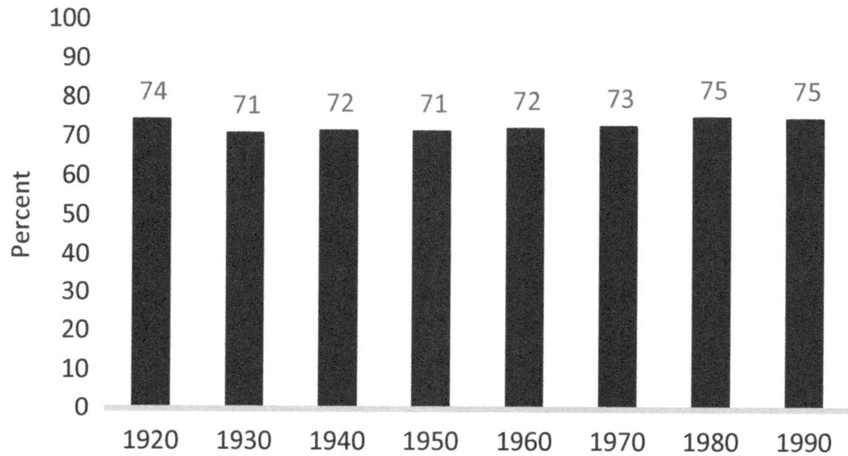

Figure 4.3 Percent Population Living in Cities Less than 100,000.

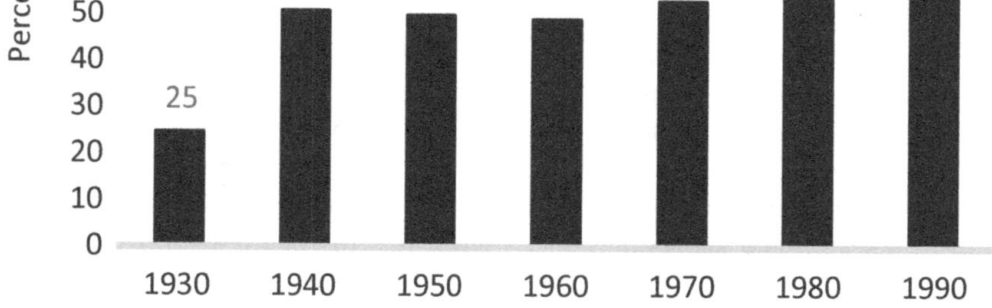

Figure 4.4 State Revenue as a Percent of Total Local and State Revenue.

Table 4.8 State Rank: Percent Population Living in Cities Less than 100,000 (1920–1990)

Rank	*State*	*<100,000*	*Rank*	*State*	*<100,000*
1	ME	100.0	25	OK	81.1
2	MT	100.0	26	UT	79.3
3	NH	100.0	27	NJ	78.0
4	ND	100.0	28	IN	77.9
5	VT	100.0	29	NE	75.7
6	WV	100.0	30	OR	75.3
7	WY	100.0	31	MN	74.9
8	SC	99.0	32	LA	74.8
9	SD	98.2	33	CT	74.6
10	ID	97.1	34	PA	73.9
11	MS	96.3	35	RI	72.7
12	AR	95.9	36	AZ	72.5
13	NC	92.6	37	TX	72.2
14	IA	91.6	38	MA	72.0
15	NV	88.6	39	WA	71.3
16	NM	88.0	40	TN	70.9
17	KY	87.5	41	MO	70.9
18	GA	86.8	42	MI	69.8
19	AL	83.9	43	CO	69.6
20	DE	83.0	44	OH	68.1
21	KS	81.7	45	MD	65.6
22	VA	81.5	46	IL	62.3
23	FL	81.3	47	CA	60.7
24	WI	81.2	48	NY	42.5

Source: Author's analysis of select datasets included in Appendix.

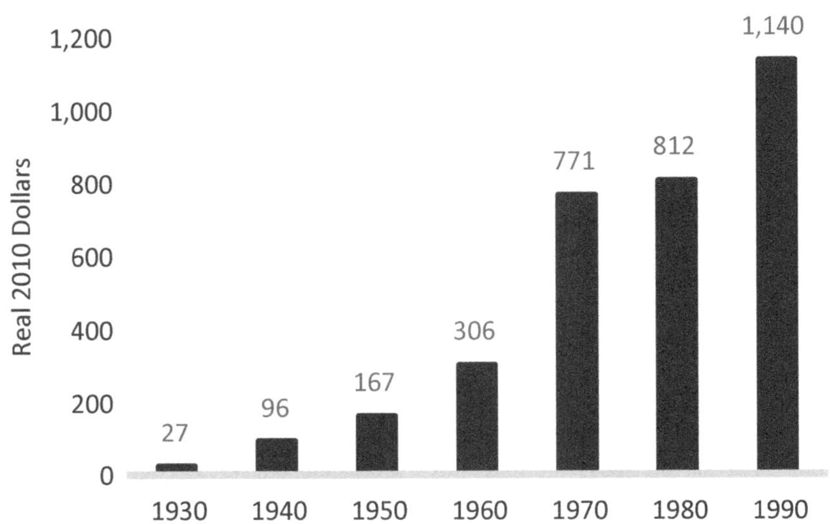

Figure 4.5 Real Intergovernmental Aid to the State Per Capita.

Table 4.9 State Rank: State Revenue as Percent of Local and State Revenue (1930–1990)

Rank	*State*	*State Revenue*	*Rank*	*State*	*State Revenue*
1	DE	71.4	25	MD	52.1
2	NM	69.3	26	MI	51.4
3	WV	66.4	27	MT	51.3
4	SC	62.5	28	GA	51.1
5	AR	61.8	29	OH	50.8
6	LA	60.8	30	CT	50.5
7	KY	60.5	31	WI	50.3
8	OK	58.5	32	NH	49.6
9	NC	58.3	33	MN	48.6
10	VT	58.3	34	IN	48.1
11	AL	58.2	35	TX	47.8
12	ME	57.8	36	CA	47.2
13	VA	57.8	37	IA	46.9
14	UT	56.2	38	MO	46.0
15	RI	56.0	39	CO	45.0
16	WA	55.9	40	TN	44.9
17	MS	55.6	41	NJ	44.6
18	ND	55.3	42	MA	44.3
19	PA	54.2	43	SD	44.3
20	WY	53.8	44	FL	43.4
21	OR	53.6	45	KS	42.8
22	NV	52.8	46	NY	41.7
23	AZ	52.2	47	IL	41.6
24	ID	52.2	48	NE	32.5

Source: Author's analysis of select datasets included in Appendix.

Voter Turnout

Voter turnout has a significant and negative effect on state debt. This study appears to be the first to include voter turnout in a general model of state debt, but the findings here are in keeping with the overarching theme of other analysis. Romer and Rosenthal find that defeated ballot measures often involve reductions in proposed spending before being resubmitted to voters.[64] Beginning his review in the mid-1960s, Matsusaka finds that states with a voter initiative (as opposed to a purely representative system) have lower and more decentralized spending patterns and that they rely more on fee for service and less on taxes.[65] He qualifies these findings for a similar analysis of the first half of the twentieth century, however, concluding that initiative states had higher aggregate levels of state and local spending but also had more decentralized expenditure.[66] Kiewiet and Szakaly[67] find that voter referendum requirements reduce guaranteed debt issue in the American states, and Feld and Kirchgassner[68] come to a similar conclusion in their analysis of Swiss municipalities. Peltzman analyzes federal and state spending trends from 1950 to 1988 and concludes that voters penalize elected officials for spending (and not just tax) increases.[69] His argument that voters do not differentiate between taxes and deficits but are focused on spending increases

Table 4.10 State Rank: Real Intergovernmental Aid to the State Per Capita (1930–1990)

Rank	*State*	*RIGSPC*	*Rank*	*State*	*RIGSPC*
1	WY	1,144	25	DE	490
2	VT	761	26	KY	479
3	MT	705	27	NH	474
4	NY	670	28	MI	467
5	NM	657	29	AZ	455
6	NV	656	30	TN	454
7	ND	645	31	GA	452
8	UT	624	32	WI	446
9	SD	614	33	SC	435
10	CA	612	34	MD	428
11	RI	578	35	NE	428
12	OR	575	36	NJ	425
13	WV	575	37	IA	422
14	LA	566	38	MO	419
15	MS	553	39	CT	419
16	ME	551	40	PA	416
17	ID	545	41	KS	408
18	MA	532	42	IL	404
19	CO	521	43	NC	398
20	WA	511	44	OH	368
21	AR	504	45	TX	365
22	MN	504	46	VA	350
23	OK	498	47	IN	349
24	AL	494	48	FL	330

Source: Author's analysis of select datasets included in Appendix.

regardless of the financing source would qualify several of the assumptions in this study. Peltzman leaves open the question, however, of why spending levels have increased so much in the face of voter opposition. He concludes that much of the increase in spending occurred early in the time period under review and that elected officials learned over time the limits to which they could push expenditure. This explanation does not give adequate weight to the rapid expansion of government debt, even at the time of Peltzman's article, and certainly in the quarter century since. Lowry, Alt, and Ferree take a more nuanced view of voter reactions to fiscal outcomes, finding that voter hostility varies according to their expectations, the party affiliation of elected officials, and the presence of unified or divided government.[70]

Another concept that can be related to voter turnout is social capital. Putnam's seminal work on social capital derived a state measure for this phenomenon.[71] His index was not longitudinal but a cross-sectional measure at the time of writing. This social capital index was compared to voter turnout numbers used in this study, and the correlation between voter turnout in 1990 and Putnam's 1993 index is very high (0.79), indicating that voter turnout may be used as a historically durable measure of social capital. Table 4.11 ranks the states by the mean of their decennial measurements of voter turnout.

Table 4.11 State Rank: Voter Turnout (1920–1990)

Rank	*State*	*Voter Turnout*	*Rank*	*State*	*Voter Turnout*
1	UT	73.0	25	MI	62.0
2	IN	69.9	26	WA	61.6
3	WV	69.9	27	OR	61.2
4	NH	69.8	28	ME	60.9
5	DE	69.4	29	VT	60.9
6	ND	69.0	30	NV	59.3
7	CT	68.8	31	NM	59.2
8	IL	68.7	32	PA	59.1
9	IA	68.2	33	CA	58.7
10	SD	68.1	34	KY	58.0
11	MN	68.0	35	OK	55.8
12	ID	67.8	36	MD	52.7
13	MA	66.4	37	AZ	48.3
14	MT	66.2	38	NC	45.0
15	RI	66.0	39	TN	39.8
16	MO	65.9	40	FL	39.7
17	NJ	65.7	41	TX	36.0
18	NE	65.6	42	LA	35.3
19	WI	65.4	43	AR	35.1
20	CO	65.0	44	VA	32.9
21	KS	64.7	45	AL	29.7
22	WY	64.1	46	GA	28.2
23	OH	64.1	47	MS	28.2
24	NY	62.5	48	SC	24.3

Source: Author's analysis of select datasets included in Appendix.

Protestant/Catholic Population Ratio

The Protestant/Catholic population ratio has a negative effect on state debt, which may support Weber's (1904–1905) thesis as it pertained to Protestant frugality.[72] The relationship of this variable also may pertain, in the most general of terms, to a Catholic emphasis on community and a Protestant emphasis on the individual. Catholicism and Protestantism both embraced the fundamental mores of American republicanism, Tocqueville argued, but Catholicism led people more readily to equality, while Protestantism led them more to independence.[73] Catholicism and Protestantism may therefore represent different ideological views of the common good, and using this variable as a measure of ideology can provide additional insight.

Wright, Erikson, and McIver developed an ideological index for the states in 1985 based on extensive survey data. Measures of ideology have been difficult to derive due to a lack of historical data, the authors note, and using various measures of party affiliation has its shortcomings.[74] While not a time series for historical application, the Wright-Erikson-McIver score for liberal ideology in a state has a fairly high negative correlation (−0.66) with the Protestant/Catholic population ratio used in this study, indicating that the religious makeup of a state may serve as a durable historical gauge of state ideology. This assumption is even more valid when considering the percent of a state's population that is Protestant (as opposed to the Protestant/Catholic ratio). The Wright-Erikson-McIver score for liberal ideology has a very high negative correlation (−0.78) with the percent of a state's population that is Protestant. The significance of the Protestant/Catholic population ratio thus may also be due to a greater Catholic emphasis on the collective and associated support for more expansive government.

Figure 4.6 illustrates the national trend in the Protestant/Catholic population ratio for 1920–1990 (1960 data is not available). Table 4.12 ranks the states by the mean of their decennial measurements of the Protestant/Catholic ratio.

Real Income Per Capita

Real income per capita has a positive effect on state debt, supporting the finding of Clingermayer and Wood, although not that of Bahl and Duncombe. Separately, Greer and Denison find that income increases the concentration of debt at the state level. The operative rationale for all three studies is that higher levels of income can sustain heavier debt burdens, just as the wealthier individual is more capable of sustaining larger levels of debt. This explanation certainly has merit, as well as higher income levels being associated with more developed economic infrastructure, much of which is funded by public debt.

Several additional considerations may be relevant as well. Lipset advanced the notion that democracy requires certain "social requisites," one of which is material well-being.[75] In this line of reasoning, a rise in personal income empowers a populace to hold government more accountable. Lipset's framework for the relationship between personal resources and government accountability cannot

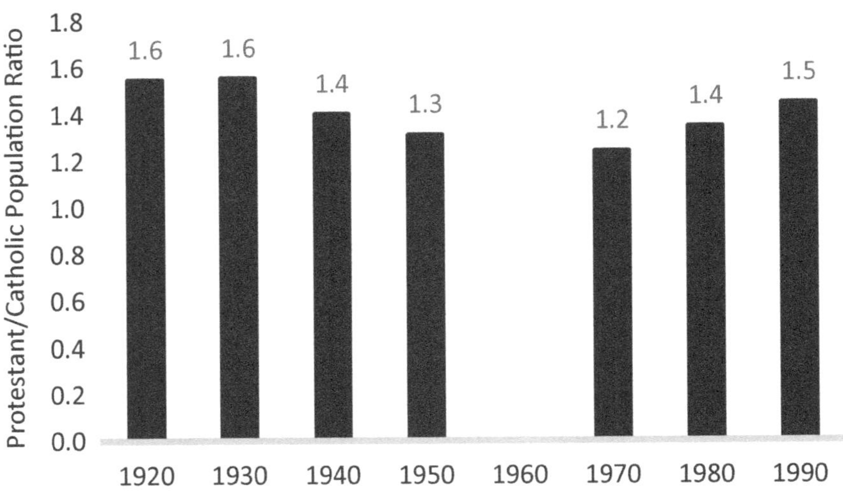

Figure 4.6 Protestant/Catholic Population.

Table 4.12 State Rank: Protestant/Catholic Population Ratio (1920–1950, 1970–1990)

Rank	*State*	*PROT/CATH*	*Rank*	*State*	*PROT/CATH*
1	NC	71.9	25	DE	1.7
2	SC	49.8	26	ND	1.7
3	GA	40.4	27	MN	1.5
4	TN	26.7	28	MD	1.4
5	AL	23.6	29	OH	1.4
6	AR	21.4	30	CO	1.3
7	UT	20.3	31	NV	1.1
8	MS	17.3	32	MT	1.1
9	VA	15.3	33	WI	1.0
10	OK	11.5	34	PA	1.0
11	ID	6.1	35	IL	0.9
12	FL	5.9	36	MI	0.9
13	WV	5.8	37	AZ	0.8
14	KY	4.4	38	LA	0.8
15	KS	3.0	39	CA	0.7
16	IN	2.7	40	VT	0.7
17	TX	2.5	41	ME	0.6
18	IA	2.4	42	NM	0.5
19	OR	2.3	43	NJ	0.4
20	WY	2.2	44	NH	0.4
21	NE	2.2	45	NY	0.4
22	SD	2.1	46	CT	0.4
23	MO	2.1	47	MA	0.3
24	WA	1.9	48	RI	0.2

Source: Author's analysis of select datasets included in Appendix.

be linear, however: if voters tend to be fiscally conservative when given the chance, rising personal income should translate into more accountability exerted upon the government and more frugal fiscal policies. Yet fiscal patterns over the course of the twentieth century show exactly the opposite pattern: rising incomes have accompanied rising debt levels.

An explanation for this may be found in research that explores the harmful effects of income on the capacity for self-government that must involve community. This theme can be discerned indirectly in Aristotle and directly in Tocqueville. Aristotle states that community is formed because of human need, material and aesthetic. To the extent that income diminishes the need of people for each other, it may promote autonomy that hinders the ascertainment of justice or the common good. Tocqueville makes this argument explicitly concerning material well-being. In the absence of norms and institutions that draw citizens into community, material interests tend to alienate individuals from each other. Bianchi and Vohs validate this hypothesis: higher levels of income are tied to more autonomous social lives.[76] As mentioned earlier, Gardner brings forward Tocqueville's concerns with equality, integrates them with Bell's important work, *The Cultural Contradictions of Capitalism*, and shows how debt has become an integral part of a democratic nihilism that is as materially profitable as it is socially corrosive.

Gardner is focused on personal credit in his essay, but his argument begins to bring into relief the theoretical and empirical ties between private and public debt. Rising income can be seen as loosening social bonds essential to self-government, or enervating the capacity for justice or the common good. To the extent that income loosens social bonds reflective of justice or the common good, it is not surprising that high income levels result in the centralization of debt at the state level (Greer and Denison) and the increased reliance on debt by state government (Clingermayer and Wood).

A theoretical view of debt based on justice not only can hold public and private debt as analogous, as the classical view does, but it can integrate both into the common theoretical framework, for a person can be unjust to himself by placing value on the wrong things, Aristotle argues. Though this study does not incorporate private debt, this is a future line of inquiry worth exploring.

Figure 4.7 illustrates the national trend in real income per capita for 1930–1990. Table 4.13 ranks the states by the mean of their decennial measurements of real income per capital.

Lawyers Per 1,000 Population

The variable for injustice, lawyers per 1,000 population, has a significant and positive relationship with state debt. The meaning of this variable is central to this book and will be discussed in the next chapter. For now, Figure 4.8 gives the total number of lawyers in the U.S. by decade, and Figure 4.9 illustrates the national trend in lawyers per 1,000 population for 1930–1990. Table 4.14 ranks the states by the mean of their decennial measurements of the lawyer population.

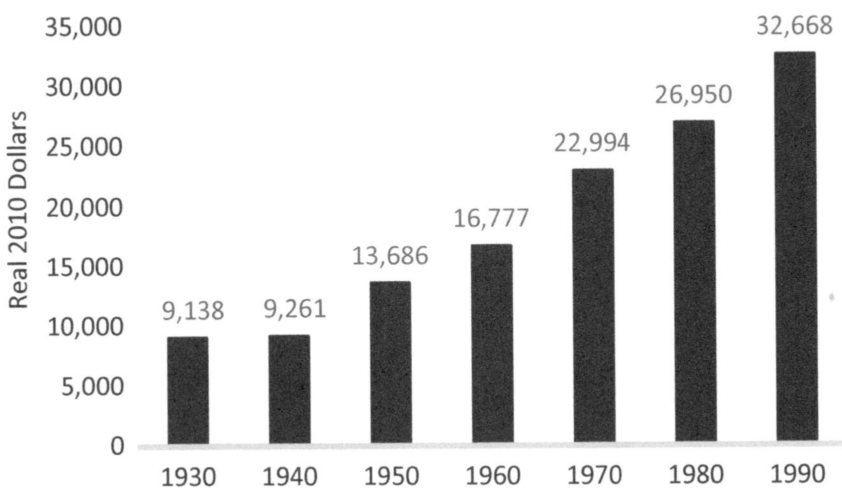

Figure 4.7 Real Income Per Capita.

Table 4.13 State Rank: Real Income Per Capita (1930–1990)

Rank	*State*	*Income*	*Rank*	*State*	*Income*
1	CT	24,647	25	MO	17,302
2	NY	23,102	26	IA	17,256
3	NJ	23,022	27	NE	17,220
4	DE	22,794	28	AZ	16,995
5	CA	22,766	29	MT	16,767
6	NV	22,583	30	TX	16,548
7	IL	21,470	31	VT	16,385
8	MA	21,388	32	ME	15,957
9	MD	21,083	33	ID	15,640
10	WA	19,920	34	UT	15,483
11	MI	19,606	35	OK	15,462
12	RI	19,462	36	SD	14,794
13	PA	19,158	37	GA	14,723
14	WY	19,142	38	ND	14,610
15	OH	19,099	39	NM	14,459
16	CO	18,869	40	NC	14,346
17	OR	18,523	41	LA	14,273
18	NH	18,445	42	TN	14,214
19	MN	18,343	43	WV	13,915
20	WI	18,172	44	KY	13,810
21	FL	17,696	45	AL	13,199
22	IN	17,494	46	SC	13,142
23	KS	17,310	47	AR	12,349
24	VA	17,309	48	MS	11,248

Source: Author's analysis of select datasets included in Appendix.

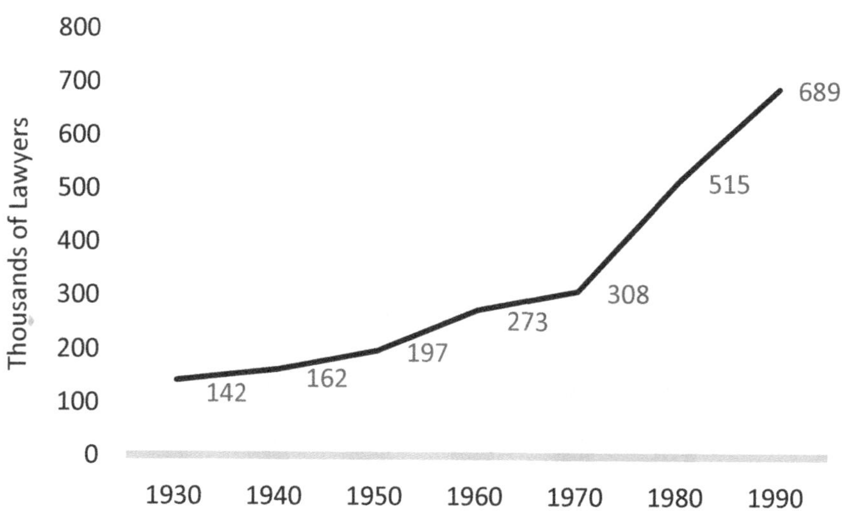

Figure 4.8 Total Number of Lawyers.

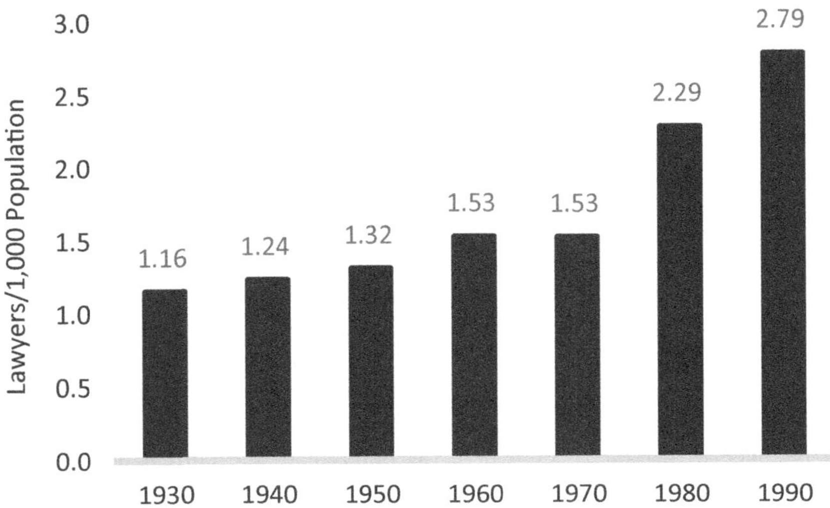

Figure 4.9 Lawyers Per 1,000 Population.

Table 4.14 State Rank: Lawyers Per 1,000 Population (1930–1990)

Rank	*State*	*Lawyers*	*Rank*	*State*	*Lawyers*
1	NY	2.89	25	RI	1.46
2	NV	2.29	26	KS	1.46
3	MA	2.28	27	WI	1.46
4	IL	2.22	28	LA	1.42
5	CO	2.11	29	VA	1.41
6	MD	1.92	30	SD	1.38
7	CT	1.90	31	UT	1.37
8	CA	1.90	32	PA	1.37
9	NE	1.87	33	GA	1.36
10	OK	1.86	34	MI	1.35
11	FL	1.84	35	ME	1.31
12	NJ	1.76	36	ID	1.30
13	MO	1.74	37	NH	1.29
14	OH	1.70	38	ND	1.26
15	OR	1.61	39	TN	1.26
16	MN	1.61	40	NM	1.24
17	WY	1.61	41	IN	1.21
18	MT	1.61	42	KY	1.20
19	WA	1.56	43	AR	1.06
20	TX	1.54	44	WV	1.05
21	AZ	1.53	45	MS	1.04
22	IA	1.51	46	AL	0.98
23	VT	1.48	47	NC	0.93
24	DE	1.47	48	SC	0.92

Source: Author's analysis of select datasets included in Appendix.

Remarks on Insignificant Variables

The age of the state, Democratic vote for president, and the number of balanced-budget rules were not significant in this study's modeling. Fiscal sclerosis does not seem to be a factor in itself in explaining state indebtedness. Democratic vote for president was used with some anticipation that it might not be significant. The null finding in this study supports Poterba's argument above that debt has not been a distinguishing issue between the two parties for much of the twentieth century. Stein and Savage also discuss in different ways this similar theme. As mentioned above, however, the Protestant/Catholic ratio (which was used in this study) and the percent Protestant population (which was not) may serve as a historically durable measure of ideology for the time period in question. Finally, balanced-budget rules are not significant in explaining state debt. This variable was used with an awareness that it is not the most appropriate measure of institutional restraint on state debt; constitutional debt limits apply more directly to the issuance of capital account debt (as opposed to the current account that balanced-budget rules typically constrain). Balanced-budget rules were used as an indicator of a general culture of thrift in a state, and, as far as this purpose goes, they do not so indicate.

A Comment on Elazar

Returning to Elazar's framework, different features of state culture can be seen as countervailing when it comes to state debt. The moralistic culture may be more inclined to consider political issues in light of the common good. Strong citizen participation may invigorate public debate and help hold government accountable. These features would tend to reduce debt. On the other hand, the moralistic culture may be inclined to realize its civic goals through the formal governmental sector. To the extent this results in centralization, public debt levels may rise. The individualistic culture esteems market-oriented principles and personal initiative. It has a high degree of tolerance that may encourage a more comprehensive view of the common good. These features would tend to reduce debt. On the other hand, government is viewed as the domain of professionals who must traffic in a certain degree of corruption. Civic participation is not as highly esteemed, and the theme of justice or the common good can be somewhat extraneous. In short, the individualistic culture may have more capacity to see the common good but less belief in its relevance as a guiding theme in political affairs. These features would tend to increase debt. Finally, the traditionalistic culture tends to resist centralization in particular and the reliance on formal governmental institutions in general. These features would tend to reduce debt. On the other hand, the dominance of an elite class of citizens discourages civic participation, which would tend to increase debt. As stated in the introduction, the modeling in this study is not designed to test Elazar's framework. If such a test is made, the countervailing influence of different features within each culture should be kept in mind.

Injustice and Public Debt

Important to this book is the significant relationship between the variable measuring injustice (the number of lawyers per 1,000 population) and state debt. An incapacity for justice or the common good, evidenced in this case by a synthetic measurement of criminal and civil strife, tends to increase the use of state indebtedness that may benefit the present at the expense of the future. Injustice or the loss of the common good in the present accompanies the loss of the common good between the present and the future. The proper specification of this variable is essential, and possible explanations for its meaning will be considered next.

Notes

1 James M. Poterba, "Do Budget Rules Work?" in *Fiscal Policy: Lessons From Economic Research*, ed. Alan Auerbach (Cambridge, MA: MIT Press, 1997), 53–86.
2 Jonathan Rodden and Gunnar S. Eskeland, "Lessons and Conclusions," in *Fiscal Decentralization and the Challenge of Hard Budget Constraints*, eds. Jonathan Rodden, Gunnar Eskeland, and Jennie Litvack (Cambridge, MA: MIT Press, 2003), 440.
3 Wallace E. Oates, *Fiscal Federalism* (New York: Harcourt Brace Jovanovich, 1972), xiv.
4 Ibid., 9.
5 Ibid., 13.
6 Charles M. Tiebout, "A Pure Theory of Local Expenditures," *Journal of Political Economy* Vol. 64 No. 5 (October 1956): 416–424.
7 Oates, *Fiscal Federalism*, 14.
8 Ibid., 54.
9 Ibid.
10 Wallace E. Oates, "An Essay on Fiscal Federalism," *Journal of Economic Literature* Vol. 37 No. 3 (September 1999): 1120–1149.
11 Jean-Paul Faguet, *Decentralization and Popular Democracy: Governance From Below in Bolivia* (Ann Arbor: University of Michigan Press, 2012), 159–198.
12 Oates, "Essay on Fiscal Federalism," 1128.
13 Robert P. Inman and Daniel L. Rubinfeld, "Making Sense of the Anti-Trust State Action Doctrine: Balancing Political Participation and Economic Efficiency in Regulatory Federalism," *Texas Law Review* 75 (1997): 1203–1299.
14 Barry R. Weingast, "The Economic Role of Political Institutions: Market-Preserving Federalism and Economic Development," *Journal of Law, Economics, and Organization* Vol. 11 No. 1 (April 1995): 1–31.
15 Ronald I. McKinnon, "Market-Preserving Fiscal Federalism in the American Monetary Union," in *Macroeconomic Dimensions of Public Finance: Essays in Honor of Vito Tanzi*, eds. Mario Blejer and Teresa Ter-Minassian (London: Routledge, 1997), 73–93.
16 Oates, "Essay on Fiscal Federalism," 1139.
17 Anwar Shah, "Fostering Fiscally Responsive and Accountable Governance: Lessons From Decentralization," in *Evaluation and Development: The Institutional Dimension*, eds. Robert Picciotto and Eduardo Wiesner (Washington, D.C.: World Bank, 1998), 83–96.
18 Oates, "Essay on Fiscal Federalism," 1140.
19 Geoffrey Brennan and James M. Buchanan, *The Power To Tax: Analytical Foundations of a Fiscal Constitution* (New York: Cambridge University Press, 1980).

20 Timothy Besley and Stephen Coate, "Centralized Versus Decentralized Provision of Local Public Goods: A Political Economy Approach," *Journal of Public Economics* Vol. 87 (2003): 2611–2637.
21 Faguet, *Decentralization*, 162.
22 Ibid., 180.
23 Jonathan Rodden, "Comparative Federalism and Decentralization: On Meaning and Measurement," *Comparative Politics* Vol. 36 No. 4 (July 2004): 481.
24 Ibid., 482.
25 Ibid., 489.
26 Ibid., 482.
27 Rodden and Eskeland, "Lessons and Conclusions," 431.
28 Nouriel Roubini and Jeffrey D. Sachs, "Political and Economic Determinants of Budget Deficits in the Industrial Democracies," *European Economic Review* Vol. 33 (1989): 903–938.
29 Francis G. Castles, "Decentralization and the Post-War Political Economy," *European Journal of Political Research* Vol. 36 (1999): 27–53.
30 Erik Wibbels, "Federalism and the Politics of Macroeconomic Policy and Performance," *American Journal of Political Science* Vol. 44 No. 4 (October 2000): 687–702.
31 Yingyi Qian and Gérard Roland, "Federalism and the Soft Budget Constraint," *American Economic Review* Vol. 88 No. 5 (December 1998): 1143–1162.
32 Lori L. Leachman, Guillermo Rosas, Peter Lange, and Alan Bester, "The Political Economy of Budget Deficits," *Economics and Politics* Vol. 19 No. 3 (November 2007): 369–420.
33 Rodden and Eskeland, "Lessons and Conclusions," 431.
34 Lynette H. Ong, "Fiscal Federalism and Soft Budget Constraints: The Case of China," *International Political Science Review* Vol. 33 No. 4 (September 2012): 455–474.
35 Jonathan Rodden and Erik Wibbels, "Beyond the Fiction of Federalism: Macroeconomic Management in Multitiered Systems," *World Politics* Vol. 54 No. 4 (July 2002): 494–531.
36 Jonathan Rodden, "Reviving Leviathan: Fiscal Federalism and the Growth of Government," *International Organization* Vol. 57 No. 4 (Autumn 2003): 695–729.
37 Robert P. Inman, "Transfers and Bailouts: Enforcing Local Fiscal Discipline with Lessons From U.S. Federalism," in *Fiscal Decentralization and the Challenge of Hard Budget Constraints*, eds. Jonathan Rodden, Gunnar Eskeland, and Jennie Litvack (Cambridge, MA: MIT Press, 2003), 35–83.
38 Rodden and Eskeland, "Lessons and Conclusions," 438–440.
39 Mark Hallerberg and Patrik Marier, "Executive Authority, the Personal Vote, and Budget Discipline in Latin American and Caribbean Countries," *American Journal of Political Science* Vol. 48 No. 3 (July 2004): 571–587.
40 Oates, "Essay on Fiscal Federalism," 1142.
41 Markus Freitag and Adrian Vatter, "Decentralization and Fiscal Discipline in Sub-National Governments: Evidence from the Swiss Federal System," *Publius* Vol. 38 No. 2 (Spring 2008): 272–294.
42 Mark Hallerberg and Sami Ylaoutinen, "Political Power, Fiscal Institutions, and Budgetary Outcomes in Central and Eastern Europe," *Journal of Public Policy* Vol. 30 No. 1 (April 2010): 45–62.
43 David O. Porter and Eugene A. Olsen, "Some Critical Issues in Government Centralization and Decentralization," *Public Administration Review* Vol. 36 No. 1 (January–February 1976): 72–84.
44 Inman, "Transfer and Bailouts," 70.
45 Jonathan Rodden and Erik Wibbels, "Beyond the Fiction of Federalism," 494–531.
46 Roy Bahl and William Duncombe, "State and Local Debt Burdens in the 1980s: A Study in Contrast," *Public Administration Review* Vol. 53 No. 1 (January–February 1993): 31–40.

47 James C. Clingermayer and B. Dan Wood, "Disentangling Patterns of State Debt Financing," *American Political Science Review* Vol. 89 No. 1 (March 1995): 108–120.
48 Robert A. Greer and Dwight V. Denison, "Determinants of Debt Concentration at the State Level," *Public Budgeting and Finance* Vol. 30 (2016): 1–20.
49 Bahl and Duncombe, "State and Local Debt Burdens," 32.
50 Ibid., 38.
51 Robert P. Inman and Daniel I. Rubinfeld, "Rethinking Federalism," *Journal of Economic Perspectives* Vol. 11 No. 4 (Autumn 1997): 43–64.
52 James C. Clingermayer, "An Intergenerational Transfer Model of State Debt Financing," *Public Choice* Vol. 72 No. 1 (October 1991): 13–21.
53 Michael A. Ellis and D. Eric Schansberg, "The Determinants of State Government Debt Financing," *Public Finance Review* Vol. 27 No. 6 (November 1999): 571–587.
54 A. Cukierman and A.H. Meltzer, "A Political Theory of Government Debt and Deficits in a Neo-Ricardian Framework," *American Economic Review* Vol. 79 (September 1989): 713–732.
55 Yilin Hou and Daniel L. Smith, "A Framework for Understanding State Balanced Budget Requirement Systems: Reexamining Distinctive Features and an Operational Definition," *Public Budgeting and Finance* (Fall 2006): 22–45.
56 Daniel L. Smith and Yilin Hou, "Balanced Budget Requirements and State Spending: A Long-Panel Study," *Public Budgeting and Finance* (Summer 2013): 1–18.
57 Gordon Johnston and Maura Stokes, "Repeated Measures Analysis with Discrete Data Using the SAS System," in *Proceedings of the Twenty-Second Annual SAS Users Group International Conference* (Cary, NC: SAS Institute, Inc., 1997), 1300–1305.
58 Rhonda R. Trautman, "The Impact of State Debt Management on Debt Activity," *Public Budgeting and Finance* (Summer 1995): 33–51.
59 Mark Skidmore, "Tax and Expenditures Limitations and the Fiscal Relationships Between State and Local Governments," *Public Choice* Vol. 99 No. 1/2 (1999): 77–102.
60 Aristotle, *Politics*, trans. Carnes Lord (Chicago: University of Chicago Press, 2013), 196.
61 David Dreyer Lassen and Soren Serritzlew, "Jurisdiction Size and Local Democracy: Evidence on Internal Political Efficacy From Large-Scale Municipal Reform," *American Political Science Review* Vol. 105 No. 2 (May 2011): 238–258.
62 Clingermayer and Wood, "Disentangling Patterns of State Debt Financing," 112.
63 Ibid., 111.
64 Thomas Romer and Howard Rosenthal, "Bureaucrats Versus Voters: On the Political Economy of Resource Allocation by Direct Democracy," *Quarterly Journal of Economics* Vol. 93 No. 4 (November 1979): 563–587.
65 John G. Matsusaka, "Fiscal Effects of the Voter Initiative: Evidence From the Last 30 Years," *Journal of Political Economy* 103 (June 1995): 587–623.
66 John G. Matsusaka, "Fiscal Effects of the Voter Initiative in the First Half of the 20th Century," *Journal of Law and Economics* Vol. 43 No. 2 (October 2000): 619–650.
67 D. Roderick Kiewiet and Kristin Szakaly, "Constitutional Limitations on Borrowing: An Analysis of State Bonded Indebtedness," *Journal of Law, Economics, and Organization* Vol. 12 No. 1 (April 1996): 62–97.
68 Lars P. Feld and Gebhard Kirchgassner, "Does Direct Democracy Reduce Public Debt? Evidence From Swiss Municipalities," *Public Choice* Vol. 109 No. 3/4 (2001): 347–370.
69 Sam Peltzman, "Voters as Fiscal Conservatives," *Quarterly Journal of Economics* Vol. 107 No. 2 (May 1992): 327–361.
70 Robert C. Lowry, James E. Alt, and Karen E. Ferree, "Fiscal Policy Outcomes and Electoral Accountability in the American States," *American Political Science Review* Vol. 92 No. 4 (December 1998): 759–774.

71 Robert D. Putnam, *Bowling Alone* (New York: Simon & Schuster, 1993).
72 Max Weber, *The Protestant Ethic and the Spirit of Capitalism*, ed. Richard Swedberg (New York: W.W. Norton, 2009).
73 Alexis de Tocqueville, *Democracy in America*, trans. Harvey C. Mansfield and Delba Winthrop (Chicago: University of Chicago Press, 2000), 276.
74 Gerald C. Wright, Robert S. Erikson, and John P. McIver, "Measuring State Partisanship and Ideology with Survey Data," *Journal of Politics* Vol. 47 No. 2 (June 1985): 469–489.
75 Seymour M. Lipset, "Some Social Requisites of Democracy: Economic Development and Political Legitimacy," *American Political Science Review* Vol. 53 No. 1 (1959): 69–105.
76 Emily C. Bianchi and Kathleen D. Vohs, "Social Class and Social Worlds: Income Predicts the Frequency and Nature of Social Contact," *Social Psychological and Personality Science* Vol. 7 No. 5 (2016): 479–486.

Bibliography

Aristotle. *Politics*. Translated by Carnes Lord. Chicago: University of Chicago Press, 2013.

Bahl, Roy and William Duncombe. "State and Local Debt Burdens in the 1980s: A Study in Contrast." *Public Administration Review* Vol. 53 No. 1 (January–February 1993): 31–40.

Barro, Robert J. "On the Determination of the Public Debt." *Journal of Political Economy* Vol. 87 No. 5 Part 1 (October 1979): 940–971.

Besley, Timothy and Stephen Coate. "Centralized Versus Decentralized Provision of Local Public Goods: A Political Economy Approach." *Journal of Public Economics* Vol. 87 (2003): 2611–2637.

Bianchi, Emily C. and Kathleen D. Vohs. "Social Class and Social Worlds: Income Predicts the Frequency and Nature of Social Contact." *Social Psychological and Personality Science* Vol. 7 No. 5 (2016): 479–486.

Brennan, Geoffrey and James M. Buchanan. *The Power To Tax: Analytical Foundations of a Fiscal Constitution*. New York: Cambridge University Press, 1980.

Castles, Francis G. "Decentralization and the Post-War Political Economy." *European Journal of Political Research* Vol. 36 (1999): 27–53.

Clingermayer, James C. "An Intergenerational Transfer Model of State Debt Financing." *Public Choice* Vol. 72 No. 1 (October 1991): 13–21.

Clingermayer, James C. and B. Dan Wood. "Disentangling Patterns of State Debt Financing." *American Political Science Review* Vol. 89 No. 1 (March 1995): 108–120.

Cukierman, A. and A.H. Meltzer. "A Political Theory of Government Debt and Deficits in a Neo-Ricardian Framework." *American Economic Review* Vol. 79 (September 1989): 713–732.

De Tocqueville, Alexis. *Democracy in America*. Translated by Harvey C. Mansfield and Delba Winthrop. Chicago: University of Chicago Press, 2000.

Ellis, Michael A. and D. Eric Schansberg. "The Determinants of State Government Debt Financing." *Public Finance Review* Vol. 27 No. 6 (November 1999): 571–587.

Faguet, Jean-Paul. *Decentralization and Popular Democracy: Governance From Below in Bolivia*. Ann Arbor: University of Michigan Press, 2012.

Feld, Lars P. and Gebhard Kirchgassner. "Does Direct Democracy Reduce Public Debt? Evidence From Swiss Municipalities." *Public Choice* Vol. 109 No. 3/4 (2001): 347–370.

Freitag, Markus and Adrian Vatter. "Decentralization and Fiscal Discipline in Sub-National Governments: Evidence from the Swiss Federal System." *Publius* Vol. 38 No. 2 (Spring 2008): 272–294.

Greer, Robert A. and Dwight V. Denison. "Determinants of Debt Concentration at the State Level." *Public Budgeting and Finance* 30 (2016): 1–20.

Hallerberg, Mark and Patrik Marier. "Executive Authority, the Personal Vote, and Budget Discipline in Latin American and Caribbean Countries." *American Journal of Political Science* Vol. 48 No. 3 (July 2004): 571–587.

Hallerberg, Mark and Sami Ylaoutinen. "Political Power, Fiscal Institutions, and Budgetary Outcomes in Central and Eastern Europe." *Journal of Public Policy* Vol. 30 No. 1 (April 2010): 45–62.

Hou, Yilin and Daniel L. Smith. "A Framework for Understanding State Balanced Budget Requirement Systems: Reexamining Distinctive Features and an Operational Definition." *Public Budgeting and Finance* (Fall 2006): 22–45.

Inman, Robert P. "Transfers and Bailouts: Enforcing Local Fiscal Discipline with Lessons From U.S. Federalism." In *Fiscal Decentralization and the Challenge of Hard Budget Constraints*, edited by Jonathan Rodden, Gunnar Eskeland, and Jennie Litvack, 35–83. Cambridge, MA: MIT Press, 2003.

Inman, Robert P. and Daniel L. Rubinfeld. "Making Sense of the Anti-Trust State Action Doctrine: Balancing Political Participation and Economic Efficiency in Regulatory Federalism." *Texas Law Review* Vol. 75 (1997): 1203–1299.

Inman, Robert P. and Daniel I. Rubinfeld. "Rethinking Federalism." *Journal of Economic Perspectives* Vol. 11 No. 4 (Autumn 1997): 43–64.

Johnston, Gordon and Maura Stokes. "Repeated Measures Analysis with Discrete Data Using the SAS System." In *Proceedings of the Twenty-Second Annual SAS Users Group International Conference*, 1300–1305. Cary, NC: SAS Institute, Inc., 1997.

Kiewiet, D. Roderick and Kristin Szakaly. "Constitutional Limitations on Borrowing: An Analysis of State Bonded Indebtedness." *Journal of Law, Economics, and Organization* Vol. 12 No. 1 (April 1996): 62–97.

Lassen, David Dreyer and Soren Serritzlew. "Jurisdiction Size and Local Democracy: Evidence on Internal Political Efficacy From Large-Scale Municipal Reform." *American Political Science Review* Vol. 105 No. 2 (May 2011): 238–258.

Leachman, Lori L., Guillermo Rosas, Peter Lange, and Alan Bester. "The Political Economy of Budget Deficits." *Economics and Politics* Vol. 19 No. 3 (November 2007): 369–420.

Lipset, Seymour M. "Some Social Requisites of Democracy: Economic Development and Political Legitimacy." *American Political Science Review* Vol. 53 No. 1 (1959): 69–105.

Lowry, Robert C., James E. Alt, and Karen E. Ferree. "Fiscal Policy Outcomes and Electoral Accountability in the American States." *American Political Science Review* Vol. 92 No. 4 (December 1998): 759–774.

Matsusaka, John G. "Fiscal Effects of the Voter Initiative: Evidence From the Last 30 Years." *Journal of Political Economy* 103 (June 1995): 587–623.

Matsusaka, John G. "Fiscal Effects of the Voter Initiative in the First Half of the 20th Century." *Journal of Law and Economics* Vol. 43 No. 2 (October 2000): 619–650.

McKinnon, Ronald I. "Market-Preserving Fiscal Federalism in the American Monetary Union." In *Macroeconomic Dimensions of Public Finance: Essays in Honor of Vito Tanzi*, edited by Mario Blejer and Teresa Ter-Minassian, 73–93. London: Routledge, 1997.

Oates, Wallace E. "An Essay on Fiscal Federalism." *Journal of Economic Literature* Vol. 37 No. 3 (September 1999): 1120–1149.

Oates, Wallace E. *Fiscal Federalism*. New York: Harcourt Brace Jovanovich, 1972.

Ong, Lynette H. "Fiscal Federalism and Soft Budget Constraints: The Case of China." *International Political Science Review* Vol. 33 No. 4 (September 2012): 455–474.

Peltzman, Sam. "Voters as Fiscal Conservatives." *Quarterly Journal of Economics* Vol. 107 No. 2 (May 1992): 327–361.

Porter, David O. and Eugene A. Olsen. "Some Critical Issues in Government Centralization and Decentralization." *Public Administration Review* Vol. 36 No. 1 (January–February 1976): 72–84.

Poterba, James M. "Do Budget Rules Work?" In *Fiscal Policy: Lessons From Economic Research*, edited by Alan Auerbach, 53–86. Cambridge, MA: MIT Press, 1997.

Putnam, Robert D. *Bowling Alone*. New York: Simon & Schuster, 1993.

Qian, Yingyi and Gérard Roland. "Federalism and the Soft Budget Constraint." *American Economic Review* Vol. 88 No. 5 (December 1998): 1143–1162.

Rodden, Jonathan. "Comparative Federalism and Decentralization: On Meaning and Measurement." *Comparative Politics* Vol. 36 No. 4 (July 2004): 481–500.

Rodden, Jonathan. "Reviving Leviathan: Fiscal Federalism and the Growth of Government." *International Organization* Vol. 57 No. 4 (Autumn 2003): 695–729.

Rodden, Jonathan and Gunnar S. Eskeland. "Lessons and Conclusions." In *Fiscal Decentralization and the Challenge of Hard Budget Constraints*, edited by Jonathan Rodden, Gunnar Eskeland, and Jennie Litvack, 431–465. Cambridge, MA: MIT Press, 2003.

Rodden, Jonathan and Erik Wibbels. "Beyond the Fiction of Federalism: Macroeconomic Management in Multitiered Systems." *World Politics* Vol. 54 No. 4 (July 2002): 494–531.

Romer, Thomas and Howard Rosenthal. "Bureaucrats versus Voters: On the Political Economy of Resource Allocation by Direct Democracy." *Quarterly Journal of Economics* Vol. 93 No. 4 (November 1979): 563–587.

Roubini, Nouriel and Jeffrey D. Sachs. "Political and Economic Determinants of Budget Deficits in the Industrial Democracies." *European Economic Review* 33 (1989): 903–938.

Shah, Anwar. "Fostering Fiscally Responsive and Accountable Governance: Lessons From Decentralization." In *Evaluation and Development: The Institutional Dimension*, edited by Robert Picciotto and Eduardo Wiesner, 83–96. Washington, D.C.: World Bank, 1998.

Skidmore, Mark. "Tax and Expenditures Limitations and the Fiscal Relationships Between State and Local Governments." *Public Choice* Vol. 99 No. 1/2 (1999): 77–102.

Smith, Daniel L. and Yilin Hou. "Balanced Budget Requirements and State Spending: A Long-Panel Study." *Public Budgeting and Finance* (Summer 2013): 1–18.

Tiebout, Charles M. "A Pure Theory of Local Expenditures." *Journal of Political Economy* Vol. 64 No. 5 (October 1956): 416–424.

Trautman, Rhonda R. "The Impact of State Debt Management on Debt Activity." *Public Budgeting and Finance* (Summer 1995): 33–51.

Weber, Max. *The Protestant Ethic and the Spirit of Capitalism*. Edited by Richard Swedberg. New York: W.W. Norton, 2009.

Weingast, Barry R. "The Economic Role of Political Institutions: Market-Preserving Federalism and Economic Development." *Journal of Law, Economics, and Organization* Vol. 11 No. 1 (April 1995): 1–31.

Wibbels, Erik. "Federalism and the Politics of Macroeconomic Policy and Performance." *American Journal of Political Science* Vol. 44 No. 4 (October 2000): 687–702.

Wright, Gerald C., Robert S. Erikson, and John P. McIver. "Measuring State Partisanship and Ideology with Survey Data." *Journal of Politics* Vol. 47 No. 2 (June 1985): 469–489.

5 Interpreting Injustice

> The special knowledge that lawyers acquire in studying the law assures them a separate rank in society; they form a sort of privileged class among [persons of] intelligence … Add to this that they naturally form *a body*. It is not that they agree among themselves and direct themselves in concert toward the same point; but community of studies and unity of methods bind their minds to one another as interest could unite their wills.
>
> —Alexis de Tocqueville, *Democracy in America*

Modeling conducted in the previous chapter showed that the variable for injustice, the number of lawyers per 1,000 population, has a significant and positive relationship with state debt. To reiterate, the argument is not that lawyers cause debt but that the size of the state bar is a synthetic measure of the level of injustice in that society as represented by criminal and civil faction. To the extent that injustice is at work in a society, as it may be in an individual person, that society will be inclined to shift its own fiscal burdens to others through public debt. It will be inclined toward a mastery that claims more than its share rather than the political rule of free and equal persons. This thesis will be defended first and then several alternative explanations will be offered. Unless otherwise noted, all figures and tables below are derived from the author's statistical analysis.

The Size of the State Bar as an Adequate Measure of Injustice

Many good things can be said about attorneys. They form the backbone of America's adversarial system of justice and guide individuals through some of the most difficult experiences in life. Because of this, attorneys are never more appreciated than when they are needed. Defendants do not tell lawyer jokes at the bar.

One thing that cannot be said of lawyers, however, is that they thrive on the common good. The profession itself has been more sensitive historically to what its services signify. Legal advertising has been restrained by norms internal to the bar and by external codes imposed by law. Those norms have broken down to some extent, and lawyers presently are not as scrupulous to avoid the appearance of fomenting legal strife. Whether they are the handlers of injustice or foment it themselves, their number is a measure of society's litigiousness.

Lawyers are the handlers of injustice, and a central assumption of the statistical modeling in this book is that the size of the state bar is a rough approximation of the level of injustice in that state, that the lawyer population reflects the demand for its services, the bulk of which are dedicated to criminal and civil proceedings. Data on criminal and civil proceedings themselves certainly would be preferable to the synthetic measure of lawyer population, but statistics for caseload burdens in state courts are a recent phenomenon and do not cover the period in question (1920–1990).

For the thesis of this book to hold, then, the first assumption to validate is that the size of the state bar is correlated over time with the level of criminal and civil strife and thus serves as an adequate measure of such faction. While data on criminal and civil proceedings in state courts does not extend very far back in time, current data can be used to begin an assessment of the correlation between a state's lawyer population and its level of injustice as reflected in caseload numbers. Consider Table 5.1.

The per capita lawyer population by state is taken for 2005 and correlated with various caseload statistics in state courts.[1] The lawyer population shows a high correlation of 0.79 and 0.85 with civil and domestic cases, respectively. Its correlation with criminal proceedings is a bit less but still fairly high at 0.61. Overall, the lawyer population per capita has a correlation of 0.77 with all civil, domestic, and criminal cases in 2005.

With this level of correlation between the lawyer population and caseload proceedings, it is reasonable to assume that the size of the state bar can serve as an approximate gauge for the level of injustice in a state—at least for 2005. This level of correlation needs to hold at times earlier in the twentieth century for lawyer population to be used as a historical gauge of state injustice. Caseload statistics are not available to validate this assumption, but the Census did gather data on divorce and prison population in the states through much of the twentieth century. The correlation of these numbers with state lawyer populations was

Table 5.1 Correlation of Lawyer Population with 2005 Litigation Data

Classes of Litigation (Incoming Cases)	*2005 Correlation*	*1930 Correlation*
Civil	0.79	
Domestic	0.85	0.76 (with divorce rate)
Criminal	0.61	0.6 (with number of prisoners)
Juvenile	0.59	
Traffic	0.61	
Total Civil, Domestic, and Criminal	0.77	
Grand Total	0.71	

measured for 1930. Referring again to Table 5.1 above, the lawyer population by state has a very high correlation with state divorce rates (0.76). Correlation between the size of the state bar and the number of prisoners by state is almost the same in 1930 (0.6) as the correlation between lawyer population and criminal proceedings in 2005 (0.61).

Correlation is not causation, but causation is not sought here. What is sought is some degree of affirmation that lawyer population is correlated with criminal and civil proceedings, that it can serve as a rough approximation of this more precise measure of injustice. The analysis above gives some reassurance that this is a valid assumption in the present and also for historical analysis.

Supporting the view that the size of the state bar is an adequate measure of injustice is statistical analysis conducted on the lawyer population itself. Model 5.1 measures the effect of different measurements of societal harmony and societal discord on the number of attorneys. Table 5.2 provides descriptive statistics for the variables used in Model 5.1.

Population density and percent population in cities greater than 100,000 are assumed to increase the lawyer population. Race is an appropriate variable to use in this model with the assumption that racial heterogeneity provides a context for greater injustice—not that racial diversity must lead to injustice but that such diversity, ceteris paribus, can present an additional obstacle to attaining the common good. Voter turnout does not have an obvious direct bearing on the lawyer population but is used as a measure of general civic health, as the previous chapter's discussion of the correlation of voter turnout with Putnam's social capital index implies. The Protestant/Catholic ratio is used with a similar assumption applied to race: that religious heterogeneity, ceteris paribus, provides a context for greater injustice as an additional obstacle to the common good. Alternatively, it could reflect a Protestant ideological orientation toward private resolution of conflict, an orientation in keeping with a Protestant aversion to expansive government. Of the positive and negative interpretations of real income per capita in the previous chapter, the negative version is assumed to apply to the use of real income per capita in this model: income gives people something to fight over and the means to fight. Income inequality is used with a similar assumption to race and religion: that income inequality, ceteris paribus, provides a context for greater injustice. Finally, a ratio of divorce to marriage (per capita) is used as a measure of domestic injustice, or the breakdown of the domestic common good.

Model 5.1: Effect of Select Variables on Lawyer Population (1920–1990)

A generalized estimating equation (GEE) through PROC GENMOD in SAS is used to regress covariates of interest on the number of lawyers per 1,000 population in the following form:

$$y_{it} = \alpha + \beta_{it} + \gamma_{it} + \mu_{it} + \delta_{it} + \theta_{it} + \vartheta_{it} + \rho_{it} + \psi_{it} + \chi_{it} + \tau_{it}$$

Table 5.2 Descriptive Statistics

	N	*Mean*	*Median*	*SD*	*Min*	*Max*	*Skewness*	*Kurtosis*
Dependent Variable								
Lawyers/1,000 Population	336	1.54	1.36	0.69	0.57	4.54	1.27	1.77
Independent Variables								
Population Density	384	124.05	54.83	189.26	0.70	1,041.95	2.70	7.37
Population Density (log)	384	3.93	4.00	1.42	–0.35	6.95	–0.23	–0.07
Population (%) in Cities > 100,000	384	18.32	18.82	15.26	0.00	66.77	0.50	–0.21
Racial Homogeneity (% White)	384	88.72	92.84	11.33	47.69	99.89	–1.34	1.20
Voter Turnout	384	57.17	61.35	15.95	7.45	83.27	–1.13	0.81
Protestant/Catholic Population	334	7.22	1.74	16.69	0.16	212.30	6.96	72.04
Protestant/Catholic Population (log)	334	0.80	0.55	1.43	–1.82	5.36	0.65	–0.23
Real Income Per Capita (2010 Dollars)	336	17,531.18	16,236.11	8,739.10	3,349.70	44,609.00	0.42	–0.62
Real Income Per Capita/1000 (2010 Dollars)	336	17.53	16.24	8.74	3.35	44.61	0.42	–0.62
Income Inequality (GINI)	384	0.45	0.44	0.07	0.24	0.67	0.14	0.47
Divorce Rate/Marriage Rate	384	0.30	0.25	0.17	0.00	0.77	0.60	–0.62

Source: Author's analysis of select datasets included in Appendix.

Where y_{it} is the number of lawyers per 1,000 population in a given state i at time t; α is the constant; β_{it} is the log of the population density of a given state i at time t; γ_{it} is the percent population in cities greater than 100,000 of a given state i at time t; μ_{it} is racial homogeneity of a given state i at time t; δ_{it} is the percent voter turnout of a given state i at time t; θ_{it} is the log of the Protestant/Catholic population ratio in a given state i at time t; ρ_{it} is real income per capita in a given state i at time t; χ is income inequality in a given state i at time t; and τ is the ratio of divorce to marriage (per capita) in a given state i at time t.

As Table 5.3 indicates, racial homogeneity, the Protestant/Catholic population ratio, real income per capita, income inequality, and the ratio of divorce to marriage are significant in Model 5.1. The error term is well-behaved, with a skewness of 0.89 and a kurtosis of 1.77. The QIC is 336.39.

The parameter estimates for each significant variable have the following interpretation: racial homogeneity has a significant and negative relationship with the lawyer population, with every unit increase in racial homogeneity decreasing the number of lawyers per 1,000 population by 0.024; the Protestant/Catholic population ratio (log) has a significant and negative relationship with the lawyer population, with every unit increase in the Protestant/Catholic population ratio (log) decreasing the number of lawyers per 1,000 by 0.16; real income per capita ($1,000 increments) has a significant and positive relationship with the lawyer population, with every unit increase in real income per capita increasing the number of lawyers per 1,000 by 0.04; income inequality has a significant and positive relationship with the lawyer population, with every unit increase in income inequality increasing the number of lawyers per 1,000 population by 1.64; and the divorce to marriage ratio (per capita) has a significant and positive relationship with the lawyer population, with every unit increase in the divorce to marriage ratio increasing the number of lawyers per 1,000 by 0.64.

Population density and percent population in cities greater than 100,000 are not significant at the 0.05 level. Voter turnout as a measure of social capital also is not significant in explaining the size of the state bar. The other variables acted as expected, however, with measures of heterogeneity (racial, religious,

Table 5.3 Regression of Lawyer Population on Select Variables (1920–1990)

Parameter	*Estimate*	*Standard Error*	*Pr* > |*Z*|
Intercept	2.4060	0.6954	0.0005
Population Density (log)	–0.0952	0.0523	0.0685
Population in Cities > 100,000 (%)	–0.0046	0.0040	0.2557
Racial Homogeneity (% White)	–0.0236	0.0070	0.0007
Voter Turnout	0.0032	0.0046	0.4849
Protestant/Catholic Population (log)	–0.1638	0.0546	0.0027
Real Income Per Capita	0.0396	0.0081	<0.0001
Income Inequality (GINI)	1.6375	0.6482	0.0115
Divorce Rate/Marriage Rate	0.6357	0.2118	0.0027

Source: Author's analysis of select datasets included in Appendix.

and economic) appearing to provide a context where the common good or justice is harder to ascertain and the number of attorneys is greater. Concerning religion, the Protestant/Catholic ratio also may simply measure a greater Protestant aversion to litigation in favor of informal means to handling injustice. Income acts in positive fashion as predicted, with increases in income leading to an increase in the number of attorneys. Finally, domestic instability measured by a higher divorce to marriage ratio also increases the number of attorneys.

The foregoing analysis shows that the size of the state bar does have a fairly high correlation with the level of criminal and civil faction and that the correlation appears to be fairly stable over time. Second, statistical evaluation of the lawyer population itself for the time period in question (1920–1990) addresses more directly the issue of causation and finds that anticipated barriers to justice or the common good do tend to increase the number of attorneys in a state.

A final justification that can be offered for the lawyer population serving as an adequate measure of societal injustice is that the primary model developed in Chapter 4 points in the direction of theoretical coherence. Taken together, the variables modeled in the last chapter point to the interaction of justice and centralization in influencing state debt. At the interpersonal level, the capacity for justice or the common good matters. Criminal and civil faction reflect less capacity for the common good in a populace that, when it comes to public policy, is inclined to take more than its share by transferring fiscal burdens to the future through higher levels of debt. Centralization is the institutional corollary to this interpersonal measure of justice or the common good. Through the cession or the seizure of the disciplines of self-government, the capacity for what Tocqueville called political freedom is diminished (although equality itself may be scrupulously preserved and even enhanced). The sinews of community essential to the realization of justice or the common good are weakened as responsibilities that should be exercised by citizens are transferred to an expanding state sector.

The Size of the State Bar as a Measure of Legal Complexity

In addition to interpreting the lawyer variable as a measure of injustice, it may be seen as a measure of legal complexity. Schuck's excellent overview of legal complexity is a helpful place to begin.[2] First of all, he readily acknowledges the definitional challenge. Complexity must be considered in context and in light of relevant actors. Furthermore, simplicity is not always a virtue, and complexity is not always a vice. Some growth in complexity must accompany increasingly intricate social and economic arrangements. Still, as a law professor, Schuck approaches the subject of legal complexity with concern, noting that complexity is increasing and has broader ramifications for effective governance than scholars typically consider. In short, complexity means more than just increasing transaction costs; in the main, it can impinge on a democracy's capacity to function. Legal complexity has to be assayed from a "political economy" standpoint that considers these larger implications for governance.

Because of institutional development associated with centralization and the incentives of actors within an increasingly centralized system, there is an inherent momentum toward greater legal complexity in American law. Normative shifts in the legal community from formalism to realism are in part responsible for this tendency. "The administrative state grew out of the effort to regulate areas of activity previously governed primarily by informal or contractual norms, and other areas previously regulated at lower levels of intensity or lower levels of government," Schuck writes.[3] Legislatures had modest goals, and courts practiced a formalism that emphasized respect for precedent and legislative intent. Schuck writes,

> The New Deal changed all that, and the change it wrought accelerated in the decades that followed. New legislative goals, largely implemented by administrative agencies, included health and safety, equal opportunity, income redistribution, financial security for the elderly, stabilization of markets, development of infrastructure, governmental reform, and many more. This transformation of public and private law invited judges to abandon even the pretense of formalism. Spurred on by many legal scholars, they openly embraced a conception of role, a style of thought, and a rhetoric of decision that legitimated judicial policymaking in a variety of areas.[4]

In addition to centralization, the incentives internal to the legal community push the law toward greater complexity. These "producers and rationalizers of the law" include, among others, litigators, legislators, judges, and legal scholars.[5] Legislators use complexity to benefit or harm particular groups, resolve collective action problems, and use the bureaucracy for political ends. Schuck validates Fiorina's[6] argument that legislators "create complex new programs and bureaucracies so that they can intervene selectively later on when problems materialize."[7] Bureaucracies are organized around technicality and issue rules to maximize compliance. Lawyers have an interest in indeterminate rules that enhance the value of their services and potential jury awards. Legal scholars have an interest in academic creativity that breaks new theoretical ground and validates their work. Driven in part by institutional centralization and the professional interest of the legal community, legal complexity can result in a system of justice that becomes incomprehensible and subject to the exploitation of special interest. Citizen attachment to the law is diminished, and government legitimacy suffers.[8]

Schuck's insightful overview of legal complexity and his expansion of that debate into the dimensions of political economy is well-complemented by Ruhl and Katz's focus on the measurement of legal complexity itself.[9] They discuss the various applications of complexity science to the legal arena to guide future research on legal complexity. They do not attempt actual measurements themselves, however. While not nearly as nuanced as their proposed metrics, various indices of political and regulatory freedom would fit generally into the kind of networks Ruhl and Katz are discussing. Table 5.4 lists the correlation of the state lawyer population[10] with measurements from the Mercatus Center of state fiscal,

Table 5.4 Correlation of Lawyer Population (2005) with Mercatus Freedom Index (2007)

Freedom Index	*Correlation*
Fiscal Freedom	–0.40
Regulatory Freedom	–0.51
Economic Freedom	–0.53

regulatory, and economic freedom.[11] The size of the state bar does have a negative correlation with each category, the largest being with regulatory and economic freedom. Of course, the results of such "freedom indexes" depend on the relative weight given to particular policies. Conservative-leaning organizations tend to be interested in such metrics (although the Mercatus Center could best be described as libertarian), and their general policy agenda must be considered when evaluating an index of this kind. Still, an index like the one from Mercatus provides a starting point to compare the correlation of the lawyer population with perceived or real areas of burdens imposed by legal complexity.

The Size of the State Bar as a Measure of the Dominance of Attorneys in the Public Square

In addition to the state lawyer population representing injustice and legal complexity, it also may represent the dominance of the bar in the elective branches of office, specifically the legislature. The dataset "Roster of United States Congressional Officeholders and Biographical Characteristics of Members of the United States Congress, 1789–1996: Merged Data" (ICPSR 7803) is used to analyze the occupations of House members.[12] Figures 5.1–5.4 illustrate the persistent dominance of attorneys in the House of Representatives over the course of American history. For each time period, lawyers comprise the largest percentage of last occupation prior to entering the House, averaging between 50 and 65 percent of the total for most parties during the first three eras. Interestingly, the percentage of lawyers falls in the final era for both parties as members have greater variety in their pre-House careers.

From 1789 to 1860 (Figure 5.1), attorneys comprise a greater proportion of Whig members, while Independents are less likely to come from a legal background. Minor parties have a pronounced presence in the professional category, while Republicans and Federalists have a higher percentage of members coming from business. Democrats and Independents have the highest percentage in agriculture, while Republicans have the lowest.

From 1870 to 1900 (Figure 5.2), the percentage of attorneys in the Democratic camp rises to roughly 65 percent while remaining at approximately the same level for Republicans. Both Democrats and Republicans continue to have less than 10 percent in the professional and agriculture categories. Interestingly, both parties have roughly equivalent proportions in business. The minor parties have noticeably less membership in law and business and more in agriculture.

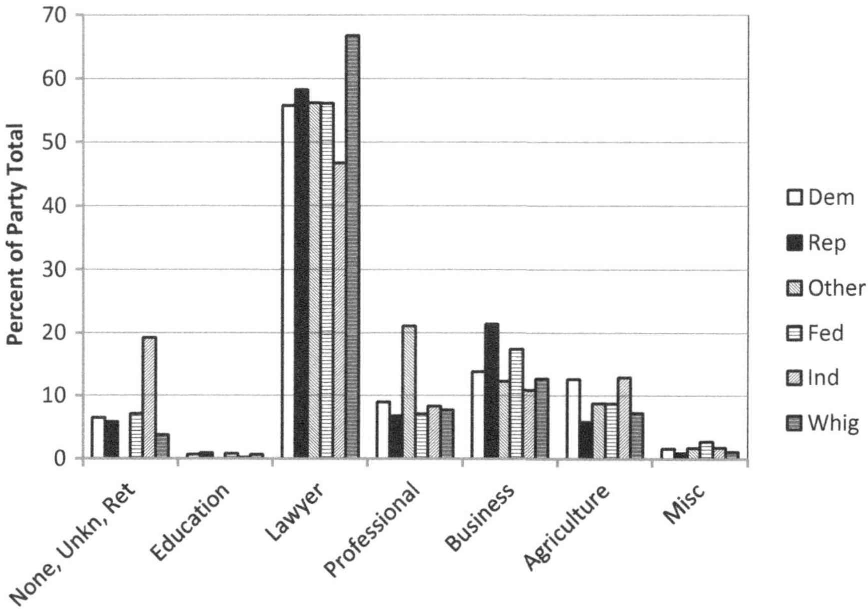

Figure 5.1 Last Occupation Prior to Service in the U.S. House (1789–1860).

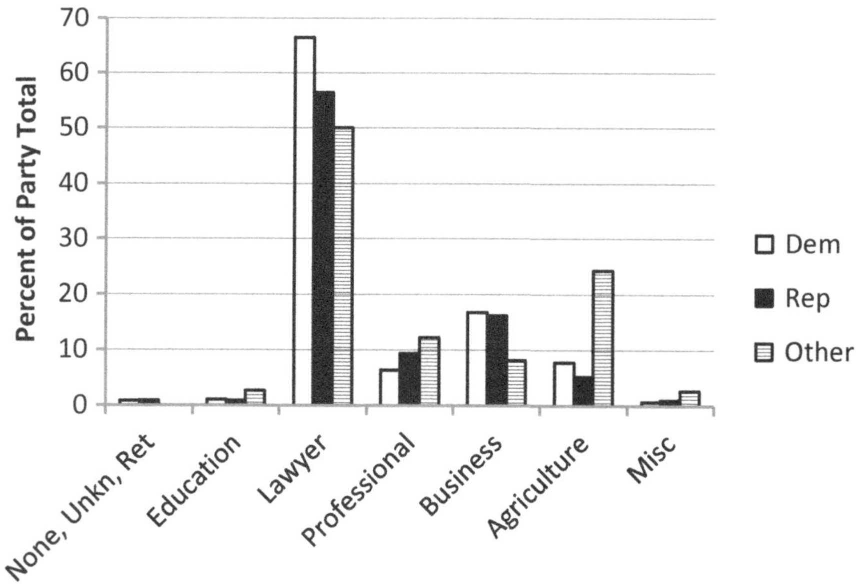

Figure 5.2 Last Occupation Prior to Service in the U.S. House (1870–1900).

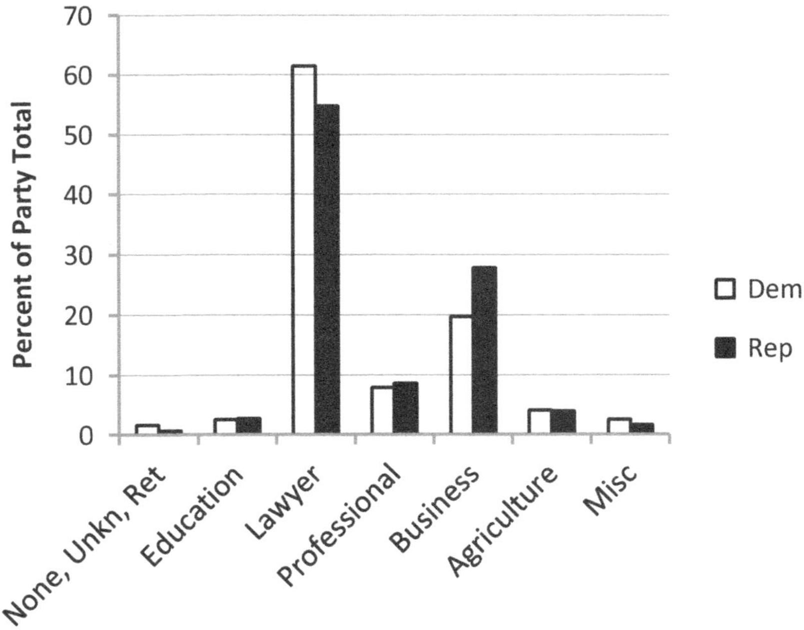

Figure 5.3 Last Occupation Prior to Service in the U.S. House (1901–1946).

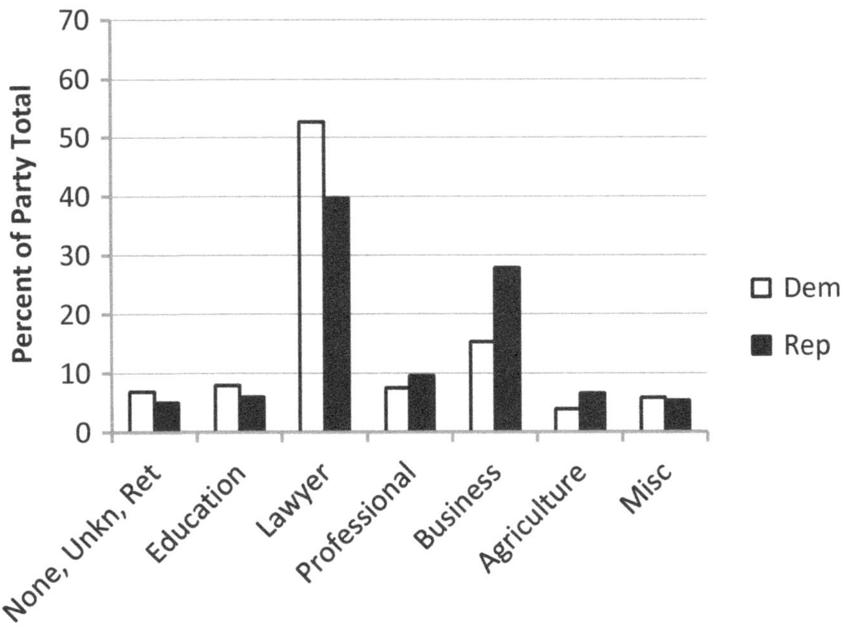

Figure 5.4 Last Occupation Prior to Service in the U.S. House (1947–1996).

From 1901 to 1946 (Figure 5.3), the percentage of Democratic attorneys declines while holding steady for Republicans. Professional and agriculture categories continue to comprise less than 10 percent for each party. Education grows slightly, and both parties increase the percent of members coming from the business sector, with Republicans beginning to show a clear edge over Democrats in this category.

The period 1947–1996 (Figure 5.4) is interesting for its greater diversity of pre-House careers. Lawyers still constitute the dominant occupation before House service, but percentages fall for both parties. Republicans register the greater decrease, however, even as they expand their lead over Democrats in business, leading to a clearer political divide between these two pre-House occupations.

Unfortunately, this very useful database of biographical information on members of the U.S. House of Representatives from 1789 to 1996 does not have a companion for state legislatures. The hypothesis that stems from this analysis of attorney dominance in the U.S. House is that lawyers dominate state legislatures in proportion to the size of the state bar. States with a higher per capita lawyer population will have a higher percentage of attorneys as state legislators and vice versa.

The dominance of a particular group in a legislature is important because that group shapes legislative procedures, norms, and outcomes. There would be a natural wariness in the public, for example, if doctors comprised 50–70 percent of the U.S. House over the course of American history. The concern would not center around the fact that these legislators are doctors but that their parochial concerns would crowd out the national interest at that level of representation.

Because attorneys are trained in the law, their dominance in legislatures may not be viewed with the same wariness. Their training in public law does not necessarily equate to a better grasp of the public interest, however. Attorneys no doubt serve in the legislature as do members from other professions: with a mixture of personal and public-mindedness. Attorneys have a distinct professional interest to enter the public square, however. The law is their craft, and the handling of the common good may proceed in tandem with private gain.

Lawyers also have what Nietzsche would call an uncanny sense of self-identity. The very fact that the number of lawyers can be tabulated from the latter decades of the nineteenth century is because of national directories that list the lawyer's name, place of residence, educational background, and practice areas. These directories themselves reveal the profession's instinctive sense of thoroughness and uniformity and a grasp of national identity and organization. Lawyers may be the only professional group better informed historically of their size and makeup than the Census. Indeed, the Census relied on attorney directories when including state lawyer totals in statistical abstracts. In short, lawyers may have been better organized in 1900 than most professional organizations are today.

In addition to a private interest in the public square and a strong internal sense of identity, the bar has potent external organizational strictures. Compulsion is a key tool in group formation and management, Olson argues, and the bar exceeds most other associations in self-enforcement. He writes,

> The self-regulating guild with compulsory membership has reached its further degree of development in many state bar associations. Many state legislatures have been induced to require *by law* that *every* practicing lawyer must be a member of the state bar association. These bar associations have closed shops enforced by government, and thus should be the envy of every labor union.[13]

Tocqueville takes with utmost seriousness the role of lawyers in America. They are the lone refuge of aristocracy and a much-needed counterweight to pervasive democratic equality. Furthermore, their legal formalism helps restrain democratic rashness. French lawyers reason from the novelties of their own opinion, but American lawyers find refuge in precedent. They are happy to frame their arguments in the parameters set by the "work of their fathers."[14]

> It was in England that this legal mind was born, which seems indifferent to the foundation of things so as to pay attention only to the letter, and which would rather depart from reason and humanity than from the law.[15]

Lawyers could check democracy's passions because they have the confidence of the people. They come from the people's ranks and are entrusted with most public offices. Lawyers have aristocratic tastes but know their eminent position rests on respect for democracy. The influence of the bar, therefore, far outweighs its visibility. Tocqueville concludes,

> Lawyers in the United States form a power that is hardly feared, scarcely perceived, that has no banner of its own, that bows with flexibility to the exigencies of the times, and lets itself go without resistance to all movements of the social body; but it envelops society as a whole, penetrates into each of the classes that compose it, works in secret, acts constantly on it without its knowing, and in the end models it to its desires.[16]

If the influence of the bar on American life begins to approach what Tocqueville described, then changes in the norms of the bar should have profound implications for the conduct of American politics. As such, the shift from formalism to realism in the legal community must be among the most significant normative changes in American society.

As will be discussed in greater detail in the next chapter, the conventional storyline associated with realism's triumph is that the judiciary was a holdout of formalism against the political branches that wanted more activist government during the New Deal. But the currency of this view may be exaggerated by the confrontation of Franklin Roosevelt with the Supreme Court, reaching a climax with the supposed switch in time that saved nine. American jurisprudence was moving toward a more realist stance prior to the pivotal cases of the 1930s. There were fits and starts, to be sure, and generational differences in the bar perhaps sharpened the contrast more at the level of the high court, where the most senior and perhaps most conservative justices sat. But the longer storyline of the latter nineteenth and early twentieth centuries is one that mirrors other eras in the Court's history: that of following, albeit erratically, the dominant and enduring political trends of the day.

The move toward political activism was therefore not in opposition to a formalist judiciary but in conjunction with more activist courts. The effect of legal realism on American jurisprudence is an obvious and much-studied topic. The effect of legal realism on the political branches is not as intuitive but worthy of more attention, for what was shared in common between the political and judicial branches were the norms of the bar that shifted toward more expansive government.

As Schuck argues, this shift in norms has broader implications for government legitimacy. The law as the express will of the people enacted through their elected representatives becomes more complex, mutable, and manipulable under a realist regime of judicial policymaking. "Intelligible only to experts, the law is likely to mystify and alienate lay citizens whose intelligence it often seems designed to mock," Schuck writes.[17]

In assessing the effect of realism on the judicial and political branches, the question is not whether lawyers were capable of hoodwinking the nation for the better part of a century to advance an agenda to which the country was opposed. Lawyers lost elections over the course of the twentieth century just like businessmen and farmers and doctors. What the historical statistics show, however, is that another lawyer would be more likely to fill that seat than a businessman or farmer or doctor. Lawyers did not have a monolithic policy agenda in any Congress, much less one sustained over many Congresses. As members of every political party, they represented the full panoply of political viewpoints. What remains, then, is the least common denominators of the bar as a profession that acted tectonically over time to shift the political ground toward centralization: the tendency toward standardization, the inclination to extend procedural controls over increasing sectors of private life, and a realist orientation that imbued the foregoing with an activist political bent through much of the twentieth century.

Furthermore, viewed in the light of legal realism, the relationship between the judicial and political branches can be seen as more cooperative than confrontational. Arguments for judicial independence, usually presented as necessary to keep the political branches in check and preserve personal liberties, give the courts more freedom to empower an expansive state because both the political branches and the judiciary are populated by a bar with shared norms. Judicial independence is a real feature in American political life and has value at a given point in time as judges have and exercise the freedom to be impartial. Historically speaking, however, and assayed over an expanse of time, judicial independence as a check on government is a bit of a sleight of hand, as realist norms operative in both the judicial and legislative branches support centralizing tendencies. Government centralization thus has proceeded hand in hand with judicial supremacy. The increasing dominance of the Supreme Court in American politics is the natural tendency of a constitutional system suffused with the interests of a particular profession that incrementally draws more political authority into the sphere over which it exercises exclusive control, that is, the judiciary.

Ironically, the administrative state that lawyers helped build may be undermining the relative influence of the bar in the legislature. As more sectors of a society organize their lives around an expansive administrative state, more sectors of that society have a vocational interest in government involvement. This may explain the decline of lawyer dominance in the 1947–1996 era in Figure 5.4.

Conclusion

This chapter has presented three different ways to interpret the important variable of lawyer population: as a measure of societal injustice seen in criminal and civil faction; as a measure of legal complexity; and as a measure of the dominance of attorneys in legislatures. The first interpretation is the one used for the underlying thesis of this book, but this viewpoint is not necessarily at odds with the latter two interpretations. All three of these viewpoints related to the size of the bar point to political implications that to some extent overlap. The theoretical construct for this model, illustrated in Chapter 3, includes two principal dimensions relating debt and injustice: mores and institutions. As it is used in modeling in Chapter 4, the lawyer population variable is seeking to assess one dimension of mores: the incapacity of a populace for justice as seen in criminal and civil faction. To the extent that the lawyer population does not adequately measure mores associated with justice, it may still be related to centralization, as this theme is present in the second and third interpretations of lawyer population presented above. Such a conclusion would not invalidate the thesis necessarily but only mean that a new measure of injustice would have to be found to sustain the argument related to mores, with the lawyer population variable being relegated to the institutional domain of centralization.

The foregoing analysis shows that this conclusion need not be reached, however. Using the lawyer population as a representative of societal injustice is defensible. With data that is currently available, it is perhaps the most defensible use of the variable. Modeling in Chapter 4 shows that the size of the bar has significance in explaining debt apart from the measures of centralization and an assortment of other socioeconomic and cultural variables. Further research on legal complexity and the parochial influence of the bar on the legislative process can give additional insight into these three interpretive dimensions related to the size and role of the legal community in American politics.

In the nascent American republic of the 1830s, Tocqueville saw the bar in an essentially positive light. The legal community provided aristocratic ballast to a society suffused with equality. Moreover, legal formalism restrained policy innovation in a rapidly changing society. Of course, it is impossible to know what Tocqueville would think of the bar today, but the growth of the bar, the shift in legal norms from formalism to realism, and the legal complexity associated with the administrative state likely would give him pause.

The discussion of the characteristics of the bar do not point toward a legal conspiracy to subvert the institutions of republican government but toward the enduring inclinations of a cohesive and capable group whose interest is advanced through a combination of strong internal identity, external enforcement, and the conflation of legal training and public service that makes the lawyer appear as a natural legislator in the public's mind. These features and others give the legal community great influence in American society. Tocqueville saw the bar as "playing the primary role in the political society that is seeking to be born."[18] The norms of the legal community therefore should be regarded as among the most important in shaping American political institutions, and the shift from formalism to realism can be seen as not only influencing the judicial but political branches through their common occupation by the bar. In light of political influence of lawyers, Madison's question of how to oblige the government to control itself may be seen in a narrower sense as directed to the bar.[19] His theory of factions being balanced in a large republic must consider the effects of one faction whose natural domain is within government and whose influence there is less perceptible because it acts as a common escort to all other factions entering the public square.

Notes

1 National Center for State Courts, "State Court Statistics, 2005," ICPSR30522-v1, Ann Arbor, MI: Inter-University Consortium for Political and Social Research (distributor), May 22, 2012. Accessed July 4, 2016 at http://doi.org/10.3886/ICPSR30522.v1.
2 Peter H. Schuck, "Legal Complexity: Some Causes, Consequences, and Cures," *Duke Law Journal* Vol. 42 No. 1 (October 1992): 1–52.
3 Ibid., 12.
4 Ibid., 14.
5 Ibid., 7.
6 Morris P. Fiorina, *Congress: Keystone of the Washington Establishment*, Second Edition (New Haven, CT: Yale University Press, 1989).
7 Schuck, "Legal Complexity," 28.
8 Ibid., 22–23.
9 J.B. Ruhl and Daniel Martin Katz, "Measuring, Monitoring, and Managing Legal Complexity," *Iowa Law Review* Vol. 101 (October 2015): 191–244.
10 American Bar Association, "ABA National Lawyer Population Survey (2015): 10-Year Trend in Lawyer Population by State (2005–2015)." Accessed November 8, 2016 at www.americanbar.org/content/dam/aba/administrative/market_research/national-lawyer-population-by-state-2005-2015.authcheckdam.pdf.
11 William P. Ruger and Jason Sorens, Freedom in the 50 States Dataset, Mercatus Center, George Mason University. Accessed November 8, 2016 at www.freedomin the50states.org/data.
12 Inter-university Consortium for Political and Social Research, and Carol McKibbin, "Roster of United States Congressional Officeholders and Biographical Characteristics

of Members of the United States Congress, 1789–1996: Merged Data," [Computer File] ICPSR07803-v10 (Ann Arbor, MI: Inter-university Consortium for Political and Social Research [distributor], 1997), Doi: 10.3886/ICPSR07803.v10.
13 Mancur Olson, Jr., *The Logic of Collective Action* (Cambridge, MA: Harvard University Press, 1965), 138.
14 Alexis de Tocqueville, *Democracy in America*, trans. Harvey C. Mansfield and Delba Winthrop (Chicago: University of Chicago Press, 2000), 256.
15 Ibid.
16 Ibid., 258.
17 Schuck, Legal Complexity," 23.
18 Tocqueville, *Democracy in America*, 252.
19 Alexander Hamilton, James Madison, and John Jay, *The Federalist* (New York: Barnes & Noble, 2006), 288.

Bibliography

American Bar Association. "ABA National Lawyer Population Survey (2015): 10-Year Trend in Lawyer Population by State (2005–2015)." Accessed November 8, 2016 at www.americanbar.org/content/dam/aba/administrative/market_research/national-lawyer-population-by-state-2005-2015.authcheckdam.pdf.

De Tocqueville, Alexis. *Democracy in America*. Translated by Harvey C. Mansfield and Delba Winthrop. Chicago: University of Chicago Press, 2000.

Fiorina, Morris P. *Congress: Keystone of the Washington Establishment*, Second Edition. New Haven, CT: Yale University Press, 1989.

Hamilton, Alexander, James Madison, and John Jay. *The Federalist*. New York: Barnes & Noble, 2006.

Inter-university Consortium for Political and Social Research, and Carol McKibbin. "Roster of United States Congressional Officeholders and Biographical Characteristics of Members of the United States Congress, 1789–1996: Merged Data." [Computer File] ICPSR07803-v10. Ann Arbor, MI: Inter-university Consortium for Political and Social Research [distributor], 1997. Doi: 10.3886/ICPSR07803.v10.

National Center for State Courts. "State Court Statistics, 2005." ICPSR30522-v1. Ann Arbor, MI: Inter-University Consortium for Political and Social Research (distributor), May 22, 2012. Accessed July 4, 2016 at http://doi.org/10.3886/ICPSR30522.v1.

Olson, Mancur Jr. *The Logic of Collective Action*. Cambridge, MA: Harvard University Press, 1965.

Ruger, William P. and Jason Sorens. Freedom in the 50 States Dataset. Mercatus Center, George Mason University. Accessed November 8, 2016 at www.freedominthe50states.org/data.

Ruhl, J.B. and Daniel Martin Katz. "Measuring, Monitoring, and Managing Legal Complexity." *Iowa Law Review* Vol. 101 (October 2015): 191–244.

Schuck, Peter H. "Legal Complexity: Some Causes, Consequences, and Cures." *Duke Law Journal* Vol. 42 No. 1 (October 1992): 1–52.

6 Progressivism and the Rise of the American Administrative State

I believe in pure democracy.

—Theodore Roosevelt, "A Charter for Democracy"

As deficits preceded Keynes, so the impetus for centralization preceded the New Deal. In the years leading up to and during the Progressive Era, the American people began to empower government to exert more public stewardship over a society being transformed by industrialization and urbanization. With the significance of centralization established in quantitative modeling in Chapter 4, this chapter reviews the rise of the American administrative state, with emphasis on Progressive Era reforms that were consolidated during the New Deal.

Ambitious political reforms outlined by the Progressive Party in the 1912 election implied an administrative apparatus out of step with traditional American views of limited constitutional government. Through its separation of powers, enumerated powers, federal structure, and natural rights tradition, limited constitutional government necessarily considers both the equal and the unequal in seeking a just society. The United States thus could be founded on the proposition that all men are created equal and then constitute a government whose "first object," according to Madison, is to protect the diverse faculties of its citizens that result in unequal outcomes.[1] The development of the American administrative state necessarily involved the diminishment of constitutional forms that provided various political platforms[2] from which to advance dissimilar, "unequal" viewpoints. Social welfare initiatives pursued in centralized fashion also conflicted with a natural rights tradition that emphasized equality of opportunity rather than equality of outcome. The growth of the administrative state was accompanied by a heightened emphasis on collective opinion as an alternative source of legitimacy in place of the constitutional structure that was being abandoned. American democracy came to rely more on a central figure to discern and lead that public opinion, as Tulis recounts of Wilson and subsequent American presidents.[3] While not dismissing the successes of the modern American administrative state, this chapter applies the theoretical arguments of Chapter 2 to the historical narrative of Progressivism to show how centralized administration more capable of programmatic achievement may be less capable of the justice that accompanies self-government.

Defining Progressivism

As Gould states, "What gives the first twenty years of the [twentieth] century their perennial fascination is the intriguing interplay of modern and traditional ideas about the direction of American society."[4] Defining the nature of this interplay and its ramifications for American politics has been the subject of intense debate, however. At one extreme is Filene's postmortem of Progressivism. Reviewing the variety, divergence, and conflict of opinion during the Progressive Era, Filene concludes the "progressive movement" never existed.[5] Rather,

> [t]he progressive era seems to be characterized by shifting coalitions around different issues, with the specific nature of these coalitions varying on federal, state, and local levels, from region to region, and from the first to the second decades of the century.[6]

In his benchmark essay, Rodgers begins with Filene and notes that definitional challenges related to Progressivism have turned the study of this period in the fruitful direction of context rather than essence.[7] With the decline of traditional parties and the pressures of economic and social change, Progressive politics comes forth as less a movement than an amalgam of "shifting, ideologically fluid, issue-focused coalitions, all competing for the reshaping of American society."[8] Amidst the plurality can be discerned three core ideas of Progressivism, or three "social languages": antimonopolism, social bonds, and social efficiency.[9] These languages often were in conflict with each other, and Progressives could be found on both sides of the major issues of the day. The Progressive Era should be understood in light of its diversity, and a contextual approach informed by assumptions of plurality is placing Progressive research on much sounder footing: as the era which inaugurated "the rise of modern, weak-party, issue-focused politics."[10]

While not dismissing the complexity of the Progressive Era, Gould tackles the definitional challenge with more optimism than Rodgers. An impetus for Progressive reform was the economic depression of 1893–1897, which sharpened social tensions over industrialization, urbanization, and various social ills. With an emphasis on "efficiency, rationality, and expertise," Progressives looked to the commission form of municipal government and commissions at the federal level where experts could formulate policy free of corrupting influences.[11] Direct democracy was central to the Progressive agenda, including the referendum, initiative, direct primary, direct election of Senators, and women's suffrage (although the internal contradiction of direct democracy with administrative efficiency was not reconciled by Progressives). The period witnessed countervailing political currents that caused the two major parties to reassess their organizing principles. Democrats began moving away from a party ideology dominated by localism and states' rights, and Republican enthusiasm for business and property was chastened by calls to restrain trusts and enact social reform. Gould writes,

> The Democrats did not resolve all their internal contradictions, as Wilson's second term and the 1920s demonstrated, but in the Progressive Era they began the slow process of erecting the base on which Franklin Roosevelt would construct the New Deal majorities.[12]

Hofstadter, Moreno, and Milkis join Gould in tracing important elements of the New Deal lineage to Progressivism. Hofstadter's "age of reform" is a bit longer than Gould's, stretching from the 1890s to the New Deal.[13] Longer still is Moreno's purview in *The American State from the Civil War to the New Deal: The Twilight of Constitutionalism and the Triumph of Progressivism.*[14] Moreno and Milkis[15] emphasize the inherent tension between limited constitutional government and Progressivism. Milkis offers the added benefit of partially alleviating Progressivism's definitional challenge by focusing on the concrete proposals of the Progressive Party in the presidential campaign of 1912. Faced with an election, the diffuse and diverse elements of the Progressive coalition had to formulate an explicit policy platform. This exercise helped define the contours of Progressivism for Progressives themselves and for the analyst seeking to evaluate the scope of their proposals.

Both Hofstadter and Rubin believe that Progressives were modest in their proposals. The Populists offer a backdrop for both scholars in their analysis of Progressive reform. Progressives lacked the originality of the Populists, Hofstadter argues, and borrowed much from the Populist agenda. The contributions of professionals and the middle class to Progressivism, however, made the movement more urban, informed, and complex than Populism.[16] Progressives had the capacity to see both sides of an issue and be on both sides of an issue, supporting Filene's thesis. Rubin likewise sees the boldest policy proposals emanating from the Populists, who came to believe that the market had fundamentally failed American farmers and that the federal government should assume direct control of the agricultural sector. By contrast, Progressives did not question the viability of the market economy but sought "marginal change" to control the excesses of capitalism.[17]

From an economic standpoint, Hofstadter and Rubin may be right, but Milkis' focus on the 1912 election brings into relief the fundamental challenge that Progressive political reform posed to constitutionalism. Having campaigned as a Republican but being blocked from the nomination at the convention, Roosevelt's newly formed Progressive Party pushed a far-reaching agenda that would require a transformation in important American political institutions and the cultural assumptions that undergirded them. Although the Progressive Party did not win the presidency, Progressive reform dominated the agenda of the campaign. Roosevelt and Wilson, the candidates most aligned with Progressivism, received more than twice the vote of the more conservative Taft.[18]

The Presidential Campaign of 1912

If not as gifted a politician as Roosevelt or Wilson, Taft was not out of touch with the times in which he governed. Taft ascended to the presidency with the support of an increasingly Progressive President Roosevelt.[19] Moreno writes, "Taft was in fact a progressive, as he claimed to be and as he was regarded in Republican ranks. The conservatives in the party feared that he was too close to Roosevelt."[20] Taft took a more aggressive posture against the trusts than Roosevelt, initiating twice as many antitrust suits in half the time. In addition, his appointments to the Supreme Court played an important role in strengthening the Sherman Antitrust Act and took a somewhat more favorable view generally of social and economic regulation.[21]

As implied in the paragraph above, Roosevelt took a different view on corporate trusts. Large corporations were a natural outgrowth of and often a prerequisite for competitiveness in contemporary economics. Strong industries were a foundation of national power and should not be penalized simply for being large. Taft's antitrust suit in 1911 against United States Steel, a company that made the acquisition of Tennessee Coal and Iron with President Roosevelt's approval in 1907, brought their two divergent antitrust policies into sharper relief, provided an occasion for personal recriminations on both sides, and served as partial pretext for Roosevelt to enter the presidential campaign of 1912.[22]

If political ties between Taft and Roosevelt were strained by the trust issue, they were completely severed by questions of constitutional governance. In contrast to Roosevelt's expansive "stewardship" theory of executive power, Taft sought to govern within constitutional bounds and offered the most traditional defense of limited constitutional government during the 1912 campaign. Conservation policy offered a precursor to what would become a full-blown struggle for the character of the Republican Party. Taft dismissed Roosevelt's Interior Secretary, James Garfield, for restricting development of government land in an extralegal fashion. When criticized, Taft defended the move as upholding proper constitutional procedures and the rule of law.[23] As Roosevelt moved toward entering the presidential contest of 1912 and then actively campaigned for the Republican nomination, Taft came to regard him as a threat to the party and sound constitutional government.

Roosevelt's Progressive Party believed that good government would follow from purer forms of democracy, or from what Aristotle would call tightening the regime. The referendum, initiative, direct primaries, direct election of Senators, and women's suffrage were political reforms that would give the American people ownership of their government, and in important ways these reforms did so, particularly with regard to women's suffrage. Support for additional avenues of citizen engagement was not balanced with a healthy respect for mediating institutions that leavened public opinion, however. Traditional parties blocked the people's will and should be removed. Roosevelt supported recall of judicial decisions at the state level, a move that cost him moderate Republican support.[24] Recall of public officials became an increasingly strident theme for Roosevelt, ending with his eventual support for recall of the president. The governmental framework outlined in the Constitution to check and refine popular opinion must give way to "We the People" in the Constitution's preamble.[25]

By contrast, Taft argued that exalting public opinion above written statutory and constitutional law would allow untrammeled majorities to violate individual liberties.[26] Durable Progressive reform only could be achieved by observing the rule of law and following proven constitutional procedures. Taft's position as the most conservative candidate and his withdrawal from the general election fray, apparently out of respect for tradition, left the race to Roosevelt and Wilson. Along with Roosevelt, Wilson adopted a modern posture of actively campaigning during the general election. Pushed by Roosevelt, Wilson came to embrace certain Progressive reforms for direct democracy, stopping short of judicial recall and the recall of public officials. "Wilson's reform message had moved very far in Roosevelt's direction by the end of the campaign. Seeking to establish his own credential as servant of the people, Wilson championed mass opinion almost as fervently as did Roosevelt," Milkis writes.[27]

Roosevelt and Wilson also shared an underlying commitment to collective national identity over the country's natural rights tradition and a belief that the executive played the key role in shaping national identity. In his New Nationalism speech in Osawatomie, Kansas, Roosevelt stated:

> The New Nationalism puts the national need before sectional or personal advantage. It is impatient of the utter confusion that results from local legislatures attempting to treat national issues as local issues. It is still more impatient of the impotence which springs from over division of governmental powers, the impotence which makes it possible for local selfishness or for legal cunning, hired by wealthy special interests, to bring national activities to a deadlock. This New Nationalism regards the executive power as the steward of the public welfare. It demands of the judiciary that it shall be interested primarily in human welfare rather than in property, just as it demands that the representative body shall represent all the people rather than any one class or section of the people.[28]

A natural rights tradition built around respect for property was a barrier to equality of opportunity. After leaving office, Roosevelt gave important speeches leading up to the 1912 election elevating human rights over property rights.[29] In his last address of the campaign, made while still recovering from an assassin's bullet, Roosevelt argued that a greater emphasis on collective well-being would not enervate American individualism but chasten it with a greater sense of national community and purpose. State rights and property rights should not stand in the way of meaningful reform.[30]

Wilson made more "cautious and ambivalent" statements about American constitutional government during his political career, but on balance the tenor of his political philosophy, particularly as expressed in his earlier academic writings, was openly hostile to the Founding and limited government.[31] In contrast to the Founding's universal precepts regarding the nature of man, his rights, and the purpose of government, Wilson believed that human progress accompanied history, that as opinion developed it would converge, and that politics would become more about defining the means rather than the ends of government. As such, a government of limited and separated powers may have been suited to its own time but was not appropriate for a developing nation.[32] "Government in such an age of unity is not a threat to the individual that has to be checked," Pestritto writes of Wilson's perspective, "rather, the state is the organ of the individuals in society."[33] History has brought the country out of its provincialism, with the Civil War completing the Union.[34] The president was in the unique position of being able to represent and speak for this national consciousness and had an obligation to transcend the separation of powers to speak for the American people.[35]

In the style of campaigning, the cultivation of public opinion, and the emphasis on national identity, Roosevelt and Wilson had important similarities. In economic policy, they sharply disagreed. Opposing the tariff and monopoly, Wilson compared Roosevelt and Taft to Tweedledee and Tweedledum.[36] The tariff was the "mother of trusts" and the fount of government privilege for big business.[37] Furthermore, monopoly cannot be made good by regulation but must be dislodged.[38] Regulation by the courts would be much more effective than government commissions.[39]

Wilson attacked Roosevelt aggressively on the issue of administrative aggrandizement to regulate trusts, exposing a deep fissure within the Progressive Party itself. Progressives were far from monolithic in their support of administrative power. Formulation of the party platform brought anti-monopoly and business elements into open conflict. The former, represented by Progressive leaders Charles McCarthy and Amos and Gifford Pinchot, were closer to Wilson's position of trust-busting and court oversight, while the latter, represented by industry magnate and Progressive Party financier, George Perkins, argued that corporations should not be penalized simply because of their size. As mentioned above, Roosevelt supported the latter view, and Democrats criticized his proposed interstate trade commission as administrative overreach that would become captive to corporate interests.[40]

Aside from the trust issue, however, Progressive language envisioned broad government mandates for social and economic welfare that implied national administrative capacity. Progressives need not be against business, for there had to be prosperity first, but the distribution of property needs as much attention as its accumulation. In his important "Charter for Democracy" speech on February 21, 1912, made right after confirming his presidential candidacy, Roosevelt said,

> The ends of good government in our democracy are to secure by genuine popular rule a high average of moral and material well-being among our citizens. It has been well said that in the past we have paid attention only to the accumulation of prosperity, and that from henceforth we must pay equal attention to the proper distinction of prosperity. This is true. The only prosperity worth having is that which affects the mass of the people. We are bound to strive for the fair distribution of prosperity.[41]

Roosevelt announced his support for presidential recall, regarded as a particularly radical step by the constitutionally minded *New York Times*, to temper

Democratic criticism of Progressive intentions for an expansive administrative state. The threat of socialism was used as a pretext to justify Progressive reform, but the reforms themselves were socialistic in nature, Wilson argued.[42] Milkis writes,

> [T]he constant attack of Wilson and Brandeis on his plan to expand the responsibilities of the executive prompted Roosevelt to elaborate on his strongly held view that the solution to America's ills was not to restrain presidential power, which the Democratic platform explicitly prescribed, but, rather, to democratize it.[43]

Theodore Roosevelt thus represented the most unabashed strain of Progressive thought in the 1912 campaign, calling for direct citizen participation at a number of points in the political process, including plebiscites on changes to the fundamental law of the Constitution. In addition, his social welfare proposals would have to rely on national administration at odds with America's tradition of limited government. Wilson pursued Progressive aims with greater respect for local government and parties than Roosevelt would have, but the overall momentum of the Progressive Era was toward centralized government and the elevation of popular opinion in government councils. Taft's traditional view of limited constitutional government was pushed to the side.

Placing the 1912 Campaign in Historical Context

Having discussed several themes from the presidential campaign of 1912, it would be helpful to place this Progressive moment in the historical context of administrative state development. Both Wilson and Roosevelt as the Progressive candidates claimed the mantle of Lincoln and regarded the nationalizing effects of the Civil War as beneficial. For Wilson, Lincoln was the ideal leader who interpreted and led public opinion.[44] For Roosevelt, Lincoln's efforts to free the slaves were akin to Progressive reforms to defend the human rights of workers against the interests of property.[45] Identifying with Lincoln has been a regular practice of progressive politicians since 1912, including Barack Obama, who wrote in 2006 that Lincoln grasped the core insight of what would become New Deal liberalism: that a strong national government was not at odds with but could be a facilitator of the market economy.[46] The Progressive celebration of the nationalizing tendencies of the Civil War aligns with contemporary scholarship portraying Lincoln as a great centralizing force in American politics.[47]

While not understating the transformational effects of the Civil War on American politics, the link between Lincoln and Progressivism is tenuous. Both Roosevelt and Wilson viewed the American tradition of natural rights and limited constitutional government as obstacles to be overcome in forming national identity. The Declaration of Independence, by contrast, was Lincoln's political lodestar. Wilson would have excised the natural rights preface of the Declaration, but for Lincoln those immutable liberties applied to all human beings at all times, even if they were not fully realized at the Founding.[48] The immutability of those liberties offered an eternal principle by which to define the purposes of government and limit its power. As discussed in Chapter 3, Lincoln's conviction that all human beings are created equal sustained him in challenging Douglas' popular sovereignty, precisely the kind of policy based on public opinion esteemed by Progressive reforms. There were certain truths concerning human freedom that could not be bartered away at the ballot box. The Progressive emphasis on public opinion had real consequences for civil liberties, both during the 1912 campaign and World War I. Roosevelt's poor treatment of black delegates to the Progressive Party convention is much more reminiscent of Douglas than Lincoln. Likewise, the infringement of civil liberties during the war confronted leading Progressives with the harmful effects of public opinion.[49]

Furthermore, Lincoln's primary aim was to preserve constitutional government rather than transform or transcend it. He affirmed constitutional protections for slavery in Southern states but believed the principles of the Founding should be interpreted as utterly against its expansion. Pestritto writes,

> What most disturbed Lincoln in the 1850s was not the actual practice of slavery in those states where it already existed (while he abhorred this, he said repeatedly that nothing could be done about it as a matter of law), but the notion that it could be extended into new territories without doing violence to the principles of the founding.[50]

In addition to Douglas, who would sacrifice unalienable rights on the altar of public opinion, the abolitionists also espoused policies contrary to the Founding. Their extra-constitutional aim of using the national government to eradicate slavery in the South was contrary to the rule of law.

The strongest claim of the extra-constitutional Progressives on Lincoln is that he exceeded constitutional bounds himself in prosecuting the war. In the early months of the conflict, Lincoln on his own authority committed the finances of the country, called for military forces, imposed a blockade on the South, and suspended the writ of habeas corpus.[51] Suspension of the writ was particularly problematic, as that power was included in Article I of the Constitution dealing with legislative powers. Against charges that Lincoln was a constitutional dictator, Kelly et al. argue that emergency powers in the Constitution are inherently contestable and that the struggle between the coordinate branches of government permits of some flexibility. Lincoln was not so much violating constitutional guidelines as he was assembling and employing constitutional powers in a creative way to preserve the government. Both Congress, in subsequent legislation, and the Supreme Court, in the *Prize Cases* (1863), would later affirm Lincoln's policies.[52]

The cataclysm of the Civil War was profound, but the transformation of American government that followed was measured, separated from the tenets of the Progressive Era by several generations of ideological and institutional change.

> The most significant constitutional change occurring between 1860 and 1880 was the extension of national power over personal liberty and civil rights through the Thirteenth, Fourteenth, and Fifteenth Amendments, the Civil Rights Act of 1866, and the Enforcement Acts of the 1870s,

write Kelly et al.[53] Nevertheless, the "nationalization of civil rights" was limited in scope. The *Slaughterhouse Cases* (1873) narrowed the Privileges and Immunities Clause to a small set of national citizenship rights, such as the right of travel, and left the corpus of civil liberties espoused in and attendant to the Bill of Rights under the jurisdiction of the states.[54] According to Justice Miller, the purpose of the Reconstruction amendments could not have been to overturn the federal system. Furthermore, a series of cases, namely *U.S. v. Cruikshank* (1876), *U.S. v. Harris* (1883), and the *Civil Rights Cases* (1883), hemmed in Congress' ability to reach private discrimination against African Americans.[55] As McPherson notes, these decisions by the Supreme Court did not take place in a political vacuum.[56] Faced with implacable opposition in the South and growing impatience with Reconstruction policies in the North, the Republican appetite for Reconstruction was surfeited. Unwilling to sustain "bayonet rule," President Hayes in 1877 withdrew federal troops protecting the last three Republican state governments in the South, leading to their imminent collapse.[57]

As Gerring expertly chronicles, the National Republicans, heirs to the Whig tradition, had a more statist political philosophy than their Democratic counterparts. Given a freer hand after the withdrawal of Southern states from Congress, Republicans passed tariff, banking, and land grant legislation.[58] "National republicans were state-builders," however, writes Gerring, "within the constitutional confines of a chronically weak state."[59] Furthermore, Republican support for economic development focused on the creation of wealth rather than its distribution. Social welfare legislation was opposed as a hindrance to economic productivity.[60] Aside from the few durable Republican interests related to protection, sound money, and internal improvement, there were at the federal level "practically no governmental controls over agriculture, commerce, industry, or labor."[61]

With these jurisprudential and political limits to national power, there were important early developments that pointed in the direction of a more expansive administrative state. The Department of Agriculture was established in 1862, becoming the first "client-oriented" department.[62] The Supreme Court laid the "cornerstone" of its regulatory jurisprudence as early as 1876, Rabin notes, with *Munn v. Illinois* and seven companion cases validating state regulation of railroads.[63] The central holding of *Munn*, that the state can regulate private property "affected with a public interest," provided an enduring constitutional basis for state and federal regulation. "Not until the New Deal era would a serious challenge be mounted to the fundamental authority for federal regulatory activity," writes Rabin.[64]

While a jurisprudential foundation for the administrative state was being laid, its ramparts also were being strengthened by halting efforts at civil service reform, an issue closely tied to the Progressive theme of administrative efficiency. A merit-based, professional bureaucracy would restrain the corrupting influence of party patronage, result in more effective government, and strengthen a relatively weak executive branch vis-à-vis Congress, reformers argued.[65] Congress opened the door to reform in 1871 by authorizing President Grant to establish entry guidelines for the civil service. Congress was antagonized by the work of Grant's Civil Service Commission, however, and cut funding for the entity in 1874. The National Civil Service Reform League, receiving critical support from business interests weary of corruption, provided a rallying point for public opinion, which was further aroused by the "the assassination of President Garfield in 1881 by a rejected office seeker."[66] The Pendleton Civil Service Act passed two years later and allowed certain bureaucratic posts to be removed from patronage considerations, enacted merit-based reforms, and protected civil servants from campaign assessments.[67]

McCloskey takes a more monochromatic view than Rabin of post-Reconstruction jurisprudence, stating that "the Court's history becomes a history of response to the advance of what was later to be called 'the general welfare state'."[68] This response was predominantly hostile to regulation and in favor of business. The Marshall Court had sought to defend the national government and the property owner. With the question of national ascendance over the states settled, the first priority of the Court shifted from issues of federalism to the protection of business, according to McCloskey.[69]

State legislation impinging on business was the primary target, but the Court also took steps to weaken the first federal forays into national administration. A denuded Privileges and Immunities Clause could not be used to restrain state regulation, as Justices Field and Bradley had lamented in their *Slaughterhouse* dissent, and the Court had not yet developed the jurisprudential apparatus to use the Due Process Clause for similar purposes. It did find in the doctrine of preemption one weapon to protect business, however, and the Court in roughly 15 cases between 1877 and 1886 used the increasingly national character of commerce to invalidate state regulation. The last of these, *Wabash, St. Louis, and Pacific Railway Company v. Illinois* (1886), prevented the states from regulating interstate rail traffic.[70]

Wabash was pivotal in prompting Congress to finally act on national rail legislation that marked the advent of the "modern age of administrative government."[71] The passage of the Interstate Commerce Act (ICA) in 1887 followed years of patchwork state legislation that left all parties dissatisfied—shippers, merchants, and the railroads themselves. Those parties looked to Congress with different interests, however. The consumers of rail services wanted to restrict pooling and discriminatory pricing between long- and short-haul routes. The rail companies, on the other hand, pushed for these things to rationalize their pricing and cover high fixed costs. Compromise was the guiding principle of the resulting legislation. It prohibited pooling and price discrimination for long- and short-haul routes but facilitated some degree of collusion by requiring the railroads to publish and maintain rates. Furthermore, railroads could set their own rates and could price discriminate between long- and short-haul routes in special cases. The Interstate Commerce Commission (ICC) created by the Act could "hear complaints, inquire into the records and accounts of railroads, compel attendance of witnesses, and issue cease-and-desist orders."[72] The ICA and the commission it established represented important ideological and institutional developments in the American administrative state. Rabin writes,

> For the first time, a national legislative scheme was enacted that provided for wide-ranging regulatory controls over an industry that was vital to the nation's economy—the railroads. Moreover, regulation of the industry was committed to an institutional mechanism that was virtually untested on the national state, an independent regulatory commission.[73]

In addition to railroads, the consolidation of industry was the other significant economic issue of the latter nineteenth century.[74] In contrast to the railroads, Congress did not establish an independent commission to regulate trusts but chose with the passage of the Sherman Antitrust Act in 1890 "the traditional method of statutory restriction and judicial enforcement."[75] The Act made illegal various business activities to restrain domestic and foreign trade. The Justice Department would enforce the Act, and individual suitors also could press their claims in court.[76]

The Court took steps to limit severely the effectiveness of the ICC. As mentioned above, a number of states had been regulating railroads with laws that presaged the federal ICA, and the Court's jurisprudence related to these state laws provided the context in which it reviewed the federal ICA. "The state cases, decided against the background of agrarian unrest, led the Court to become increasingly distrustful of legislative and administrative determinations of railroad rates," Rabin writes.[77] Congress did not give the ICC explicit authority to set rates, but the ICC derived that power implicitly from its authority to review the reasonableness of such rates. In two cases, *Cincinnati, New Orleans, and Texas Pacific Railway Company v. ICC* (1896) and *ICC v. Cincinnati, New Orleans, and Texas Pacific Railway Company* (1897), the Court ruled that the ICC did not have rate-setting authority.[78] It further weakened the ICC by holding that circuit courts can hear rail cases *de novo* (*ICC v. Alabama Midland Railway Company* [1897]) and that rate bureaus (a form of pooling to control prices) were invalid under the Sherman Act (*United States v. Trans-Missouri Freight Association* [1897]). Taken together, these decisions undermined the ICC, according to Justice Harlan, who dissented in *Midland* and other railroad rate cases.[79]

Prompted in part by "state abdication" in restraining trusts,[80] the Sherman Act suffered at the federal level from inconstant enforcement. The Cleveland and McKinley administrations neglected the measure.[81] As discussed above, Roosevelt favored a regulatory rather than an antitrust approach to large corporations and used the Act selectively. Taft was much more aggressive, dramatically increasing the number of suits and targeting high-profile offenders such as U.S. Steel. The subject matter of the legislation also defied straightforward judicial guidelines. The Court limited the reach of the statute in *United States v. E.C. Knight* (1895) by distinguishing between manufacturing within a state and the actual transport and marketing of those goods in interstate commerce. Federal antitrust law could not be used against the intrastate manufacturing of monopolies. In addition, the Court distinguished between direct and indirect effects on commerce to leave a domain of business regulation for state control.[82] In addition to the pooling prohibition in *United States v. Trans-Missouri Freight Association* (1897) and *United States v. Joint Traffic Association* (1898), the Court also invalidated loose price-fixing schemes in *Addyston Pipe and Steel Company v. United States* (1899).[83]

Unpredictable application and complex judicial interpretation (finally arriving at the "rule of reason" under *United States v. Standard Oil* [1910]) led the business community to push for a trade commission to help regularize government policy on corporate consolidation. Corporate interests, represented by the National Civic Federation, wanted a federal commission to provide a business-friendly forum and give advance guidance on business activity. Smaller businesses, led by the National Association of Manufacturers (NAM), opposed such an entity and governmental oversight of the business sector in general.[84]

Wilson's extra-constitutional flexibility allowed him, once in office, to shift toward the more regulatory approach of Roosevelt's New Nationalism.[85] In addition to the Clayton Antitrust Act that sought to define certain unfair business practices, Wilson supported the Federal Trade Commission Act of 1914, establishing a commission to hear evidence and issue cease-and-desist orders against unfair trade practices.[86] The Federal Trade Commission (FTC) and the Federal Reserve Board, also established in Wilson's first term, were milestones in the development of the national administrative state. The FTC in particular amplified the constitutional issues raised by the ICC, for the expansion of federal power and the consolidation of separated powers now applied to the entire economy rather than to just the railroads.[87]

Wilson began his term with a powerful new revenue-raising tool authorized by the Sixteenth Amendment. The *Pollock* cases[88] invalidated the income tax provisions of the Wilson-Gorman Act by disregarding "100 years of decisions by the Court itself in which the meaning of a direct tax had been narrowly and definitely established."[89] Income tax proposals had been offered as a perennial counterbalance to Republican tariffs. When attachment of an income tax proposal to a tariff bill looked likely in 1909, Republican leaders sought to deflect the effort in part by sending to the states a constitutional amendment authorizing the income tax, assuming the amendment would not receive requisite state support. The amendment was enacted, however, and quickly became the primary means of raising federal revenue.[90]

Regarding spheres of influence that had been reserved to the states, Kelly et al. write,

> No constitutional principle was more fundamental than that which gave the federal government specific powers to deal with matters of general national

> import, while reserving to the states the general power to govern the social and economic affairs of the people in their local communities.[91]

The Progressive Era witnessed the growing use of this "police power," typically reserved to the states, by the federal government under the commerce and taxing provisions of the Constitution. The Pure Food and Drug Act of 1906, the Meat Inspection Act of 1906, the Mann Act of 1910 (prohibiting the transport of prostitutes in interstate commerce), and the Keating-Owen Act of 1916 (restricting the interstate commerce of products made with child labor) reflected the reformist impulse of the age and the willingness to use national authority to regulate affairs heretofore addressed at the local level.

While scholars such as McCloskey may portray the Court primarily as a bulwark resisting Progressive reform, its jurisprudence can be seen as more accommodating than reactionary. Constitutional separation of powers presented an obstacle to consolidated powers of administrative agencies, but the Court in *Buttfield v. Stranahan* (1904) sanctioned congressional delegation to the executive of "minor policy-making decisions." It also accorded administrative rulings the force of law in *United States v. Grimaud* (1911). These cases built upon the 1892 ruling in *Field v. Clark* that legitimized the congressional delegation of authority to the president that was of a mere fact-finding nature.[92] *Champion v. Ames* (1903), *McCray v. United States* (1904), and *Hoke v. United States* (1913) validated, respectively, federal use of the police power to restrict the interstate shipment of lottery tickets, discourage through taxation a particular food product, and prohibit interstate transport of prostitutes.[93] Furthermore, between 1889 and 1918, the Court "approved the exercise of the state police power in 369 of 422 cases.[94]

Congress also passed legislation to rationalize rail operation and buttress the ICC. The Elkins Act of 1903 was a cartel-facilitating measure requiring railroads to stay with the published rate and not offer rebates. In addition, Congress gave the ICC rate-setting powers in the Hepburn Act of 1906 (rate-setting upon complaint) and the Mann-Elkins Act of 1910 (original rate-setting). Recognizing congressional persistence in strengthening the ICC, the Court in *ICC v. Illinois Central Railroad* (1910) narrowed the scope of its own judicial review, validated the rate-setting powers of the agency, and affirmed the authority of Congress to delegate such authority to the commission.[95] "The holding was deservedly regarded as a landmark," writes Rabin, "The days of de novo review of ICC decisions were over … *Illinois Central* adopted a position that, in hindsight, is recognizable as the modern administrative law position on limited judicial review."[96]

The Court drew important boundaries to national regulation in *Adair v. United States* (1908) and *Hammer v. Dagenhart* (1918), however.[97] As restrictions on working hours for bakers were invalidated at the state level in *Lochner v. New York* (1905), so *Adair* held that freedom of contract was violated by the Erdman Act's prohibition of "yellow-dog" contracts in which an employee agreed not to join a union as a condition of employment.[98] Furthermore, *Hammer v. Dagenhart* invalidated federal child labor legislation on the distinction between manufacturing and commerce.[99]

While world war led to violations of civil liberties that troubled some Progressives, it also augmented centralized authority in a way that appealed to reformers. Congress quickly made use of its new powers under the Sixteenth Amendment, raising tax rates several times in anticipation of and during the war, with the highest rates reaching 67 and 77 percent by 1918.[100] In addition, Congress delegated extensive war-time powers to Wilson, most importantly through the Lever Act of 1917 and then with other significant pieces of legislation related to selective service, trade, and administrative organization. With the Lever Act provisions to protect the supply of food and fuel, Wilson could reach most of the economy through regulation, price fixing, or assumption of outright control of assets.[101] In the Overman Act of 1918, Wilson gained a virtual free hand in administrative organization. As the Lever Act did before it, the Overman Act prompted vociferous congressional debate, with criticism of the measure as a complete abdication of legislative responsibility.[102] These statutes were not utilized to their full extent, and with administrators such as Herbert Hoover and Bernard Baruch, the administration adopted a more cooperative than confrontational approach with the private sector.[103] Nevertheless, "[t]he First World War did much to accustom the American people to an enlarged conception of federal authority," facilitating the enactment of assertive New Deal measures in response to economic crisis.[104]

The "return to normalcy" in the 1920s was characterized by a slowdown in Progressive reform but not a departure from the trend toward consolidated national power. The Transportation Act of 1920 strengthened the authority of the ICC over railroad rate setting and earnings. The Court validated this additional rate-setting authority in *Railroad Commission of Wisconsin v. Chicago, Burlington, and Quincy* (1922) and the recapture provision in *Dayton-Goose Creek Railway Company v. United States* (1924).[105] While expansive ICC authority was upheld, the FTC was reined in, supporting Rabin's thesis that the Court resisted new regulatory regimes. In *Federal Trade Commission v. Gratz* (1920) and *Federal Trade Commission v. Curtis Publishing Company* (1923), respectively, the Court undermined the commission's independent capacity to define unfair trade practices and investigate such practices.[106]

Grants-in-aid became an increasingly important way for the federal government to exert influence over state policy. Land grants had been used in this manner for some time, but the modern form of grants-in-aid took shape under the Weeks Act of 1911, a bill to encourage state fire prevention programs. Other grant-in-aid legislation was passed in subsequent years to shape state policy in the areas of transportation, agriculture, and veterans' care.[107] The most important of these from a jurisprudential perspective was the Sheppard-Towner Act related to maternity care. In dismissing the suit against the Act, the Court affirmed the concept of grants-in-aid, precipitating heightened demand for such benefits.[108]

Important new bureaucracies were established, such as the Federal Power Commission in 1920 and the Federal Radio Commission in 1927. Passage of the

Eighteenth Amendment prohibiting intoxicating liquors and the amendment's implementing legislation (the Volstead Act) marked the most significant intrusion of federal power into national life, however. "Alcoholic beverage production was the fifth-largest American industry, which made prohibition the largest uncompensated taking of property since the abolition of slavery," writes Moreno.[109]

Consumed by the onset of economic depression, the presidency of Herbert Hoover was anything but passive. He offered perhaps the most "influential and coherent regulatory philosophy between the Progressive era and the New Deal," argues Rabin.[110] Having served as a key administrator for Wilson during the war, Hoover viewed the federal government as an active economic facilitator. He supported the Agricultural Marketing Act to extend credit to and support prices in the farm sector. The Federal Employment Stabilization Act of 1931 and the Reconstruction Finance Corporation (RFC) presaged ambitious New Deal programs and were used by New Dealers as blueprints.[111]

In his inaugural address, Franklin Delano Roosevelt asked for the equivalent of war powers to address the domestic economic crisis, and Congress responded with zeal.[112] The Emergency Banking Act legitimized the president's dubious use of the Trading with the Enemy Act to suspend bank operations.[113] Going further, the executive branch was authorized through the RFC to buy bank stock and did so in "half of American banks, totaling one-third of all bank capital."[114]

McNary-Haugen legislation to benefit farmers with government price supports and equalization fees was turned back by President Coolidge on grounds of being unconstitutional,[115] but the New Deal's Agriculture Adjustment Act authorized greater federal control of the agricultural sector. Farmers were paid to reduce the acreage in production, and an excise tax was imposed on processors to fund food price levels at a more profitable pre-war level (1909–1914).[116] "No previous act tried so overtly to promote private interests—higher income for farmers—rather than public goods," writes Moreno.[117]

The National Industrial Recovery Act (NIRA) was the second major piece of New Deal legislation and gave the president plenary regulatory authority over the national economy. The executive branch could accept from trade groups "codes of fair competition" or impose such codes if they were not forthcoming.[118] As discussed above, Congress had given Wilson extensive economic oversight powers in the context of war, but the peacetime delegation of legislative power under NIRA was more expansive and accompanied with few restraining guidelines. "In many ways the law … was like an enabling act in a formal constitutional dictatorship," write Kelly et al.[119]

The Agricultural Adjustment Act (AAA) and the NIRA as "supply-side" measures did not restore economic confidence,[120] however, and Roosevelt moved further left in a "Second New Deal" that embraced more government spending. Funded with almost $5 billion by Congress, the Works Progress Administration (WPA) employed millions in a variety of public works.[121] The Social Security Act, establishing the most durable and best-known of New Deal programs, provided grants-in-aid to the states for unemployment insurance and "a completely national program of old-age insurance."[122] Finally, the National Labor Relations Act (NLRA) made company unions illegal and required all employees of a company to be represented by the union supported by a majority of those employees.[123] As Moreno states, "The Wagner Act [NLRA] represented the transformation of traditional constitutional liberalism into entitlement-based statism," providing "not *freedom* of association, but an *entitlement to* association—compulsory collective bargaining."[124]

Several early Court decisions seemed to indicate an openness to the New Deal. Impairment of mortgage contracts was authorized in *Home Building and Loan Association v. Blaisdell* (1934), and *Munn's* distinction between public and private spheres was erased in *Nebbia v. New York* (1934).[125] The Court cut out the heart of Roosevelt's agenda, however, with a series of decisions beginning in January 1935. Eight out of ten major cases ruled some element of New Deal legislation unconstitutional, with the most important decisions invalidating the NIRA and the AAA. Extensive delegation of legislative authority without clear guidelines, the role of private individuals in exercising that delegated power, and the intrastate nature of the commerce in question were the principal complaints of the Court against the NIRA in *Schechter v. United States* (1935).[126] In a less coherent ruling in *United States v. Butler* (1936), the Court invalidated the AAA on the grounds that Congress' taxing power had been misused for merely regulatory ends and that federal government could not "impose conditions on those who accepted its grants,"[127] in apparent contradiction to important precedents such as *Massachusetts v. Mellon* (1923).

Roosevelt was stung by these judicial setbacks but for the most part moderated his criticism until after the 1936 election. He forwarded a judicial reorganization plan to Congress in 1937 that would have expanded the number of Supreme Court justices to 15, with the additional appointments presumably inclining the Court to affirm New Deal policies. His proposal encountered immediate resistance on Capitol Hill, and the Court's about face on important New Deal cases seemed to diminish the need for a confrontational approach.[128] The NLRA, the unemployment tax and grant provisions of the Social Security Act, and the Fair Labor Standards Act were upheld by the Court in *NLRB v. Jones & Laughlin* (1937), *Steward Machine Company v. Davis* (1937), and *United States v. Darby* (1941), respectively.[129]

Along with Roosevelt's court-packing plan, executive branch reorganization and the purge campaign of 1938 were the principal elements of a "Third New Deal" aimed at diminishing party influence and consolidating the expanded powers of the presidency.[130] Wary of further executive branch aggrandizement, Congress blocked both the court-packing plan and the initial executive branch reorganization proposal. Conservative Democrats posed an obstacle to these reforms, and Roosevelt took unprecedented steps to support liberal opponents in the 1938 Democratic primaries.[131] The purge campaign was for the most part unsuccessful, but Roosevelt was able to secure passage of a scaled-down administrative reform bill in 1939 that "laid the institutional foundation for the creation of the modern presidency."[132]

Applying Themes from Aristotle and Tocqueville

With eventual Court validation of New Deal policies and the institutional support such policies received through executive branch reorganization, the modern administrative state was firmly established in American politics. "For over a generation progressive and liberal reformers had called for the creation of a state in the European sense of the term, in order to correct the injustices of industrialization and achieve social and economic democracy," write Kelly et al.[133] In the presidential campaign of 1912, Progressives supported a regulatory approach to deal with corporate consolidation and espoused social welfare programs that implied an administrative structure much larger than the one envisioned for management of the trusts. The New Deal represented the consummation of much of this agenda (although it should be noted that the Progressive vision of national health insurance has yet to be realized). The federal police power that began to be developed in the Progressive Era with legislation such as the Pure Food and Drug Act of 1906 went so far as to embrace a national pension program in the Social Security Act of 1935. Whereas the Court previously had invalidated various state laws on wages and hours, it affirmed a national minimum wage law in *United States v. Darby* (1941), also upholding in that case federal restrictions on child labor and overruling *Hammer v. Dagenhart* (1918) in the process. Distinctions between manufacture and commerce and between direct and indirect effects of commerce kept the federal government from reaching monopolies in *E.C. Knight* (1895), but Congress under *Wickard v. Filburn* (1942) could control farm products not disposed of in interstate or even intrastate commerce but on the originating farm itself.

The tremendous change in governmental forms between the latter nineteenth century and the New Deal accompanied a change in fundamental assumptions related to politics and law. The rise of an expansive administrative state proceeded in tandem with a prolonged "intellectual struggle against the legal foundations of the old order."[134] "The Progressive attack on Classical Legal Thought developed, above all, into a challenge to the world view that endowed nineteenth century orthodoxy with legitimacy," Horwitz writes.[135] Classical Legal Thought, or formalism, elevated the defense of property above other constitutional considerations to defend a shrinking world of decentralized politics and individual liberty. A formalist understanding of freedom of contract was based on the assumption of two assenting, equally well-positioned parties, an assumption that became increasingly tenuous in an integrated economy with complex business entities. The law of agency became unrealistically confined as jurists sought to limit corporate liability. Redistributionist tendencies were seen working their way through a host of legal and political channels. Eminent domain, taxes, contracts, and agency all were eyed warily by formalist jurists eager to ensure that social reform did not undermine capitalism.

Horwitz makes his argument in terms that are perhaps too stark. As noted above, the Court approved the exercise of state police power in an overwhelming majority of cases in and around the Progressive Era. The *Lochner* (1905) decision, the bane of Progressive legal thought, was after all preceded by *Holden v.*

Hardy (1898) upholding a Utah law prescribing an eight-hour workday in "mines, smelters, and ore refineries" and followed by *Muller v. Oregon* (1908) validating an Oregon law limiting to ten hours the workday for women in "factories and laundries."[136] Horwitz is on his firmest ground when talking about the Court's questionable ruling in *Pollock* (1895) and the national repudiation of those decisions with ratification of the Sixteenth Amendment. He writes,

> Here we see clear evidence of the dramatic defeat that ratification of the Income Tax Amendment in 1913 represented for the orthodox goal of creating a clean distinction between a tax and a taking. Not only had the constitutional legitimacy of the progressive income tax muddied that distinction but, even more important, it had discredited the Classical notion that a neutral state entailed opposition to redistribution.[137]

Setting aside the question of degree, Horwitz can be used as a pretext to put the Progressive complaint against formalism in Aristotelian terms: Classical Legal Thought was not keeping the whole of justice in view but defending the mastery of property and laissez-faire economics. Progressives were quick to perceive the fundamental changes taking place in an industrializing, urbanizing society and stayed several steps ahead of the judiciary in recognizing that social reform was needed for the common good of a more integrated society. The Progressive prescription for social reform aligned with Aristotelian themes: justice is formed in the context of community, and national economic and political life was changing dramatically. Aristotle's emphasis on justice considering both the equal and the unequal would have led him to recognize more readily than the *Lochner* Court that bakers and their employers did not stand on equal footing in contract negotiations.

Progressivism may have perceived the need for beneficial reforms that would come closer to the whole of justice, but it responded in kind to the real or perceived mastery of the judiciary. A masterful judicial branch would be checked by the mastery of the executive branch. As formalist jurists sought to keep politics out of law,[138] so the Progressives would try to keep politics out of administration. Court invalidation of safeguards for workers as in *Lochner* would be met with coercive union authority in the NLRA. Formalist channels to limit the reach of the Commerce Clause in *E.C. Knight* would be flooded with national power in *Wickard* that reached all the way to agricultural products harvested and consumed on the same farm.

Aristotle's view of the whole of justice was not balanced in Progressive politics by his understanding of different degrees of unity. A family had more unity than a city, and a city more unity than a nation. When drafting the Constitution, the Founders may have been more concerned with excessive national power than Aristotle's view of unity, but the governmental structures they put in place are informed by Aristotle's insight nonetheless. A nation, and certainly one as large as the United States, would be able to move in unison on a much narrower range of issues than a state or city. Elevating too broad a set of policy issues to the national level would of necessity impose uniformity where flexibility would be preferable, which is a core argument of Oates' Decentralization Theorem.

The strength of free market and natural rights traditions in American politics prevented the formation of a European-style, collectivist state. Franklin Roosevelt achieved his goal of administrative centralization by couching his agenda in the language of rights that Theodore Roosevelt had shunned. "Roosevelt gave legitimacy to progressive principles by imbedding them in the language of constitutionalism and interpreting them as an *expansion* of rights rather than a *subversion* of the natural rights tradition," writes Milkis.[139] Social Security is a good example. The program had redistributionist aims but was financed by payroll taxes for primarily political reasons, to give taxpayers a stake in the program and create a government obligation in return.[140]

American-style interest group pluralism came to define national councils and inverted Madison's theory of the large republic restraining faction. Whereas constitutional devices such as separation of powers and enumerated powers, alongside extra-constitutional institutions such as localized political parties and federalism, ensured that national policy would only be formed through sustained and widespread public support, the administrative state gave a national platform to narrow interests. In Aristotelian terms, the Founders' Constitution required an arduous effort to comprehend the whole of justice before national policy could be influenced. The expansive administrative state, by contrast, created an institutional refraction chamber designed to produce only partial views of the common good. As mentioned in Chapter 2, Socrates argues that a tyrant intentionally promotes divisions within his polity. Tyranny was not the goal of New Deal centralizers, but there is something akin to tyranny in the practical effect of the administrative state. As Moreno notes, the Agricultural Adjustment Act "was more than just interest-group or 'class legislation'; it was an attempt to bring classes or interest groups into being."[141]

Aristotle, aided by Tocqueville, would offer another check to Progressivism by arguing that democracy can be as tyrannical as oligarchy. A unifying theme of Progressive thought was direct democracy. Direct primaries, popular election of United States Senators, women's suffrage, the recall of judicial decisions at the state level, and the recall of state and federal officials, including the president himself, were supported by the Progressive Party in the 1912 campaign. The benefit of these proposed reforms in giving citizens more avenues for engagement was not balanced with a healthy respect for the role of mediating institutions in leavening public opinion. The authors of *The Federalist* sought to demonstrate how each of the powers of the national government were derived from the people, but the mutability of public opinion and the potential abuse of national authority obliged the Founders to create a system of separated and enumerated powers where only sustained and refined public will would shape national policy. Madison's institutional defenses against majority tyranny draw on the classical insight of democratic mastery.

Bringing in Tocqueville, democracies have a particular liability when it comes to governing by public opinion. He discusses two types of centralization, governmental and administrative, as reviewed in Chapter 2. Democracies naturally have a high degree of governmental centralization (the capacity to address national interests) because of the importance of public opinion. Governmental centralization is not necessarily a threat to democratic liberty unless combined with administrative centralization, or the capacity to control local interests from the center. America had more governmental centralization than any other country due to the unity of public opinion but almost no administrative centralization. While Tocqueville thought the lack of administrative centralization had been carried too far in America, he saw decentralization in general as a great bulwark of liberty, in addition to such cultural features as associations, religion, and the family. Progressive efforts to elevate a host of issues to the national level and rely on public opinion to enact policy through an expansive administrative state would not chasten democracy, as Tocqueville wanted, but amalgamate some of its worst tendencies.

A disposition toward equality undergirds the importance of public opinion in democracy. It also is a pretext, along with political crisis, for the centralization of governmental power, according to Tocqueville. Rising inequality was the animating force for many centralizing Progressive reforms, and crisis, whether apparent or real, was used to justify the expansion of federal authority. Theodore Roosevelt compared his struggle to help workers to Lincoln's efforts to free the slaves, Wilson assumed vast new executive branch powers in the context of World War I, and Franklin Roosevelt sought to govern in a perpetual state of emergency to push through New Deal policies. Kelly et al. write,

> Roosevelt's reliance on a World War I statute as the basis for the bank holiday in 1933 was followed in the next six years by thirty-five instances in which he referred to emergency, crisis, or national peril as justification for legislative or executive action.[142]

Aristotle's distinction between the primary goods of the soul and secondary material goods may help explain the underlying sense of crisis and haste in Progressive politics. Theodore Roosevelt's "human rights," Pound's "law in action," and Franklin Roosevelt's "economic rights" were synonymous, to varying degrees, with concerted government action over and against a natural rights tradition and a constitutional form of government that restrained national power. Natural rights are derived from the Creator; the emphasis is on property in oneself; and the political assumption is equality of opportunity. Economic rights are derived from government; the emphasis is on material well-being; and the political assumption is equality of outcome. To distinguish between the primary goods of the soul and the secondary goods of the body, or by rough approximation between natural and economic rights, is not to deny the inextricable tie between the two. Aristotle himself recognized the need for a certain measure of material well-being, and modern liberalism's view of liberty was bound thoroughly to property by Locke. Aristotle's point is not that material goods do not matter but that they are of secondary importance. To integrate Aristotle with

Locke, if one does not have property in oneself, other forms of property have little value, or as Christ would say, "What good is it for a man to gain the whole world, yet forfeit his soul?"[143]

Lincoln placed the Civil War in the context of immutable principles regarding the nature of man. His statement that we choose the man over the dollar was used by Theodore Roosevelt,[144] but in the context of Roosevelt's Progressivism the comment meant something totally different. Roosevelt's human rights were an empty vessel that could be filled with any transitory meaning of the majority's momentary will. Empowering government to pursue human rights understood in this way necessarily will involve an infringement on natural rights, as Progressive reformers would learn and lament during wartime violations of civil liberties. Such concerns led Croly to try and rebuild mediating institutions to replace the ones he had worked so assiduously to destroy.[145] Lincoln was no Progressive. What he did at the edges of constitutional law was to preserve its essence, while Wilson's most conservative statements about the Constitution conveyed no durable meaning about the document.

Echoing the theme of Aristotle's degrees of unity, Oates recognizes that some national policy challenges require a centralized solution. To use an example from this chapter, only the federal government could have addressed management of railroads through the ICC. A centralized response does not fit every policy context, however. Decentralization offers the benefit of flexibility, policy innovation, and a combination of efficiency and accountability as local control matches available resources and expenditures more effectively.[146] This last benefit of decentralization, a matching of resources and expenditures, pertains directly to the question of fiscal imbalance at the national level. To the extent that centralization obscures the value of what is being exchanged, institutional controls would need to be augmented to provide the accountability that a loss of citizen engagement has removed.

Considerations such as these may explain in part why local and state debt levels are much better rationalized to the tax base and why federal revenue is much better rationalized to the tax base than federal debt. These considerations also may explain why centralized redistributive programs are the source of fiscal imbalance at the national level. It is not the Federal Communications Commission or the Federal Aviation Administration that is breaking the American budget. From a budgetary standpoint, these elements of the administrative state are not problematic, although their improper functioning may undermine justice or the common good in a secondary way. It is entitlement programs related to retirement security and healthcare that are the source of the nation's budgetary woes. These programs comprise roughly two-thirds of the federal budget, and their true cost is concealed by an administrative apparatus that obliges interested parties to seek their own exclusive good.

Justice rests on the capacity to determine value. It is not necessarily against redistribution. Indeed, Aristotle's proportional reciprocity is inherently redistributive, be it related to money or honor or anything else of value that two unequal parties exchange in a transaction that both regard as just. What is essential is that both parties are able to determine the value of what is exchanged to arrive at the common good.

The Progressive impulse for reform can be seen as an Aristotelian effort to comprehend better the whole of justice in a changing society. The great error of Progressivism was pursuing that reform in centralized fashion. An increasingly integrated and complex American society required the expansion of national administration. Aristotle's different degrees of unity would be satisfied by the creation of the ICC and a host of other agencies that administer truly national problems. The Progressive vision of national social welfare without stringent institutional controls, however, led to centralized programs that obscured rather than clarified the common good by using debt to push current obligations to the future.

It matters whether political failure is systemic or isolated. The Founders believed that the establishment of a viable union was essential to secure the blessings of liberty. They feared that a loss of confidence in national governing institutions would cause Americans to lose faith in self-government itself. Relative to the Articles of Confederation, their response was to centralize, to establish a stronger national government. If a weak national government could undermine public faith, however, so too can expansive national authority. To the extent that unrestrained borrowing undermines the solvency of the national government, the pursuit of the human rights of pension and healthcare security is threatening the natural rights of life, liberty, and the pursuit of happiness.

Notes

1 Alexander Hamilton, James Madison, and John Jay, *The Federalist* (New York: Barnes & Noble, 2006), 53.
2 Keith Whittington, *Constitutional Construction: Divided Powers and Constitutional Meaning* (Cambridge, MA: Harvard University Press, 2001), 223–224.
3 Jeffrey K. Tulis, *The Rhetorical Presidency* (Princeton, NJ: Princeton University Press, 1987).
4 Lewis L. Gould, "Introduction: The Progressive Era," in *The Progressive Era*, ed. Lewis L. Gould (Syracuse, NY: Syracuse University Press, 1974), 9.
5 Peter G. Filene, "An Obituary for 'The Progressive Movement'," *American Quarterly* Vol. 22 No. 1 (Spring 1970): 20.
6 Ibid., 33.
7 Daniel T. Rodgers, "In Search of Progressivism," *Reviews in American History* Vol. 10 No. 4, The Promise of American History: Progress and Prospects (December 1982): 114.
8 Ibid.
9 Ibid., 123.
10 Ibid., 117.
11 Gould, "Introduction," 4.
12 Ibid., 7.
13 Richard Hofstadter, *The Age of Reform: From Bryan to F.D.R.* (New York: Alfred A. Knopf, 1974).
14 Paul D. Moreno, *The American State From the Civil War to the New Deal: The Twilight of Constitutionalism and the Triumph of Progressivism* (New York: Cambridge University Press, 2013).

15 Sidney M. Milkis, *Theodore Roosevelt, the Progressive Party, and the Transformation of American Politics* (Lawrence: University Press of Kansas, 2009).
16 Ibid., 133.
17 Robert L. Rabin, "Federal Regulation in Historical Perspective," *Stanford Law Review* Vol. 38 No. 5 (May 1986): 1218.
18 Hofstadter, *The Age of Reform*, 133.
19 Lewis L. Gould, "The Republicans Under Roosevelt and Taft," in *The Progressive Era*, ed. Lewis L. Gould (Syracuse, NY: Syracuse University Press, 1974), 70–72.
20 Moreno, *The American State*, 114.
21 Hofstadter, *The Age of Reform*, 244n; Moreno, *The American State*, 116–117.
22 Moreno, *The American State*, 116–118.
23 Ibid., 115.
24 Gould, "The Republicans," 80.
25 Milkis, *Theodore Roosevelt*, 14.
26 Ibid., 89.
27 Ibid., 271.
28 Theodore Roosevelt, New Nationalism Speech, August 31, 1910. Osawatomie, Kansas. Accessed March 6, 2018 at http://teachingamericanhistory.org/library/document/new-nationalism-speech/.
29 Ibid., 32, 55.
30 Ibid., 250.
31 Moreno, *The American State*, 3.
32 Ronald J. Pestritto, "Woodrow Wilson and the Meaning of the Lincoln Legacy," in *Constitutionalism in the Approach and Aftermath of the Civil War*, eds. Paul D. Moreno and Johnathan O'Neill (New York: Fordham University Press, 2013), 185–187.
33 Ibid., 186.
34 Ibid., 188.
35 Ibid., 192.
36 Milkis, *Theodore Roosevelt*, 205.
37 Moreno, *The American State*, 132.
38 Milkis, *Theodore Roosevelt*, 205.
39 Moreno, *The American State*, 133.
40 Milkis, *Theodore Roosevelt*, 177–181.
41 Theodore Roosevelt, "A Charter for Democracy," February 21, 1912. Columbus, Ohio. Accessed March 6, 2018 at http://teachingamericanhistory.org/library/document/a-charter-for-democracy/.
42 Ibid., 133.
43 Milkis, *Theodore Roosevelt*, 218.
44 Pestritto, "Woodrow Wilson and the Meaning of the Lincoln Legacy," 193.
45 Milkis, *Theodore Roosevelt*, 94.
46 Pestritto, "Woodrow Wilson and the Meaning of the Lincoln Legacy," 184.
47 Ibid.
48 Ibid., 194.
49 Milkis, *Theodore Roosevelt*, 278–279, 285.
50 Pestritto, "Woodrow Wilson and the Meaning of the Lincoln Legacy," 198.
51 Alfred H. Kelly, Winfred A. Harbison, and Herman Belz, *The American Constitution: Its Origins and Development*, Seventh Edition, Vol. 1 (New York: W.W. Norton, 1991), 293.
52 Ibid., 292–298.
53 Ibid., 361.
54 Robert G. McCloskey, *The American Supreme Court*, Fifth Edition (Chicago: University of Chicago Press, 2010), 79.
55 Kelly et al., *American Constitution*, Vol. 1, 356–357.

56 James M. McPherson, *Abraham Lincoln and the Second American Revolution* (New York: Oxford University Press, 1991), 148.
57 Ibid., 149.
58 Ibid., 12.
59 John Gerring, "Party Ideology in America: The National Republican Chapter, 1828–1924," *Studies in American Political Development* Vol. 11 (Spring 1997): 69.
60 Ibid., 62.
61 Kelly et al., *American Constitution*, Vol. 1, 311.
62 Moreno, *The American State*, 22.
63 Rabin, "Federal Regulation in Historical Perspective," 1208.
64 Ibid., 1209.
65 Alfred H. Kelly, Winfred A. Harbison, and Herman Belz, *The American Constitution: Its Origins and Development*, Seventh Edition, Vol. 2 (New York: W.W. Norton, 1991), 368–369.
66 Ibid., 369.
67 Ibid.
68 McCloskey, *The American Supreme Court*, 81.
69 Ibid., 69.
70 Ibid., 82–84.
71 Rabin, "Federal Regulation in Historical Perspective," 1189, 1209.
72 Kelly et al., *American Constitution*, Vol. 2, 374–375.
73 Rabin, "Federal Regulation in Historical Perspective," 1189.
74 Kelly et al., *American Constitution*, Vol. 2, 373.
75 Ibid., 378.
76 Ibid.
77 Rabin, "Federal Regulation in Historical Perspective," 1212.
78 Kelly et al., *American Constitution*, Vol. 2, 373.
79 Rabin, "Federal Regulation in Historical Perspective," 1215.
80 Moreno, *The American State*, 38.
81 Rabin, "Federal Regulation in Historical Perspective," 1217.
82 Kelly et al., *American Constitution*, Vol. 2, 379.
83 Moreno, *The American State*, 70.
84 Rabin, "Federal Regulation in Historical Perspective," 1221–1223.
85 Moreno, *The American State*, 145.
86 Kelly et al., *American Constitution*, Vol. 2, 423.
87 Moreno, *The American State*, 144–145.
88 *Pollock v. Farmers' Loan and Trust Co.* (1895); *Pollock v. Farmers' Loan and Trust Co.* (1895).
89 Kelly et al., *American Constitution*, Vol. 2, 402.
90 Ibid., 431–432.
91 Ibid., 416.
92 Ibid., 413.
93 Ibid., 417–418.
94 Ibid., 446n.
95 Ibid., 425.
96 Rabin, "Federal Regulation in Historical Perspective," 1234.
97 Kelly et al., *American Constitution*, Vol. 2, 419.
98 Moreno, *The American State*, 71–72.
99 Kelly et al., *American Constitution*, Vol. 2, 419.
100 Ibid., 166.
101 Kelly et al., *American Constitution*, Vol. 2, 434.
102 Ibid., 439.
103 Rabin, "Federal Regulation in Historical Perspective," 1237–1238.

104 Kelly et al., *American Constitution*, Vol. 2, 440–441; Hofstadter, *The Age of Reform*, 304 footnote 2.
105 Kelly et al., *American Constitution*, Vol. 2, 445.
106 Ibid., 461.
107 Ibid., 459–460.
108 Moreno, *The American State*, 182.
109 Ibid., 203.
110 Rabin, "Federal Regulation in Historical Perspective," 1237.
111 Moreno, *The American State*, 219.
112 Ibid., 231.
113 Kelly et al., *American Constitution*, Vol. 2, 470.
114 Moreno, *The American State*, 233.
115 Ibid., 182–184.
116 Kelly et al., *American Constitution*, Vol. 2, 471.
117 Moreno, *The American State*, 235.
118 Rabin, "Federal Regulation in Historical Perspective," 1243.
119 Kelly et al., *American Constitution*, Vol. 2, 473.
120 Moreno, *The American State*, 235, 241; Kelly et al., *American Constitution*, Vol. 2, 474.
121 Rabin, "Federal Regulation in Historical Perspective," 1249.
122 Moreno, *The American State*, 258.
123 Ibid., 261–262.
124 Ibid., 263.
125 Rabin, "Federal Regulation in Historical Perspective," 1253–1254.
126 Kelly et al., *American Constitution*, Vol. 2, 476–477.
127 Ibid., 478.
128 Ibid., 481–486.
129 Rabin, "Federal Regulation in Historical Perspective," 1260; Kelly et al., *American Constitution*, Vol. 2, 488.
130 Sidney M. Milkis, *The President and the Parties: The Transformation of the American Party System Since the New Deal* (New York: Oxford University Press, 1993), 100.
131 Ibid., 4.
132 Kelly et al., *American Constitution*, Vol. 2, 499.
133 Ibid., 503.
134 Morton J. Horwitz, *The Transformation of American Law, 1870–1960: The Crisis of Legal Orthodoxy* (Oxford: Oxford University Press, 1992), 3.
135 Ibid., 4.
136 Kelly et al., *American Constitution*, Vol. 2, 444.
137 Horwitz, *Transformation of American Law*, 165.
138 Ibid., 11, 15, 51.
139 Milkis, *President and the Parties*, 43.
140 Ibid., 145.
141 Moreno, *The American State*, 235.
142 Kelly et al., *American Constitution*, Vol. 2, 504.
143 *The Holy Bible*, New International Version (Grand Rapids, MI: Zondervan, 1978), Mark 8:36.
144 Milkis, *Theodore Roosevelt*, 94.
145 Ibid., 285.
146 Wallace E. Oates, *Fiscal Federalism* (New York: Harcourt Brace Jovanovich, 1972), 13.

Bibliography

Filene, Peter G. "An Obituary for 'The Progressive Movement'." *American Quarterly* Vol. 22 No. 1 (Spring 1970): 20–34.

Gerring, John. "Party Ideology in America: The National Republican Chapter, 1828–1924." *Studies in American Political Development* Vol. 11 (Spring 1997): 44–108.

Gould, Lewis L. "Introduction: The Progressive Era." In *The Progressive Era*, edited by Lewis L. Gould, 1–10. Syracuse, NY: Syracuse University Press, 1974.

Gould, Lewis L. "The Republicans Under Roosevelt and Taft." In *The Progressive Era*, edited by Lewis L. Gould, 55–82. Syracuse, NY: Syracuse University Press, 1974.

Hamilton, Alexander, James Madison, and John Jay. *The Federalist*. New York: Barnes & Noble, 2006.

Hofstadter, Richard. *The Age of Reform: From Bryan to F.D.R.* New York: Alfred A. Knopf, 1974.

The Holy Bible. New International Version. Grand Rapids, MI: Zondervan, 1978.

Horwitz, Morton J. *The Transformation of American Law, 1870–1960: The Crisis of Legal Orthodoxy*. Oxford: Oxford University Press, 1992.

Kelly, Alfred H., Winfred A. Harbison, and Herman Belz. *The American Constitution: Its Origins and Development*, Seventh Edition, Vols. 1–2. New York: W.W. Norton, 1991.

McCloskey, Robert G. *The American Supreme Court*, Fifth Edition. Chicago: University of Chicago Press, 2010.

McPherson, James M. *Abraham Lincoln and the Second American Revolution*. New York: Oxford University Press, 1991.

Milkis, Sidney M. *The President and the Parties: The Transformation of the American Party System Since the New Deal*. New York: Oxford University Press, 1993.

Milkis, Sidney. *Theodore Roosevelt, the Progressive Party, and the Transformation of American Politics*. Lawrence: University Press of Kansas, 2009.

Moreno, Paul D. *The American State From the Civil War to the New Deal: The Twilight of Constitutionalism and the Triumph of Progressivism*. New York: Cambridge University Press, 2013.

Oates, Wallace E. *Fiscal Federalism* (New York: Harcourt Brace Jovanovich, 1972).

Pestritto, Ronald J. "Woodrow Wilson and the Meaning of the Lincoln Legacy." In *Constitutionalism in the Approach and Aftermath of the Civil War*, edited by Paul D. Moreno and Johnathan O'Neill, 183–201. New York: Fordham University Press, 2013.

Rodgers, Daniel T. "In Search of Progressivism." *Reviews in American History* Vol. 10 No. 4, The Promise of American History: Progress and Prospects (December 1982): 113–132.

Roosevelt, Theodore. "A Charter for Democracy." February 21, 1912. Columbus, Ohio. Accessed March 6, 2018 at http://teachingamericanhistory.org/library/document/a-charter-for-democracy/.

Roosevelt, Theodore. New Nationalism Speech. August 31, 1910. Osawatomie, Kansas. Accessed March 6, 2018 at http://teachingamericanhistory.org/library/document/new-nationalism-speech/.

Rubin, Robert L. "Federal Regulation in Historical Perspective." *Stanford Law Review* Vol. 38 No. 5 (May 1986): 1189–1326.

Tulis, Jeffrey K. *The Rhetorical Presidency*. Princeton, NJ: Princeton University Press, 1987.

Whittington, Keith. *Constitutional Construction: Divided Powers and Constitutional Meaning*. Cambridge, MA: Harvard University Press, 2001.

7 Conclusion

> For in time from things falsely good there must result a true evil.
>
> —Aristotle, *Politics*

Public debt at all levels of government has grown significantly over the course of the twentieth century. Trends since 1990, the point in time at which the analysis of this book ends, lend additional, perhaps conclusive, support to the argument that public debt is being used in an unsustainable way. The federal debt of $3.23 trillion[1] (nominal dollars) in 1990 has grown to $20.49 trillion[2] as of January 2018, a six-fold increase that has outstripped Keynesian and Ricardian rationales and left few theoretical threads to cover the nakedness of its injustice.

Political liberalism has a better grasp of human equality than classical thought, but classical thought has a more consistent view of justice that may facilitate a better ethical and theoretical understanding of debt. Justice is not an abstract concept for Aristotle but the common good. It is not equality but the equalizing of distinct interests of distinct parties. Justice must therefore consider dimensions of equality and inequality. It is proportional and contextual, not a rigid theory that pursues rationality at the expense of reality but an empirical empowerment of society through sustainable relationships. In light of the circumstances, the just person takes only what is due him. He does not take more than his share.

Tocqueville brings a classical sense of justice to bear in the American context and adds important insights related to mores and institutions in democratic societies. There is a difference between equality and political freedom. The former may be achieved in a variety of political settings, including the debased equality that attends tyranny. Political freedom is a rarer bloom, however, and is cultivated primarily by local government that imparts the requisites of liberty through involvement with political objects that are near and dear. Centralization diminishes this capacity and should be guarded against. It can advance due to crisis (such as economic depression or war) or democracy's incessant push for ever greater levels of equality that tend to enable an expansive administrative state at the expense of local government.

Aristotle distinguishes between political rule of free and equal persons and mastery. Socrates shows how the tyrant is the most wretched of persons, ruling by a regime of terror and living in fear as a result. Tocqueville echoes this theme, arguing that mastery in its various forms is always degrading, whether it be the tyranny of a master over a slave (that degrades both) or the tyranny of the democratic majority that dulls the conscience of its citizens. Modernity's milieu of mastery stands against these classical assumptions. Reason is elevated as master and discovery is pursued as an end in itself. The arts, or technology, are divorced from philosophy, or the love of wisdom that seeks to integrate human endeavor into broader considerations of what ennobles humanity. The strong form of mastery represented by Marx and Nietzsche dismisses justice as an illusion. Echoing Thrasymachus, justice is only the advantage of the strong. The weak form of mastery represented by Kant and Rawls abjures the use of force but holds a view of the citizen that is unencumbered, a sovereign in choosing the obligations that bind.[3] Maintaining the sovereignty of the citizen and a view of justice with independent normative force tends to sever a public understanding of justice from private connotations of virtue, however, a hollowing out of justice in the public square that leaves it as little more than a proxy for equality. Whether by the strong or weak form, modernity's milieu of mastery influences the character of the modern state: rational, expansive, and guided more by the cultivation of dependence than the use of force.

The capacity of a people for justice and the institutional setting in which this people operates politically, that is, their mores and institutions, can help inform contemporary explanations for the usage of public debt. Keynesianism posits a rationale for when debt should be used, and Barro updates Ricardo to equate debt and taxes in contemporary politics. The countercyclical dimension of Keynesianism clearly is not manifested in the presence of the mature administrative state, however. In a clear departure from nineteenth- and early twentieth-century practice, federal debt is not paid down and continues to be issued in good times as well as bad. From the standpoint of budget balance, Barro makes it clear that debt is really a future tax, but he does not give a compelling rationale for why a citizen would want debt or taxes.

Further explanation for the proclivity to use debt is thus needed, and understanding debt in terms of political freedom may be of help. Figure 3.9 illustrates the interaction of mores and institutions to assess a society's capacity for political freedom. The mores curve is a measure of the capacity to integrate considerations of equality and inequality to attain justice or the common good. The centralization curve is a measure of the capacity to institutionally integrate elements of democracy and oligarchy to avoid the extremes of each that result in mastery. Underlying the theoretical construct is the assumption that injustice or the incapacity for the common good explains in part the usage of public debt, that a society less capable of justice based on an ethic of self-sufficiency will seek to transfer more of its own obligations to the future. Through cession or seizure of the prerogatives of self-government, centralization is an institutional representation of injustice. It reflects the withering of local politics and the exertion of independent institutional influence on public debt levels by diminishing accountability and obscuring valuation. To the extent that public debt can be explained in terms of injustice and centralization, the decline in political freedom can serve as a measure of a society's proclivity to use debt.

These assumptions are tested in longitudinal modeling of state indebtedness through most of the twentieth century and found to have some merit. Civil and criminal strife have a strong correlation with the size of the state bar and provide some justification for using the lawyer population as a measure of societal injustice, or the incapacity of a society for the common good. When this variable is incorporated into a model with other socioeconomic factors, it has a significant and positive effect on indebtedness. Measures of centralization likewise have a significant and positive effect on debt. Most importantly, the concentration of government at the state (as opposed to the local) level and the tendency of that state to look to the central government for aid, both increase levels of state debt.

Political freedom as illustrated in Figure 3.9 also may provide a more durable theoretical framework for fiscal federalism. Oates' economic perspective helped political science break out of a rule-bound approach to federalism, and political theory may return the favor by giving Oates a unifying theme in the midst of the conflicting messages of federalism research. First, the complex interaction of mores and institutions underscores a central message in recent studies: context matters. Depending on the circumstances, what goes on under the name of decentralization may simply be the transfer of mastery to the local level. Second, an Aristotelian understanding of centralization recognizes a democratic and oligarchic path to mastery. Adding Tocqueville, political freedom and democracy are not the same thing, just as voting is not the sum and substance of self-government. Decentralization therefore is not defined by democratic institutions alone but by various integrations of democratic and oligarchic elements to achieve a republican form of government that is context specific. Finally, it is possible for a society to travel up both sides of the centralization curve simultaneously. In U.S. politics, for example, features such as the direct election of Senators, the expansion of primary elections, and the increasing importance of public opinion can be seen as moving the country toward a purer form of democracy. On the other hand, the growth of the administrative state, the centrality of campaign contributions in the electoral process, and the dominance of well-established lobbies in the halls of power can be seen as moving the country toward a more oligarchical form of government. What does centralization and decentralization mean in light of the complexity of these issues? A unifying theme like political freedom can offer a matrix to more consistently answer that question. A focus on political freedom thus adds theoretical depth to Faguet's contention that decentralization is primarily defensible in terms of facilitating accountable, responsible government.

The theoretical challenge to Oates posed by Besley and Coate offers one example of applying a political freedom matrix to questions of fiscal federalism. If the assumptions of Oates' Decentralization Theorem are relaxed, they argue, if central government can provide tailored services or there are spillover effects from local expenditures that make them Pareto inefficient, then decentralization becomes less attractive relative to centralization. But the pendulum can swing the other way. If assumptions of Musgrave's are relaxed, if local government can be seen as the proper venue through which to provide public welfare instead of central authority, then decentralization becomes more attractive relative to centralization.

A concern for equality is what underlies Musgrave's assignment of redistribution efforts to the central government instead of localities. Oates accepts this when he should question it (other assumptions of Musgrave's, that central authority is best suited to provide for national defense and manage the money supply, appear unassailable). When the theoretical forces of centralization open a front on the Decentralization Theorem, a flanking maneuver is possible. The matrix of political freedom espouses a view of justice that considers not only equality but inequality in attaining the common good. If a top-heavy, national administrative state is ill-equipped to manage aspects of public welfare, then political freedom would counsel greater tolerance for redistributive inequality to address the more serious threat of unrestrained public debt.

Several interpretations of the injustice variable were considered. The lawyer population can be seen as a synthetic measure of the level of injustice in society, as this book assumes. It also can be seen as a measure of legal complexity and influence of the bar in the legislature. Observations pertaining to these three interpretations do not necessarily conflict and, indeed, complement each other in some ways. The change in legal norms from formalism to realism that contributes to legal complexity, taken together with the dominance of the bar in legislatures, explains in part the joint movement of the judicial and legislative branches toward more activist, expansive government.

This book was conceived with the intent of informing the broader discussion of public debt. The statistical analysis herein can support the argument that centralization tends to increase debt in state government. The analysis was not designed to and therefore cannot prove that centralization is responsible for debt at the federal level. But it can be more than silent on the question. Chapter 6 provides important context by which to apply the theoretical and quantitative themes of this study to the development of the American administrative state. The Civil War profoundly altered American federalism, opening vistas of centralized power that social reformers worked for decades to consolidate. America's tradition of decentralized, limited constitutional government posed formidable obstacles to the development of a modern American administrative state capable of implementing national social reform, however. The separation of powers, enumerated powers, and federal structure provided different political platforms from which to espouse varying, "unequal" perspectives. In addition, America's heritage of immutable natural rights implied certain immutable boundaries for governmental authority. There was a tension between "human rights" and natural rights in Theodore Roosevelt's rhetoric, for inviolable liberties posed an obstacle to unrestrained and assertive national action to alleviate social ills. Franklin Roosevelt remedied the semantics by presenting social welfare as an expansion of rights, but the underlying conflict was not resolved, for both Progressive "human rights" and New Deal "economic rights" were empty vessels to be filled with any transitory meaning of the majority's momentary will. Direct democracy reforms constituted the heart of the Progressive Party platform in the 1912 campaign and were the means to empower majority opinion against statutory and constitutional barriers to reform. Theodore Roosevelt's support for the recall of state judicial decisions shared an affinity with Franklin Roosevelt's plan to pack the U.S. Supreme Court. It was not coincidental that the fundamental domestic conflict of both Roosevelts was with the courts, the branch of government most directly responsible for defending the rule of law. In Aristotelian terms, the real or perceived mastery of the judiciary would be overcome by the mastery of the executive shaping and responding to immediate public opinion.

The Progressive impulse for reform can be seen as an Aristotelian effort to comprehend better the whole of justice in a changing society. Progressivism's error was pursuing that reform in centralized fashion. An increasingly integrated and complex American society required the expansion of national administration. Aristotle's different degrees of unity would be satisfied by the creation of the Interstate Commerce Commission and a host of other agencies that administer truly national problems. The Progressive vision of national social welfare without stringent institutional controls, however, led to centralized programs that obscured rather than clarified the common good by using debt to push current obligations to the future.

Summary of Findings

This book offers the longest quantitative review of state debt in the literature (1920–1990). It does this by taking decennial measurements of important variables, as annual data is not available for this time period. Drawing on classical themes, institutional analysis is integrated with dimensions of culture to define the parameters of political freedom in a theoretically coherent way. Quantitative analysis supports the essence of the theoretical framework: centralization and injustice, or the incapacity for the common good, can help explain state indebtedness. Centralization is the primary institutional feature measured in statistical modeling and is shown to have a significant, positive relationship with state debt. A unifying classical theme of self-sufficiency allows for different measures of centralization to be seen in a common light. Centralization within a state and the reliance of a state on intergovernmental aid both can be seen as a loss of the self-sufficiency that attends political freedom: the first a measure of less self-sufficient local governments and the second a measure of a state's tendency to depend on central national authority. Both of these indices have a positive relationship with state debt levels. A synthetic measure of injustice is derived and shown to have a significant, positive relationship with state debt. Also, important cultural measures such as voter turnout and religious composition are integrated into state debt modeling for the first time and shown to have significant explanatory power.

Using these variables, this book posits a contribution to public debt theory by offering an explanation in terms of mores for the proclivity to use debt. Injustice can be measured in societal faction and understood as reflective of not only the incapacity for the common good among the living but a lack of common good between the older and younger or between present and future generations. This finding begins to operationalize the moral dimension of Buchanan's neoclassical argument against public debt as benefiting the present at the expense of the future. The study also points to one step beyond Buchanan's argument that public and private debt are analogous (as directed against Keynesian theory that holds them to be dissimilar). As an explanation in terms of mores, injustice may provide a common explanation for the proclivity to use public and private debt, not just see them as analogous. This is so because a person may be unjust to himself as well as others, Aristotle argues. Gardner does not draw on classical themes in his essay on debt and democratic nihilism, but his thesis points in this direction. "Equality is not just a right; it's a burden, as individuals must demonstrate to themselves and their contemporaries that they are not inferior but just as good as anyone else or even better," writes Gardner. He continues,

> To show oneself as "equal" or better, one must also show that one is autonomous, independent, or self-determined, if not self-created. In this context, democracy's addiction to debt, personal and sovereign, may be understood as a strategy of deferral that underwrites myths of freedom of popular culture. Dangerous as this might be for the long-term health of the economy or polity, this structure of postponement can scarcely be avoided as a condition of democracy ...[4]

The inflamed materialism that journeys alongside democratic nihilism points to a crisis of values, of a misunderstanding of what is truly important, which is the basis of being unjust with others (contributing to public debt) and with oneself (contributing to private debt). Finally, this book posits a contribution to fiscal federalism theory. The market-oriented assumptions undergirding Oates' Decentralization Theorem do not lend themselves to a variety of contexts as well as the more comprehensive view of political freedom that integrates institutions and mores.

Areas for Further Research

Obviously, the first step that could be taken to improve this book is to extend analysis to incorporate recent decades. For the study as it is presently structured, other improvements would be to incorporate constitutional debt limits as an additional institutional variable. A historical taxonomy of such restrictions, along the lines of Hou and Smith's classification of balanced-budget rules, would be needed to assess reliably the influence of this variable. At the very least, this book points to the need for more systematic research on the bar as an institution in American politics. It is the most enduring and yet unperceived lobby in American government, spanning generations, the federal structure, and branches of government with persistent force. Measuring the influence of the bar in state legislatures is a specific item raised in the previous chapter. In addition, the general question of changing mores within the bar and the effect of those changes on American politics points in a variety of fruitful directions. As a start, to further test the hypothesis that a lack of justice or the common good explains in part the proclivity to use debt, this study can be retooled with annual data in recent decades on civil and criminal faction (as measured in court proceedings) instead of the synthetic measure of size of the state bar. Aside from further study on the bar, local government can be integrated in various ways to better assess the influence of community size and intergovernmental relations within a state on public debt. Finally, delineating between types of state debt, as Bahl and Duncombe do, may provide, additional, important insight.

A Qualification

This book's critique of centralization should proceed hand in hand with a recognition that centralization has taken place to secure social goods of great value, the most important being national survival. Enduring the Great Depression, prevailing in World War II, persevering through the Cold War, and advancing civil rights are several of the most important political successes due to centralization.

Oakeshott's essay "Rationalism in Politics" offers a caution and an affirmation to the thrust of this study. It affirms wariness of a modern administrative state driven by an extreme rationality that does violence to the organic nature of society. It cautions against making the same error in reverse, however. Oakeshott criticizes Hayek's "plan to resist all planning" as driven by the same ideological rigidity as rational politics.[5] For better or worse, the administrative state has grown as an integral part of American society, and decentralization will not be the answer for every political difficulty. Neither Tocqueville nor Oates would counsel such a course. Federalism's purpose is not decentralization per se but discerning "which functions and instruments are best centralized and which are best placed in the sphere of decentralized levels of government."[6]

Likewise, it has not been argued here that public debt is always bad. Indebtedness to preserve the nation during war is the most obvious example of the just use of debt. A variety of other enduring national interests, infrastructure comes readily to mind, also make debt a just fiscal course. All of this is to say that a return to some decentralized state of balanced-budget bliss is not what is being advocated. Still, the fiscal trends documented in this study point to very real concerns with centralization.

The American Administrative State: A Hypothesis

The statistical significance of centralization contributing to state indebtedness provides context that points the debate on national debt in a particular direction, a different direction from the trend of twentieth-century American politics. Indeed, the direction of decentralization does not seem to be on the compass of many political analysts.

Why does centralization not factor more prominently in analysis of the American administrative state? A Hartzian explanation is offered. That Hartz did not perceive the significance of centralization may reinforce his own thesis that aspects of America's liberal culture blind us to certain political perils. It was not only from European feudalism that America was spared but the centralization of government power in Europe.

This is why Tocqueville feared the combination of governmental centralization and administrative centralization in America. Governmental centralization, or a cohesive national government focused on national issues, naturally has strong support in a democracy due to the great influence of majority opinion. The power of the majority, or negatively, the tyranny of the majority, is restrained to the extent that it is not combined with administrative centralization that enables government to infringe on the liberties of its citizens. By Tocqueville's account, decentralization must be counted as one of the great institutional bulwarks against democratic tyranny.

And yet centralization does not seem to receive its due in contemporary political analysis, even though viewing important issues through the prism of centralization can offer additional insight. Fiorina and others point to various reasons for vanishing marginal districts but do not give adequate weight to centralized government's role in overtaxing institutions and diminishing political flexibility.[7] Barnett laments the erosion of constitutional limits on governmental power in twentieth-century jurisprudence—the shift from "islands of government powers in a sea of liberty" to "islands of liberty rights in a sea of governmental power"—but does not recognize that the lost Constitution will not be restored without the decentralized form of government that sustained it.[8]

Mann and Ornstein critique the decline of collegiality in Congress and the institution's general dysfunction without emphasizing centralization's contribution to congressional maladies.[9] The 535 members of Congress have had transferred to their shoulders over the course of the last century most of the political weight of the country. They thrive on the power that crushes them. With one House member representing over half-a-million people conditioned by centralization to look to the federal government for answers on any given policy issue, it is no wonder that collegiality has declined—there is little time for friendship. The ethic of every man for himself in Congress reflects centralized strain on the institution. Furthermore, as the administrative state expands, the stakes of control rise. Winning and losing become paramount, and partisanship is a means of survival in the more brutal politics of centralized government. Mann and Ornstein recommend many reforms for Congress but leave out the most important: taking pressure off the institution through decentralization.

Ceasar,[10] Tulis,[11] Kernell,[12] and Schlesinger[13] highlight related themes for the executive branch. The presidency has become more powerful and isolated, alternating between imperial and imperiled. To the extent that this alternation is perceived and not real is due to the continuing durability of the Constitution whose enumerated powers do not depend on political context. To the extent that this alternation is real and not perceived is due to the expansion of centralized government that depends more on public opinion than constitutional norms and thus must rely on a key figure to marshal that public opinion.

Contemporary political analysis thus seems to evince a degree of shortsightedness in perceiving some of the ways in which centralization may be enervating political freedom in America. Tocqueville's experience with administrative control in France gave him an instinctive wariness of centralization, a wariness that was more pronounced in earlier eras of American politics and that perhaps would be good to recall. A Hartzian case can be made that the American public, its policymakers, and its political scholars do not perceive the hazards of centralization because they have not felt the full weight of its yoke. American society since the New Deal has been sustained by centralization's successes and has been the beneficiary of centralization's largesse. The duress of centralization's mastery has not been discerned, however, and this is in no small part due to an indebtedness that has transferred present obligations to the future. The bill certainly will come due, however, and by that time it may be too late for the American people to recall their heritage of self-government, having been moved imperceptibly toward dependence, as a Frenchman warned them almost two centuries ago.

Notes

1 United States Department of Treasury, "Historical Debt Outstanding: Annual." Accessed March 7, 2018 at http://treasurydirect.gov/govt/reports/pd/histdebt/histdebt.htm.
2 U.S. Department of Treasury, "The Debt to the Penny and Who Holds It." Accessed March 7, 2018 at https://treasurydirect.gov/NP/debt/current.
3 Michael J. Sandel, *Democracy's Discontent: America in Search of a Public Philosophy* (Cambridge, MA: Belknap Press, 1996), 12.
4 Stephen L. Gardner, "Democracy's Debt: Capitalism and Cultural Revolution," in *Debt*, eds. Peter Y. Paik and Mary Wiesner-Hanks (Bloomington: Indiana University Press, 2013), 95–96.
5 Michael Oakeshott, *Rationalism in Politics and Other Essays* (Indianapolis, IN: Liberty Fund, 1991), 26.
6 Wallace E. Oates, "An Essay on Fiscal Federalism," *Journal of Economic Literature* Vol. 37 No. 3 (September 1999): 1120.
7 Morris P. Fiorina, *Congress: Keystone of the Washington Establishment*, Second Edition (New Haven, CT: Yale University Press, 1989).
8 Randy E. Barnett, *Restoring the Lost Constitution: The Presumption of Liberty* (Princeton, NJ: Princeton University Press, 2004), 1.
9 Thomas E. Mann and Norman J. Ornstein, *The Broken Branch: How Congress Is Failing American and How to Get It Back on Track* (Oxford: Oxford University Press, 2006).
10 James W. Ceaser, *Presidential Selection: Theory and Development* (Princeton, NJ: Princeton University Press, 1979).
11 Jeffrey K. Tulis, *The Rhetorical Presidency* (Princeton, NJ: Princeton University Press, 1987).
12 Samuel Kernell, *Going Public: New Strategies of Presidential Leadership* (Washington, D.C.: CQ Press, 1986).
13 Arthur M. Schlesinger, Jr., *The Imperial Presidency* (Boston: Houghton Mifflin, 1973).

Bibliography

Barnett, Randy E. *Restoring the Lost Constitution: The Presumption of Liberty*. Princeton, NJ: Princeton University Press, 2004.

Ceaser, James W. *Presidential Selection: Theory and Development*. Princeton, NJ: Princeton University Press, 1979.

Fiorina, Morris P. *Congress: Keystone of the Washington Establishment*, Second Edition. New Haven, CT: Yale University Press, 1989.

Gardner, Stephen. "Democracy's Debt: Capitalism and Cultural Revolution." In *Debt*, edited by Peter Y. Paik and Mary Wiesner-Hanks, 94–115. Bloomington: Indiana University Press, 2013.

Kernell, Samuel. *Going Public: New Strategies of Presidential Leadership*. Washington, D.C.: CQ Press, 1986.

Mann, Thomas E. and Norman J. Ornstein. *The Broken Branch: How Congress Is Failing American and How to Get It Back on Track*. Oxford: Oxford University Press, 2006.

Oakeshott, Michael. *Rationalism in Politics and Other Essays*. Indianapolis, IN: Liberty Fund, 1991.

Oates, Wallace E. "An Essay on Fiscal Federalism." *Journal of Economic Literature* Vol. 37 No. 3 (September 1999): 1120–1149.

Sandel, Michael J. *Democracy's Discontent: America in Search of a Public Philosophy*. Cambridge, MA: Belknap Press, 1996.

Schlesinger, Arthur M. Jr. *The Imperial Presidency*. Boston: Houghton Mifflin, 1973.

Tulis, Jeffrey K. *The Rhetorical Presidency*. Princeton, NJ: Princeton University Press, 1987.

United States Department of Treasury. "Historical Debt Outstanding: Annual." Accessed March 7, 2018 at http://treasurydirect.gov/govt/reports/pd/histdebt/histdebt.htm.

United States Department of Treasury. "The Debt to the Penny and Who Holds It." Accessed March 7, 2018 at https://treasurydirect.gov/NP/debt/current.

Appendix

Data Sources

Data closest to the decennial measurement is used from the following sources.

State Area

1870–1990: Carter, Susan B., Scott Sigmund Gartner, Michael R. Haines, Alan L. Olmstead, Richard Sutch, and Gavin Wright, eds. *Historical Statistics of the United States: Millennial Edition Online*. New York: Cambridge University Press, 2006.

State Population

1870–1990: Carter, Susan B. et al. *Historical Statistics of the United States*.

State Racial Composition

1870–1990: Carter, Susan B. et al. *Historical Statistics of the United States*.

State Voter Turnout

1870–1990: Carter, Susan B. et al. *Historical Statistics of the United States*.

State Democratic Vote for President

1870–1990: Carter, Susan B. et al. *Historical Statistics of the United States*.

State Religious Composition

1920: ARDA state file, 1916.
1930: ARDA state file, 1926.
1940: ARDA state file, 1936.
1950: ARDA state file, 1952.
1960: –
1970: ARDA state file, 1971.
1980: ARDA state file, 1980.
1990: ARDA state file, 1990.

State Population by City Size

1920: U.S. Census. *Statistical Abstract: 1962*, pp. 22–23.
1930: U.S. Census. *Statistical Abstract: 1962*, pp. 22–23.
1940: U.S. Census. *Statistical Abstract: 1962*, pp. 22–23.
1950: U.S. Census. *Statistical Abstract: 1962*, pp. 22–23.
1960: U.S. Census. *Statistical Abstract: 1962*, pp. 22–23.
1970: U.S. Census. *Statistical Abstract: 1972*, pp. 21–23.
1980: U.S. Census. *Census of Governments: 1982*, pp. 31–132.
1990: U.S. Census. *Census of Governments: 1992*, pp. 31–132.

State Inequality Index

1920–1990: Frank, Mark. Atkinson Index, GINI Coefficient, Relative Mean Deviation, Theil Index Dataset "Frank_GINI_2013." Sam Houston State University. Accessed March 18, 2016 at www.shsu.edu/eco_mwf/inequality.html.

State Marriages

1920: U.S. Census. *Statistical Abstract: 1926*, p. 85.
1930: U.S. Census. *Statistical Abstract: 1933*, p. 81.
1940: U.S. Census. *Statistical Abstract: 1942*, p. 121.
1950: U.S. Census. *Statistical Abstract: 1953*, p. 82.
1960: U.S. Census. *Statistical Abstract: 1973*, p. 66.
1970: U.S. Census. *Statistical Abstract: 1984*, p. 85.
1980: U.S. Census. *Statistical Abstract: 1984*, p. 85.
1990: U.S. Census. *Statistical Abstract: 2002*, p. 88.

State Divorce

1920: U.S. Census. *Statistical Abstract: 1926*, p. 85.
1930: U.S. Census. *Statistical Abstract: 1933*, p. 91.
1940: U.S. Census. *Statistical Abstract: 1942*, p. 121.
1950: U.S. Census. *Statistical Abstract: 1962*, p. 70.
1960: U.S. Census. *Statistical Abstract: 1962*, p. 70.
1970: U.S. Census. *Statistical Abstract: 1984*, p. 86.
1980: U.S. Census. *Statistical Abstract: 1984*, p. 86.
1990: U.S. Census. *Statistical Abstract: 2002*, p. 88.

State Prison Population

1930: U.S. Census. *Statistical Abstract: 1931*, p. 76.

State Bar Population

1920: –
1930: *Martindale-Hubbell Law Directory*, 1932 (author's estimate).
1940: *Martindale-Hubbell Law Directory*, 1941 (author's estimate).
1950: U.S. Census. *Statistical Abstract: 1961*, p. 150.
1960: U.S. Census. *Statistical Abstract: 1982–83*, p. 186.
1970: U.S. Census. *Statistical Abstract: 1982–83*, p. 186.
1980: U.S. Census. *Statistical Abstract: 1992*, p192.
1990: U.S. Census. *Statistical Abstract: 1992*, p. 192.

Local Debt

1910: U.S. Census. *Wealth, Debt, and Taxation: 1913*, Volume 1, p. 238.
1920: –
1930: U.S. Census. *Financial Statistics of State and Local Govts.: 1932*, pp. 51–56.
1940: U.S. Census. *Revised Summary of State and Local Govt. Fin. in 1942*, pp. 23–27.
1950: U.S. Census. "GOVT_FINANCES" Dataset.
1960: U.S. Census. "GOVT_FINANCES" Dataset.
1970: U.S. Census. "GOVT_FINANCES" Dataset.
1980: U.S. Census. "GOVT_FINANCES" Dataset.
1990: U.S. Census. "GOVT_FINANCES" Dataset.

State Debt

1910: U.S. Census. *Wealth, Debt, and Taxation: 1913*, Volume 1, p. 37.
1920: –
1930: U.S. Census. *Statistical Abstract: 1941*, pp. 247–249.
1940: U.S. Census. *Statistical Abstract: 1941*, pp. 247–249.
1950: U.S. Census. "GOVT_FINANCES" Dataset.
1960: U.S. Census. "GOVT_FINANCES" Dataset.
1970: U.S. Census. "GOVT_FINANCES" Dataset.
1980: U.S. Census. "GOVT_FINANCES" Dataset.
1990: U.S. Census. "GOVT_FINANCES" Dataset.

Local Revenue

1910: U.S. Census. *Wealth, Debt, and Taxation: 1913*, Volume 2, pp. 462–469.
1920: –
1930: U.S. Census. *Financial Statistics of State and Local Govts.: 1932*, pp. 7–17.
1940: U.S. Census. *Revised Summary of State and Local Govt. Fin. in 1942*, pp. 5–14.

1950: U.S. Census. "GOVT_FINANCES" Dataset.
1960: U.S. Census. "GOVT_FINANCES" Dataset.
1970: U.S. Census. "GOVT_FINANCES" Dataset.
1980: U.S. Census. "GOVT_FINANCES" Dataset.
1990: U.S. Census. "GOVT_FINANCES" Dataset.

State Revenue

1910: U.S. Census. *Wealth, Debt, and Taxation: 1913*, Volume 2, p. 36.
1920: –
1930: U.S. Census. *Financial Statistics of State and Local Govts.: 1932*, pp. 7–17.
1940: U.S. Census. *Revised Summary of State and Local Govt. Fin. in 1942*, pp. 5–14.
1950: U.S. Census. "GOVT_FINANCES" Dataset.
1960: U.S. Census. "GOVT_FINANCES" Dataset.
1970: U.S. Census. "GOVT_FINANCES" Dataset.
1980: U.S. Census. "GOVT_FINANCES" Dataset.
1990: U.S. Census. "GOVT_FINANCES" Dataset.

Intergovernmental Aid to State Government

1920: –
1930: U.S. Census. *Financial Statistics of State and Local Govts.: 1932*, pp. 7–17.
1940: U.S. Census. *Revised Summary of State and Local Govt. Fin. in 1942*, pp. 5–14.
1950: U.S. Census. "GOVT_FINANCES" Dataset.
1960: U.S. Census. "GOVT_FINANCES" Dataset.
1970: U.S. Census. "GOVT_FINANCES" Dataset.
1980: U.S. Census. "GOVT_FINANCES" Dataset.
1990: U.S. Census. "GOVT_FINANCES" Dataset.

State Per Capita Income

1920: –
1930–1990: U.S. Census. *Statistical Abstract: 2003*, p. 67.

Index

AAA see *The Agricultural Adjustment Act*
accountability 69, 89, 96, 144, 151; fiscal 68, 71; personal 88; that comes with mutual exchange 88
accumulation of property and wealth 31, 129
Acts and Regulations: *The Agricultural Adjustment Act* 138–139, 142; *The Clayton Antitrust Act 1914* 135; *The Elkins Act 1903* 136; *The Emergency Banking Act* 138; *The Fair Labor Standards Act* 139; *The Federal Employment Stabilization Act 1931* 138; *The Hepburn Act 1906* 136; *The Income Tax Amendment 1913* 141; *Interstate Commerce Act* 133–134; *The Interstate Commerce Act* 133–134; *The Lever Act 1917* 137; *The Mann-Elkins Act 1910* 136; *The Meat Inspection Act 1906* 136; *The National Industrial Recovery Act 1937* 138–139; *The National Labor Relations Act 1935* (The Wagner Act) 139, 141; *The Overman Act 1918* 137; *The Pure Food and Drug Act 1906* 136, 140; *The Social Security Act* 139–140; *The Trading with the Enemy Act 1917* 138; *The Transportation Act 1920* 137; *The Volstead Act* 138; *The Wilson-Gorman Act* 135
Adair v. *United States 1908* 136
Addyston Pipe and Steel Company v. *United States 1899* 135
administrations 2, 25, 54, 134; centralized 9, 124; national 130, 133, 145, 154; public 25
administrative agencies 114, 136
'administrative centralization' (Tocqueville) 23–24, 27, 142–143, 157
administrative state 9, 24, 27–28, 34, 56, 114, 122, 124–145, 152, 156–157
"age of reform" (Hofstadter) 126
agencies 136, 140, 145, 154
aggregate debt 44
The Agricultural Adjustment Act 138–139, 142
agriculture 115, 118, 132, 137
aid 53, 68, 72, 89, 152; decennial measurements of intergovernmental 90; extent of intergovernmental 70–71; figures for intergovernmental 89; public 16
Alchian, Armen A. 41
Alt, James E. 93
Amendments 141; Eighteenth 138; Fifteenth 132; Sixteenth 135, 137–138, 141
American administrative state 9, 124, 134, 153, 156–157
American banks 138
American Civil War 32, 35
American constitutional government 128
American democracy 3, 9, 22, 24–25, 41, 124
American federalism 4, 71, 153
American government 41, 65, 131, 155
American history 9, 77, 115, 118
American jurisprudence 119–120
American politics 3, 9, 54, 119, 121, 125, 130, 140, 142, 155, 158; and the bar as an institution in 155; and changing mores within the bar 156; and the effects of the Civil War 130; and free market and natural rights traditions in 142; and the increasing dominance of the Court in 121; and the legal community in 121; twentieth-century 156
American society 119, 122, 125, 145, 154, 156, 158
American states 3, 66, 92, 126

ARDA *see* Association of Religious Data Archives
aristocracy 14, 18, 22, 25–26, 119
Aristotelian 7, 10, 20–21, 29–30, 32, 58, 72, 88, 141–142, 145, 152, 154; concepts 29; contribution to federalism theory 72; effort to comprehend justice in a changing society 20, 32, 145, 154; ethic of self-sufficiency 88; premises 21; reading of Rawls "justice and fairness" 29; themes 7, 141–142, 154; understanding of centralization 152; uses of terminology 30
Aristotle 5–7, 13–22, 25–27, 30, 32–35, 40–41, 55, 57, 61, 88, 96–97, 140–145, 150, 154–155; anticipates contemporary issues 15; distinction between mastery and the political rule of free and equal persons 28–29, 143; emphasis on justice 30, 141; and the ethic of self-sufficiency 18; and justice as the common good 30, 141; and Machiavelli 40; and the placement of equality in the broader concept of justice 20; and themes of decentralization in 25; and Tocqueville 33, 55, 61, 72, 140; and treatises on ethics and politics in antiquity 34
Association of Religious Data Archives 77
attorneys 9, 108, 110, 113, 115, 118; Democratic 118; dominance of 9, 115, 118, 121; Republican 118; in state legislative councils 9

Bahl, Roy 73–74, 84, 86, 95, 156
balanced-budget rules 65, 75, 78, 80–81, 83–84, 100, 155
bar 79, 108–109, 115, 118–122, 153, 155–156; associations 119; and the influence on American politics 9; and the size of the 121
Barnett, Randy E. 157
Barro, Robert 7, 48–50, 52, 60–61, 74, 151; case for a Ricardian equivalence between debt and taxes 88, 151; contemporizes the Ricardian theory of equivalence between debt and taxes 55
Baruch, Bernard 137
benefits 3, 7–8, 21, 23–24, 31, 34–35, 40, 53, 55–56, 67–70, 89, 101, 137, 144; of centralization 69; of decentralization 70, 144; of equality 22–23; political 71; potential 68
bequests 50–51, 60–61
Besley, Timothy 69, 152
Bianchi, Emily C. 96
Bradley, Justice 133
Breit, William 40–41, 54
Brennan, Geoffrey 68
Buchanan, James 7–8, 48–49, 52–55, 61, 64, 68
budget balance 40–41, 44, 53, 60, 64–65, 78, 151; description of 40–41; norm of 2, 54, 60, 64
budget deficits 48
budget rules 8, 65, 71
bureaucracies 4–5, 114; Federal Power Commission 138; Federal Radio Commission 138

candidates for office 77, 126
capitalism 16, 96, 126, 140
cases: *Adair* v. *United States 1908* 136; *Addyston Pipe and Steel Company* v. *United States 1899* 135; *Buttfield* v. *Stranahan 1904* 136; *Champion* v. *Ames 1903* 136; *Dayton-Goose Creek Railway Company* v. *United States 1924* 137; *Federal Trade Commission* v. *Curtis Publishing Company 1923* 137; *Federal Trade Commission* v. *Gratz 1920* 137; *Field* v. *Clark 1892* 136; *Hammer* v. *Dagenhart 1918* 136–137; *Hoke* v. *United States 1913* 136; *Holden* v. *Hardy 1898* 141; *Home Building and Loan Association* v. *Blaisdell 1934* 139; *ICC* v. *Alabama Midland Railway Company 1897* 134; *ICC* v. *Cincinnati, New Orleans, and Texas Pacific Railway Company 1896* 134; *ICC* v. *Illinois Central Railroad* 136; *Lochner* v. *New York 1905* 136; *Massachusetts* v. *Mellon 1923* 139; *McCray* v. *United States 1904* 136; *Muller* v. *Oregon 1908* 141; *Nebbia* v. *New York 1934* 139; *NLRB* v. *Jones & Laughlin 1937* 139; *Railroad Commission of Wisconsin* v. *Chicago, Burlington, and Quincy 1922* 137; *Schechter* v. *United States 1935* 139; *Steward Machine Company v Davis 1937* 139; *United States* v. *Butler 1936* 139; *United States* v. *Darby 1941* 139; *United States* v. *E.C. Knight 1895* 135, 140–141; *United States* v. *Grimaud 1911* 136; *United States* v. *Joint Traffic Association 1898* 135; *United States* v. *Standard Oil 1910* 135; *United States* v. *Trans-Missouri Freight Association 1897* 134–135

Castles, Francis G. 70
Catholic population (ratio) 81, 84, 112
Catholics 78, 94
Census 42, 78, 109, 118
Census data 42–43, 45–47
Census records 8, 75, 78
centralization 4, 8–9, 22–24, 57–58, 69–72, 74, 86, 88–89, 113–114, 120–121, 124, 142–144, 150–154, 156–158; crisis in 48; of debt 97; and decentralization 72, 152; federal 47; of government power 143, 157; hazards of 88, 158; and injustice 154; institutional 114; measures 48, 58; political 86; of population 86; of power 4
Champion v. *Ames 1903* 136
cities 14–16, 18, 20, 32, 64, 75–76, 79–84, 86, 88–90, 110–112, 141–142; smaller 89
citizen engagement 68, 144
citizens 8–9, 15–19, 21, 23–28, 30, 34, 36, 48–53, 55–57, 60, 66–67, 69, 88, 151; democratic 23, 25; direct participation in the political process 130; private 35; rights of 132
citizenship 14, 19, 21, 27
city size 8, 86, 88
civic participation 100
civil factions 8, 78, 108, 113, 121
civil liberty 131–132, 137, 144
Civil War 31, 53, 126, 129–131, 144, 153
'class legislation' 142
classes 25, 29, 109, 119, 128, 142; elite 100; middle 19, 23, 26, 126; privileged 108
classical legal thought 20, 28, 52–53, 140–141, 150; *see also* formalism
classical thinkers 21, 49, 53
The Clayton Antitrust Act 1914 135
Clingermayer, James C. 73–74, 84, 86, 89, 95, 97
Coate, Stephen 69, 152
commerce 26, 35, 132–133, 135–137, 139–140; interstate 135–136, 140; intrastate 140
commissions 125, 134–137
community 6, 10, 15–18, 20, 29, 32–34, 36, 88, 94, 96, 108, 113; context of 10, 22, 141; legal 114, 119, 121–122; size 87, 156
comparative studies of developed democracies 71
Congress 65, 115, 120, 131–134, 136–140, 157; authority of 136; collegiality in 157; members of 157; reforms for 157; taxing power of 139
congressional delegations 136
congressional maladies 157
congressional persistence 136
constitutional democracy 34
constitutional procedures 127–128
constitutionalism 126, 142
constitutions 6, 30, 34, 40, 127, 130–131, 136, 141, 144, 157
corruption 4–5, 14, 18, 28, 100, 133
courts 25, 31, 41, 64, 114, 120, 129, 133–137, 139–141, 154; in America 25; dispensing justice 6; state 109
credit 1, 34, 40–45, 47–61, 138
credit debt 73
creditors 2, 41, 53, 55–56
criminal proceedings 8, 109–110
criminals 8, 78, 101, 108–110, 113, 121
"The Crisis of the Tax State" 1
cultural capacity 17, 56, 59–61; for justice 61; for political freedom 59–60

data sources 75
Dayton-Goose Creek Railway Company v. *United States 1924* 137
de Tocqueville, Alexis 3, 108
debt 3–4, 6–8, 32–34, 41–44, 48–57, 59–61, 64–65, 70–75, 77–78, 87–89, 95–97, 100, 121, 150–156; aggregate 44; capital account 100; concentration 74, 84, 87, 95; equating 52; external 49; and injustice 121; internal 48; issues 52, 74, 88, 92; limits 65, 73, 78, 100, 155; non-guaranteed 73; and party affiliation 77; repaying 61; repayments 52, 60; and revenue 43, 54; servicing 66; and taxes 49, 52, 55, 60–61, 88, 151; unsustainable 64; uses of 8, 55, 58, 151–152, 154, 156
debt levels 55, 72–74, 78, 95; federal 42; public 4, 73, 100, 151; rising 2, 61, 96; state 5
decennial measurements 8, 42, 75, 84, 86, 90, 93, 95, 97, 154
decentralization 25, 50, 66–74, 88, 143–144, 152–153, 156–157; administrative 24; in Aristotle 25; degree of 25; direct effect of 69; and federalism 69
"Decentralization Theorem" 67, 153, 155
decentralized systems 66, 68–69
deficits 2, 9, 40, 54, 70–71, 92, 124
democracy 15–16, 18–19, 22, 24–25, 27,

33–35, 59–60, 71–72, 124, 127, 129, 142–143, 152, 155; contemporary 13–14, 21; developed 71; extreme 57–58; and oligarchy 18–19, 22, 58–59, 72, 151; procedural 33
Democracy in America 22, 108
democratic citizens 23, 25
Democrats 2, 77, 115, 118, 125–126, 129, 139; and presidential candidates 80–81, 83; states held by 77; voting for president 81–82, 84, 100
Denison, Dwight V. 73–74, 84, 87, 95, 97
dependent variables 8, 75–76, 79, 81, 111
Depression 43–45, 47–48, 54
divorce 109–110, 112–113
doctors 9, 17, 118, 120
Douglas, Stephen Arnold 32, 131
Duncombe, William 73–74, 84, 86, 95, 156
Durkheim, Emile 57–58

economic policies 129
economic thinking on public debt 8
economists 2, 41, 44
economy 48, 55, 66, 69, 72, 135, 137, 155; dimensions of political 114; integrated 140; of the market 126, 130; modern 2; national 134, 138; and society 69
Eighteenth Amendment 138
Elazar, Daniel J. 4–5, 10, 100
elections 9, 24–25, 65, 74, 77, 124, 126, 128, 139
The Elkins Act 1903 136
Ellis, Michael A. 75
The Emergency Banking Act 138
employees 137, 139
equality 6, 10, 13–17, 19–20, 22–25, 27, 29–31, 34–35, 58–60, 94, 96, 150–151, 153, 155; of conditions 6, 22; considerations of 58–60, 151; in democracies 22; human 7, 14, 35, 150; in John Rawls 30; of outcomes 9, 124, 143; pervasive democratic 119; and political freedom 22, 27, 150
Erikson, Robert S. 94
Eskeland, Gunnar 70–71
ethics 34–35, 89, 157
ethnic conflicts 69
Europe 22–23, 25–26, 157
evaluation of public debt 30
external debt 49

factions 5, 28, 36, 78, 109, 122, 142
Faguet, Jean-Paul 68–69, 73, 152
The Fair Labor Standards Act 139
fairness 30–33
families 23, 26, 32, 35, 50–51, 75, 141, 143
family estates 33
farmers 17–18, 120, 138
federal budgets 54, 144; *see also* budgets
federal debt 42–44, 46, 50, 52, 75, 144, 150–151; *see also* debt
The Federal Employment Stabilization Act 1931 138
federal government 2, 43–45, 47–48, 54–55, 66, 73, 78, 89, 126, 136–140, 144, 157; centralization of 45; and the revenue expansion of the states over 44; reviews of 3
Federal Net Outlays 48
federal power (intrusion into national life) 138
Federal Power Commission 138
Federal Radio Commission 138
federal revenue 43–44, 47, 50, 52, 135, 144
federal structures 9, 68–70, 124, 153, 155
federal systems 67–68, 70, 132
Federal Trade Commission 135, 137
Federal Trade Commission v. *Curtis Publishing Company 1923* 137
Federal Trade Commission v. *Gratz 1920* 137
federalism 65–70, 72–73, 133, 142, 152; research on 65, 67–69, 89, 152; theory of 67, 71–72
The Federalist 16, 142
Federalists 115
Feld, Lars P. 92
Ferree, Karen E. 93
Field, Justice 133
Field v. *Clark 1892* 136
Fifteenth Amendment 132
Filene, Peter G. 125
finances 2, 33, 131; deficit 55; review of fiscal 50; state 78
Fiorina, Morris P. 157
fiscal autonomy 71
fiscal decentralization 70–71
fiscal federalism 65–66, 73–74, 152
fiscal imbalance 71, 144
fiscal policies 7, 55, 66, 88, 96
fiscal trends 8, 42–44, 64, 156; and economic thought on public debt 8; twentieth-century 7
formalism 140–141
Founders 4, 34, 57, 141–142, 145

freedom 13, 18, 23, 25, 36, 120, 139, 155; economic 115; regulatory 114–115; spirit of 24–25, 88
Freitag, Markus 72
FTC *see* Federal Trade Commission
funds 48–49, 52–53, 56; *see also* public funds

Gardner, Stephen L. 6, 10, 96–97, 155
Garfield, James 127
GDP *see* gross domestic product
GEE *see* Generalized Estimating Equations
Generalized Estimating Equations 79–81, 83, 110
Gerring, John 132
Gettysburg Address 31
Giovannini, Alberto 2
Gould, Lewis L. 125–126
government 4–5, 7–9, 14–15, 40–45, 48–51, 54–57, 66–68, 70–71, 87–89, 127–129, 131, 143–144, 152, 154–158; accountability of 69, 95; activists 119; administrative 133; central 23, 66, 68–70, 130, 152–153, 157; constitutional 33, 127, 131; contemporary 23; debt and deficits 42; decentralized 35, 50; democratic 24, 43; divided 74, 93; expansive 95, 110, 120, 153; expenditures 53; finance 41, 52; good 8, 69, 71, 127, 129; land 127; legitimacy 114, 120; municipal 125; neutrality 5; obligations 142; officials 69; operations 4; powers 157; recipient 68; Republican 122; subnational 68
Government, intervention in society 4
government debt 48, 93; local 43; new 2
government expenditures, funding of 53
governmental centralization (Tocqueville) 23–24, 27, 44, 143, 157
governmental institutions 35, 100
governmental structures 65, 67, 141
Greer, Robert A. 73–74, 84, 87, 95, 97
gross domestic product 48

Hallerberg, Mark 71–72
Hammer v. *Dagenhart 1918* 136–137
Harlan, Justice 134
The Hepburn Act 1906 136
Hobbes, Thomas 20
Hofstadter, Richard 126
Hoke v. *United States 1913* 136
Holden v. *Hardy 1898* 141
Home Building and Loan Association v. *Blaisdell 1934* 139
honor 1, 15, 29–30, 144; constructs of 29; and morality 15, 29
Hoover, Herbert 54, 137–138
Horwitz, Morton J. 140–141
Hou, Yilin 78
House of Representatives 9, 115, 118
human relationships 6–7, 16
Hume, David 49, 52–53

ICA see *Interstate Commerce Act*
ICC *see* Interstate Commerce Commission
ICC v. *Alabama Midland Railway Company 1897* 134
ICC v. *Cincinnati, New Orleans, and Texas Pacific Railway Company 1896* 134
ICC v. *Cincinnati, New Orleans, and Texas Pacific Railway Company 1897* 134
ICC v. *Illinois Central Railroad* 136
ideology 74, 77, 94, 100; liberal 94–95; political 77
incentives 66, 68–70, 75, 114
income 52, 65, 68, 74, 95–96, 110, 113; inequality 110–112; levels of 95–96; measuring 78
The Income Tax Amendment 1913 141
income tax proposals 135
indebtedness 3, 48, 60, 65, 70–71, 73–74, 87, 152, 156, 158; public 7, 34, 75
independence, judicial 120
independent variables 8, 65, 70, 75–76, 79, 81, 111
inequality 15, 17, 26, 59–60, 150–151, 153; considerations of equality and 59–60, 150–151; of income 110–112; redistribution of 153; rising 143
injustice 3, 8, 34, 36, 53, 55, 64, 78–79, 97, 108–110, 113, 115, 121, 150–155; avoidance of 16; and centralization 152; domestic 110; handling of 113; and legal complexities of 115; measures 78, 101; racial 32; variable 8, 64–65, 79, 153
Inman, Robert P. 68, 71–72, 74
interests 9, 17–18, 20, 23, 30–31, 34–35, 53, 55–56, 60, 65–66, 72–73, 80–81, 114, 121–122; corporate 129, 133, 135; individual 5; local 23, 143; national 3, 56, 118, 143, 156; private 14, 18, 22–24, 27, 77, 118, 138; Republican 132; special 114; taxpayer's 56
intergovernmental aid 67–68, 70, 72, 74, 78–82, 84, 86, 88–91, 93, 154; federal 74, 89; figures for 89; function and

scope of 67; inefficient 72; national trend in 90; per capita 79, 81, 83; real 82–83; role of 68; scope of 67; uncircumspect 89
interstate commerce 135–136, 140
The Interstate Commerce Act 133–134
Interstate Commerce Commission 134–137, 144–145, 154

Jaffa, Harry V. 32
Jefferson, Thomas 16, 34, 36
judiciary 119–121, 128, 141, 154
jurisdiction size (Lassen and Serritzlew) 88–89
jurisdictions 36, 66–68, 132
justice 2–4, 6–10, 13–36, 41, 55–56, 59–61, 64, 72–73, 88–89, 96–97, 113–114, 141–142, 144–145, 150–151; background to 31, 33; and centralization 113; and debt 64; diminished 35; and morality 21; viewed as the common good 7
"justice as fairness" (John Rawls) 13, 29–30

Kant, Immanuel 16, 20–21, 35
Kelly, Alfred H. 131–132, 135, 138, 140, 143
Kernell, Samuel 157
Keynes, John Maynard 7, 40–45, 47–61, 74; and the historical constraints on the thought of 53; impetus for centralization precedes the New Deal 9; influence the decade of depression 54; and the publication of *General Theory* 48
Keynesianism 7, 49, 52–53, 55, 61, 151; central assumptions of 8, 49; flagging 52; in mitigating recession 55
Keynesians 7–8, 48, 52–54, 60, 150
Kiewiet, Roderick 92
kurtosis 75, 79, 81–83, 112

labor 23, 26, 28–29, 132
languages 125, 142
law 6, 8–9, 15–17, 19, 22–24, 58–60, 78, 108–109, 114–115, 118–120, 127–128, 131, 134, 140–141; of agency 140; constitutional 128, 144; fundamental 130; and informal judgments 78; national minimum wage 140; private 114; public 118
Lawson, Gary 3
lawyer population 8, 97, 109–110, 112–113, 115, 121, 152–153; and caseload proceedings 109; and criminal proceedings 110; per capita 109; by state 109–110
lawyers 8, 79–84, 97–99, 101, 108–110, 112, 114–115, 118–122; light of political influence of 122; national trend in 97; role of 119; by state 79; total number of 97–98
Leachman, Lori L. 70
legislation 31, 131, 133, 135, 137, 140; class 142; grant-in-aid 137; implementing 138; invalidated federal child labor 137; land grant 132; national rail 133; New Deal 138–139; self-interested 31; social welfare 132
Lerner, Abba P. 48
The Lever Act 1917 137
liberal ideology 94–95
liberty 22, 24–28, 31–34, 71, 131, 143, 145, 150, 157; civil 131–132, 137, 144; human 32–33; personal 22, 24, 74, 120, 132
Lieske, Joel 5
Lincoln, Abraham 31–32, 35, 130–131, 144
Lipset, Seymour M. 95
local governments 24, 43–45, 47, 58, 66–67, 69–70, 72, 86–89, 130, 150, 153, 156; in China 70; competition 68; and parties 130; reliance of 68; responsiveness 43; self-sufficient 154
Lochner v. *New York 1905* 136
Locke, John 16, 20, 143–144
Lowry, Robert C. 93

Machiavelli 14–15, 20, 40
Madison, James 9, 16, 23, 124, 142
Mafioso 41
Mann, Thomas E. 157
The Mann-Elkins Act 1910 136
Marier, Patrik 71–72
marriage 26, 110, 112–113
Marx, Karl 16, 20–21, 26, 35, 151
Massachusetts v. *Mellon 1923* 139
Matsusaka, John G. 92
McCloskey, Robert G. 133, 136
McCray v. *United States 1904* 136
McIver, John P. 94
McKinnon, Ronald I. 68
McPherson, James M. 132
measurements 58, 110, 114; of centralization 8, 47, 78, 89, 121, 152, 154; of debt 75; quantitative 3
The Meat Inspection Act 1906 136

Mencken, Carson 57–58
Milkis, Sidney 3–4, 126, 128, 130, 142
Miller, Justice 132
money 1–2, 18, 56, 60, 66, 144; creation of 68; supply 153; transferring 60
monopolies 66, 129, 135, 140
Moreno, Paul D. 126–127, 138–139, 142
"mores" 6, 25, 28, 56, 58–60, 72, 121, 155; explanation in terms of 154–155; and institutions 3, 35, 56, 121, 150–152
Muller v. *Oregon 1908* 141
municipalities 74, 87, 89
Musgrave, Peggy B. 65–66, 153

NAM *see* National Association of Manufacturers
National Association of Manufacturers 135
national debt 2–3, 44, 48, 50, 156
national government 2–4, 24, 42, 45, 54, 131, 133, 142, 145; cohesive 157; strong 130; weakness of 145
The National Industrial Recovery Act 1937 138–139
national interests 3, 56, 118, 143, 156
The National Labor Relations Act 1935 (The Wagner Act) 139, 141
national power 127, 132, 141
National Republicans 132
natural rights 20–21, 130–131, 143–145, 153; immutable 153; and the relationship with natural right 21; traditions 9, 124, 128, 142–143
Nebbia v. *New York 1934* 139
New Deal 9, 40, 53–54, 64, 114, 119, 124, 126, 130, 132, 138–140, 142, 153, 158; legislation 138–139; policies 139–140, 143
New Nationalism 128
New York Times 130
newspapers, *New York Times* 130
Nietzsche 16, 20–21, 29, 35, 118, 151
NIRA *see* National Industrial Recovery Act
NLRA see *National Labor Relations Act*
NLRB v. *Jones & Laughlin 1937* 139
non-guaranteed debt 73

Oakeshott, Michael 156
Oates, Wallace E. 65–69, 72, 144, 152–153, 156
Oates' Decentralization Theorem 69, 142, 152
Olsen, Eugene A. 72
Ong, Lynette H. 70
Ornstein, Norman J. 157
The Overman Act 1918 137

Peltzman, Sam 92–93
Perkins, George 129
personal liberty 22, 24, 132
Pestritto, Ronald J. 129, 131
policies 1, 3, 35, 48–49, 66, 68, 70, 115, 125, 131, 140, 143; expansionary government 48; helping regularize government 135; national 142
political conventions 41
political culture 4–5
political freedom 10, 22–23, 25, 27, 29, 33–34, 55–57, 59–60, 72–73, 113, 150–155, 158; and centralization 27; in democracy and oligarchy 59
political ideology 77
political institutions 16, 55, 59, 70, 72, 126
political liberalism 6, 10, 13–14, 27, 29, 32–33, 150
political parties 4–5, 40, 120
political power 25, 70
political reforms 124
political rule 15, 19, 21, 27, 33, 41, 57, 72
political systems 71, 86
political theory 6, 72, 152
political tribunals 22
population (in cities) 79, 83–84, 110, 112
population density 73–76, 80–84, 86–87, 110–112; decennial measurements of 86; independent variables 81; national trend in 86; and population change 73
Porter, David O. 72
Poterba, James M. 65
powers 4–5, 19, 21, 23–25, 66, 68, 129, 131, 134, 136, 138, 142, 152–153, 157; enumerated 4, 9, 124, 142, 153, 157; executive 127–128; governmental 25, 128, 143, 157; social 23, 25, 27; wartime 137
The President and the Parties 3
presidential campaigns 126–127, 130
presidents 3, 72, 77, 81–82, 84, 100, 127, 129, 136, 138, 142
prisoners 109–110
private citizens 35
private debt 40, 48–49, 52, 97, 155
private interests 14, 18, 22–24, 27, 77, 118, 138
Progressive candidates 130
Progressive Era 9, 124–126, 130, 132, 136, 138, 140–141

Progressive Party 9, 124, 126–127, 129, 131, 142, 154
Progressive reforms 125–126, 130–131, 136–137, 143
Progressives 9, 124–145, 153; contours of Progressivism for 126; errs by pursuing reform in a centralized fashion 145; extra-constitutional 131; great error of 145, 154; and tension between limited constitutional government and the 126
prohibition 135, 137–138
Protestant/Catholic population ratio 76–77, 80–84, 94–96, 111–112
Protestant/Catholic ratios 95, 100, 110, 113
Protestants 78, 81, 84, 94–95, 112
public debt 2–3, 5, 7–8, 10, 32–36, 48–50, 52–53, 55, 59–61, 64, 71–72, 74–75, 150–151, 155–156; economic thinking on 8; evaluation of 30; for present benefit at the expense of future taxpayers 61; to profit taxpayers 53; repaid 50; and taxes 49; theory 154; to transfer present obligations to future generations 59; unrestrained 153; usage of 64, 151
public funds 7, 65
public officials 24–25, 49, 68, 74, 127–128
public opinions 9, 124, 128–131, 133, 142–143, 152, 154, 158
Public Principles of Public Debt 52
Putnam, Robert D. 7, 16, 93, 110

Rabin, Robert L. 132, 134, 136, 138
racial composition 77
racial homogeneity 111–112
Railroad Commission of Wisconsin v. *Chicago, Burlington, and Quincy 1922* 137
railroads 132–136, 144
Rawls, John 5–6, 13, 20–21, 29–33, 35; contemporary democracy by 21; distinction between "rational" and "reasonable" 30, 32; and liberalism that distinguishes between democratic society and community 6, 35
Reconstruction Finance Corporation 138
reform 128, 130, 133, 139, 141, 145, 154, 157; civil service 133; governmental 114; merit-based 133; political 127; progressive impulse for 126, 145, 154
regulation 6, 31, 129, 133–134, 137; companion cases validating state 132; invalidating state 133; restraining state 133
relationship 16, 21, 58, 64, 73, 77–78, 94–95, 120; of democracy and oligarchy 58; justice's 32
Republicans 2, 77, 115, 118, 126, 132
revenue 7, 42–44, 66, 68, 87–88; figures 43; intergovernmental 8; per capita 73–74; sharing 45, 47
RFC *see* Reconstruction Finance Corporation
Ricardo, David 49–52
Rodden, Jonathan 69–71
Rodgers, Daniel T. 125
Romer, Thomas 92
Roosevelt, Franklin 54, 119, 126–131, 134, 138–140, 142–144, 153–154
Roosevelt, Theodore 124, 130, 142–144, 153
Rosenthal, Howard 92
Rubin, Robert L. 126
Rubinfeld, Daniel I. 68, 74
Ruhl, J.B. 114
rules 5–6, 14–15, 19, 21, 28, 68, 78; for balanced-budgets 65, 75, 78, 80–81, 83–84, 100, 155; "bayonet" 132; indeterminate 114; popular 129; *see also* budget rules

Sachs, Jeffrey D. 70
Sandel, Michael J. 1, 6, 14, 21
Savage, James D. 54, 100
Schechter v. *United States 1935* 139
Schuck, Peter H. 8, 113–114, 120
Schumpeter, Joseph 1
self-government 9–10, 14, 22, 27, 29, 31–32, 34–35, 97, 113, 124, 145, 151–152, 158; capacity for 23–24, 27, 60, 88, 96; and the exercise of civic powers for 10
self-sufficiency 17–18, 21, 26, 34, 88–89, 151, 154
Sharkansky, Ira 5
Sixteenth Amendment 135, 137–138, 141
Smith, Adam 49, 52–53, 78
social capital 16, 93, 112
social planning 65
social reform 125, 140–141
The Social Security Act 139–140
societal injustice 78, 113, 121; measure of 121, 152; synthetic measure of 8
society 4–5, 9, 13–14, 17–18, 24–28, 30, 33–34, 59–61, 64, 72–73, 108, 121–122,

society *continued*
124, 150–153; capacity for political freedom 60, 151; democratic 6, 26, 30, 32, 34, 60, 150; penchant for debt 61; political 33, 122; proclivity for debt 57
Socrates 20–21, 28–29, 64, 142, 150
state and federal debt 42, 44
state and federal levels of government 44
state and local debt 44, 50
state and local governments 86
state and local revenue 45, 74, 78
state and local spending 92
state bar 8–9, 108–110, 112–113, 115, 118, 152, 156; associations 119; size of the 8; *see also* bar
state courts 109
state debt 44, 46, 73–75, 77–79, 84, 86–87, 89, 92, 94–95, 97, 100–101, 152, 154, 156; levels 8, 51, 86, 144, 154; modeling 154
state governments 23, 45, 47, 73, 87, 89, 97, 153; centralization 45, 47; debt 43
state indebtedness 42, 44, 73, 75, 89, 100–101, 152, 154, 156
state legislatures 9, 118–119, 155
state revenue 8, 43–45, 47, 74, 76, 78, 80–84, 90, 92
Stein, Herbert 54, 100
Steward Machine Company v Davis 1937 139
Strauss, Leo 21
Suicide 57
Supreme Court 119, 127, 131–132, 139, 154
Swiss Municipalities 92
Szakaly, Kristin 92

Taft, William Howard 126–130, 135
tax base 50–52, 144
tax proposals 135
taxes 7, 49–52, 54–55, 60–61, 65–68, 75, 87–89, 92, 140–141, 151; and debt 49, 52, 55, 60–61, 88, 151; excise 138; payroll 142; significant 64
Theory of Justice 30
Thrasymachus 28–29, 41, 151
Tiebout, Charles M. 65, 67
Tocqueville 3, 5–6, 15–16, 22–29, 32–35, 55, 57–58, 94, 96, 119, 121–122, 142–143, 150–152, 156–157; and American society 22; and Aristotle 33, 55, 61, 72, 140; distinction between morality and honor 15; and John Rawls 33; lauds township government 25; and tyranny 24
The Trading with the Enemy Act 1917 138
The Transportation Act 1920 137
Trautman, Rhonda R. 87
Tulis, Jeffrey K. 157
tyranny 15, 18–19, 21–22, 24–25, 28, 57–58, 60, 142, 150–151, 157; as Aristotle had in mind 24; democratic 57, 157

United States Congress *see* Congress
United States v. *Butler 1936* 139
United States v. *Darby 1941* 139
United States v. *E.C. Knight 1895* 135, 140–141
United States v. *Grimaud 1911* 136
United States v. *Joint Traffic Association 1898* 135
United States v. *Standard Oil 1910* 135
United States v. *Trans-Missouri Freight Association 1897* 134–135
urbanization 9, 75, 124–125
usage of public debt 64, 151

Vaughn, Karen I. 49, 53
virtue 6, 14–16, 18–19, 30–33, 35, 113, 151; and the dependency of justice 16; and the link with justice 14
Vohs, Kathleen D. 96
The Volstead Act 138
voters 74, 92, 96; initiatives 92; turnout 8, 65, 76–77, 80–84, 92–94, 110–112, 154

Wagner, Richard E. 49, 53
Wealth, Debt, and Taxation (Census report) 42
Weingast, Barry R. 68, 70
welfare state 66, 133
Wibbels, Erik 70
Wilson, Woodrow 9, 124, 126–131, 135, 137–138, 143–144
The Wilson-Gorman Act 135
Wood, B. Dan 73–74, 84, 86, 89, 95, 97
workers 26, 48, 130, 141
World War I 54, 143
World War II 8, 44–45, 47, 156
Wright, Gavin 94

Ylaoutinen, Sami 72

For Product Safety Concerns and Information please contact our
EU representative GPSR@taylorandfrancis.com Taylor & Francis
Verlag GmbH, Kaufingerstraße 24, 80331 München, Germany